D1105563

Great Britain and the Caribbean,

1901–1913

A Study in Anglo-American Relations

Great Britain and the Caribbean, 1901–1913

A STUDY
IN ANGLO-AMERICAN RELATIONS

WARREN G. KNEER

MICHIGAN STATE UNIVERSITY PRESS

Copyright © 1975
MICHIGAN STATE UNIVERSITY PRESS
Library of Congress Card Catalog Number: 74–15582
ISBN: 0–87013–187–7
Manufactured in the United States of America

Southern Cross

Quotations from Crown-copyright records in the Public record Office appear by permission of the Controller of the HM Stationery Office.

Preface

Although the Caribbean and Central America were the crucial
testing grounds of Anglo-American friendship from 1901–1913, relatively little has been written about British diplomacy during these
years within this United States' "sphere of influence." The difficulties
arising from the Venezuelan blockade and the Mexican revolution
are the only aspects of Anglo-American relations in the area after
1901 that have received much attention from historians. This study,
I feel, will contribute to a fuller understanding of the nature of
Britain's relationship with the United States in the Caribbean during
this period. Throughout, my emphasis is on the problems of the
British Foreign Office adjusting to the new Anglo-American "entente" in Latin America that resulted from the pre-World War I
rapprochement between the two countries. Enough has been written about the benefits—both real and imagined—that the British
gained from their strategic "withdrawal" from the Caribbean. My
aim is to balance this picture by recounting some of the trials suffered
by the Foreign Office during the era of the "big stick" and "dollar
diplomacy."

With the exception of the settlement of the Guatemalan debt in
1913, I have not gone beyond the Roosevelt and Taft years because
British-American relations in the Caribbean during the Wilson administration is a subject worthy of separate treatment. British policy
in Mexico has been ably analyzed in recent years and needs no
retelling here. On the other hand, I have devoted considerable space
to the Venezuelan intervention of 1902–1903 because of its importance to my general theme and because many past accounts of Britain's role in this affair have been marred by dubious interpretations
and factual errors.

My research in England for this study was greatly facilitated by the
courteous and invaluable help given me by the staffs of the Public
Record Office, the Foreign Office Library, the Bodleian Library, and
the British Museum. I would also like to thank the State Department's Office of Educational Exchange for the grant that made this

research possible, and the British Foreign Office for giving me access to certain records on Central America that were not then open to the public. I owe a particular debt of gratitude to Paul A. Varg for his valuable advice and unfailing encouragement.

Table of Contents

Introduction

During the early years of the twentieth century, British foreign policy was undergoing a significant transformation. British power was overextended, and "splendid isolation" was giving way to a policy of alliances and ententes aimed at the protection of British interests in a world of increasingly dangerous rivalries and competition. Although Britain could not secure any alliance or even a formal understanding with the United States, a very real Anglo-American rapprochement was underway by the turn of the century. Friendship with the United States became one of the major goals of British diplomacy. It was a policy few would question, and it transcended Conservative and Liberal party differences.

Such a policy inevitably affected Britain's diplomacy in Latin America. British deference to the United States in the Western hemisphere was the first prerequisite to any friendship between the two countries. Caution was particularly necessary in the Caribbean and Central America, for American activity there during these years centered around the Isthmus of Panama and the countries dominating the sea approaches to the site of the proposed canal. Americans talked of the Monroe Doctrine, but to Europeans schooled in traditional power politics, the United States was creating a sphere of influence and transforming the Caribbean into an American lake. British sympathy in the Spanish-American War and British concessions in the canal treaty of 1901 played a significant part in forging the new Anglo-American friendship, but were not enough to maintain it. The United States expected Britain to continue a policy of acquiescence to the expansion of American influence into this crucial region.

In attempting to carry out this policy, Britain had to sacrifice little strategic or political interests in the Caribbean. British influence there had been declining for decades, and even before Sir John Fisher's reorganization of the fleet in 1904 British naval power in the Western hemisphere was far from formidable.[1] Britain's decision to accept the Hay-Pauncefote Treaty of 1901, by which the United

States rid itself of earlier treaty restrictions against an American owned and operated isthmian canal, was an important step in the shifting power relationship of the United States and Britain in the Caribbean, but it hardly represented any dramatic change in British policy. During negotiations, the Admiralty did point out that "from a purely naval and strategical point of view" it was "not really in the interests of Great Britain" that an isthmian canal be constructed,[2] but by 1901 the British navy had in fact come to accept the inevitability of an American canal and American naval supremacy in the Caribbean.[3] In any event, the British statesmen responsible for the treaty were not unhappy with the results. As Ambassador Pauncefote reported from Washington:

> The success of the Canal Treaty has been a great blow to my "chers collegues" here. Not one of them has offered congratulations, & throughout they have maintained a lugubrious silence. It was hoped no doubt that the Treaty would again be mangled in the Senate & that the entente cordiale would perish with it. If we now settle the Alaska trouble they will be in despair & I shall be able to say with infinite satisfaction "nunc dimittis."

And Lord Lansdowne agreed: "How delightful it would be if you should be able, before you leave Washington, to give us that clean slate we all so much desire."[4]

The decline of British political and strategic interests in Latin America did not mean that Britain no longer had significant commercial and financial interests there. On the contrary, British exports and investments were increasing. According to the Board of Trade, British exports to all of South America averaged slightly over £19,000,000 a year from 1895–99, rising to almost £40,000,000 by 1906.[5] From 1880 to 1900 British investments in Latin America had increased from almost £180,000,000 to about £540,000,000.[6] Was it possible for Great Britain to "withdraw" from the Western hemisphere in favor of the United States without jeopardizing her enormous economic interests there? In the last analysis, the viability of the "entente cordiale" depended to a great degree on the answer to this question.

Fortunately for the Foreign Office, British trade and investments in the Caribbean and Central America were relatively small compared with theirs in South America,[7] but there were still possible points of friction between Britain and the United States within the American "sphere of influence." While Britain was still well ahead of her major rivals, the United States and Germany, in the export trade to South America, the Americans already dominated trade in Central America, Mexico, and the island republics of the Caribbean by 1900.[8] Would this trend continue to the detriment of existing British trade in the Caribbean? Would it eventually affect the more lucrative markets of the South American continent? American successes were disturbing enough when they resulted from "fair" competition, but were the Americans willing to rely on this? Worried British exporters would view with alarm any signs of the Latin American "open door" closing.

In investments, as in the field of trade, the United States—although still a large debtor to British investors—was beginning to provide serious competition in some areas of Latin America. In both Cuba and Mexico, American investments pulled ahead of the British. In 1902 Americans had invested half a billion dollars in Mexico; by 1910 the total was over one billion. In Cuba, American investments climbed from an estimated $50,000,000 at the time of the Spanish-American War to more than $200,000,000 in 1911.[9] American investments in the other nations of the Caribbean and Central America seem to have been rather small in 1900,[10] and, despite the American commercial lead there, they were still behind the British. But it was obviously only a matter of time before the United States would become a formidable investment rival in those countries as well.[11]

In addition to maintaining an economic "open door" in Latin America, the Foreign Office was also committed to a policy of securing "fair treatment" in the settlement of British claims. In the past, the arbitrary actions of dictators, legislators, and government troops and the vagaries of Latin American justice had resulted in innumerable controversies over outrages against British subjects, violations of contracts, and the seizure or confiscation of British property. Like other "civilized" nations, Great Britain always reserved the right of diplomatic intervention in such cases. As the British minister to

Venezuela put it in 1902, the theory that "foreigners can have in Venezuela no rights save those of natives" was "preposterous."[12]

Of course, behind diplomatic intervention there always lurked the ultimate threat of force. "Gunboat diplomacy" and periodic calls by men-of-war were traditional procedures in Latin American waters. For example, in 1842 and 1844 the British blockaded the port of San Juan de Nicaragua; Britain joined France in intervention against Argentina in the 1840s by a blockade of the Rio de la Plata; in 1851 the entire coast of El Salvador was blockaded; in 1862 and 1863 the British navy seized Brazilian ships in Brazilian waters in reprisal for the plundering of a British vessel; in 1861 Britain for a brief time joined France and Spain against Mexico for the payment of claims; in 1887 Britain sent an ultimatum to Venezuela and threatened a blockade over the seizure of two British ships. As late as 1895 the British had seized the customs house at Corinto in Nicaragua and exacted an indemnity for the expulsion of the British consul. Obviously, the growth of American naval power in the Caribbean and an expanding Monroe Doctrine would eventually restrict diplomatic and naval activity by European powers. Would the United States accept the responsibility for fair treatment of British claims? Or would she make such settlements more difficult to obtain?

One category of British claims promised to be particularly troublesome. A high percentage of British investments in the nineteenth century went into government securities, and the long history of debt defaults in Latin America was punctuated by fraud, chicanery, heavy losses for the unwary, refunding arrangements, and fresh defaults. The annual report of the Council of Foreign Bondholders for 1901–1902 listed seven Latin American nations in default—Argentina, Colombia, Costa Rica, Guatemala, Honduras, Santo Domingo, and Venezuela—for securities totaling £36,948,075 principal, with interest in arrears of £15,723,433.[13] Six of the seven defaulters were within the Caribbean "sphere of influence" of the United States.

The Foreign Office could not possibly ignore the problem of debt defaults in Latin America as long as the Corporation of Foreign Bondholders, the quasi-official British bondholders' protective association, exerted pressure. The Corporation's Council was both persistent and influential. It had direct ties with the powerful financial and commercial interests of London, with twelve of the twenty-one members of the Council being nominated by the Central Association of Bankers and the London Chamber of Commerce and the rest co-opted by the Council as a whole. Its membership during these years included several Privy Councillors and members of both houses of Parliament.[14]

The Council's arsenal against defaulting governments ranged from mere protests and advice to legal actions, press campaigns, and the use of its influence to stop the quotation of a country's bonds on the London Stock Exchange.[15] But if these devices were unsuccessful there was always the hope of assistance from the British government, and the Council was never at a loss to think of ways to appeal for help. For example, there was nothing modest in the "few suggestions as to certain steps which might be taken in order to put pressure on the defaulting Governments" that the Council sent to Lansdowne in 1901. The bondholders wanted a vigorous government policy of immediate formal protests to defaulting countries, warnings to the investing public, the suspension of diplomatic courtesies, the use of investigating commissions, the breaking of diplomatic relations, and "concerted action" with other countries affected.[16] As Lansdowne noted, the British government "could not possibly assent" to some of the suggestions, and he had no intention of creating "the impression that such measures were regarded by me as likely to be accepted." But while the problem of pressure from this influential source remained, the Foreign Secretary also wanted "to avoid saying anything which might seem to make light" of the bondholders' grievances.[17]

The Council of Foreign Bondholders encountered its greatest difficulties trying to overcome the traditional feeling within the Foreign Office that the highly speculative nature of such investments precluded strong governmental support. The government generally had a laissez-faire attitude toward foreign investments, and nothing was done to interfere with loans to Latin American countries, but the Foreign Office realized that they were a fertile source of troublesome controversies. "High interest means bad security," one Under Secretary of State wrote in 1901, "and it has been the policy of this country for a very long time past not to encourage British investors to put their money into these Foreign Loans which offer such tempting inducements never or hardly ever realized."[18] Claims arising from these loans usually did not receive the same sympathy at the Foreign Office as other claims.

On the other hand, the Foreign Office was not immune to the pleas of the bondholders. Although the British government had not resorted to actual armed intervention to help the bondholders during the nineteenth century, the Foreign Office had extended diplomatic aid to them in a number of ways. British policy statements on the subject in the nineteenth century were not always consistent,[19] but the diplomats could use, if they desired, Lord Palmerston's famous "doctrine" that it was simply "a question of discretion" whether the British government would intervene diplomatically in support of the bondholders, and "the decision of that question of discretion turns entirely upon British and domestic considerations."[20] Thus, by the time Lansdowne took over the Foreign Office, past attitudes and practices could either justify help for the bondholders or a policy of inaction.

As the new Anglo-American "entente cordiale" was to be subjected to its first serious strain over the settlement of British claims in Venezuela, the attitude of Lansdowne and the Foreign Office in 1901–1902 toward British claimants in the Caribbean is particularly important. The record shows that Britain's new relationship with the United States did not cause any immediate shift to a more passive policy. On the contrary, Lansdowne and his subordinates were on the verge of inaugurating a more vigorous claims policy. For example, in 1901 and 1902 the Foreign Office helped or attempted to help in various ways the British bondholders and other claimants in Venezuela, Guatemala, Costa Rica, Honduras, and Santo Domingo. There was nothing anti-American in any of this, for Lansdowne wanted no part of any policy hostile to the United States.[21] He was, however, slow to realize the potential dangers in aiding British claimants in their quarrels with Latin American nations. The Foreign Office did not yet grasp the full implications of their political and strategic withdrawal from the Caribbean. The fact that British claims would have to be settled in a new environment was brought into focus for the first time by the Venezuelan intervention of 1902–1903.

NOTES AND REFERENCES

1. According to *The Naval Annual,* British naval strength in American waters in 1899 consisted of one battleship, seven second- and third-class cruisers, and eight smaller craft. After 1900 the largest British ship on the North American station was a first-class cruiser.

2. Admiralty to Foreign Office, January 5, 1901. Quoted in Charles S. Campbell, Jr., *Anglo-American Understanding, 1898–1903* (Baltimore, 1957), pp. 357–60.

3. See Kenneth Bourne, *Britain and the Balance of Power in North America, 1815–1908* (Berkeley, 1967), pp. 342–51.

4. Pauncefote to Lansdowne, December 19, 1901; Lansdowne to Pauncefote, December 31, 1901. Lord Lansdowne Papers (Foreign Office Library, London), U.S., vol. 28. Cited hereafter as Lansdowne Papers.

5. Great Britain, *Parliamentary Papers,* "Exports to China and South America," 1906 (131) cx; 1917 (351), lxxxi.

6. By 1913 British investments in Latin America would reach nearly £1,000,000,000. These figures are taken from J. Fred Rippy's *British Investments in Latin America, 1822–1949* (Minneapolis, 1959), pp. 25, 36–41, 45. A United Nations study of 1955 uses considerably lower estimates. See Marvin D. Bernstein (ed.), *Foreign Investment in Latin America, Cases and Attitudes* (New York: 1966), p. 36.

7. British exports to the Caribbean area in 1901 ranged from a high of £1,959,770 to Cuba to a low of £57,919 to Honduras. See "Annual Statement of Trade of the United Kingdom with Foreign Countries and British Possessions," *Parliamentary Papers,* Cd. 2626 (1905), lxxx. With the exception of Mexico, all the major Latin American recipients of British investments were in southern Latin America. For a breakdown of British Latin American investments by country in 1890, see Rippy, *British Investments,* p. 37.

8. For American export values to each country, see *Statistical Abstract of the United States, 1911* (Washington, D.C.: U.S. Department of Labor and Commerce, 1912), pp. 364–80.

9. J. Fred Rippy, *The Caribbean Danger Zone* (New York: 1940), p. 224; Alfred P. Tischendorf, *Great Britain and Mexico in the Era of Porfirio Diaz* (Durham, N. C.: 1961), pp. 139, 142; Dana G. Munro, *Intervention and Dollar Diplomacy in the Caribbean, 1900–1921* (Princeton, 1964), pp. 16–17.

10. Munro, *Intervention and Dollar Diplomacy,* p. 16. Rippy estimates that there was probably not much over a hundred million dollars invested by Americans in the whole Caribbean region in 1900. This figure excludes Mexico but includes Cuba. Rippy, *The Caribbean Danger Zone,* p. 224.

11. In his *Globe and Hemisphere* (Chicago: 1958), Rippy places the total United States' investment in Latin America in 1897 at probably more than $320,000,000, with $278,000,000 of this in northern Latin America. By 1914 the total exceeded $1,600,000,000, with $1,241,500,000 in the northern Latin countries. See pp. 30–38.

12. Haggard to Lansdowne, February 19, 1902. F. O. 80/443. The rejection of the

"Calvo Doctrine" by the United States and Europe is discussed in Donald R. Shea, *The Calvo Clause* (Minneapolis: 1955), pp. 16–20.

13. *Annual Report of the Council of the Corporation of Foreign Bondholders for the Year 1901–1902* (London: 1902), p. 456. Cited hereafter as *Annual Report.*

14. The Corporation of Foreign Bondholders was founded in 1868 and was the first national organization dedicated to the protection of bondholders' interests. Similar French and Belgian associations were formed in 1898. Germany and the United States did not have such organizations in the years before World War I.

The British Council usually acted through affiliated bondholders' committees chosen at appropriate times for particular countries. The Council was always represented on these committees as its President and Vice President were ex officio members of all of them, and at times other members of the Council would also be appointed to them. The complete membership lists of the Council and the various committees can be found in the Council's *Annual Reports.* In addition, see Edwin Borchard and William H. Wynne, *State Insolvency and Foreign Bondholders* (New Haven: 1951), I, 192–216; Herbert Feis, *Europe the World's Banker* (New Haven: 1930), pp. 113–17; and D.C.M. Platt, "British Bondholders in Nineteenth Century Latin America—Injury and Remedy," *Inter-American Economic Affairs,* 14 (Winter 1960).

15. Platt, *loc. cit.,* pp. 26–36.

16. C. of F. B. to Lansdowne, November 26, 1901. Great Britain, Public Record Office, Foreign Office Papers, F. O. 15/344.

17. Lansdowne's minute on the C. of F. B.'s of November 26, 1901. F. O. 15/344.

18. Memorandum by Francis Bertie, November 29, 1901. F. O. 15/344.

19. See Platt, *loc. cit.,* pp. 39–41.

20. Feis, *op. cit.,* pp. 103–104.

21. For example, one of the reasons that Lansdowne no longer favored an alliance with Germany was fear that it might jeopardize relations with the United States. Although his limited cooperation with Germany in Venezuela showed a certain obtuseness, Lansdowne certainly did not view it as a challenge to the United States. For Lansdowne's views toward Germany in 1901–1902, see George Monger, *The End of Isolation, British Foreign Policy, 1900–1907* (London: 1963), pp. 21–45, 63–66, and 99–103.

Chapter I

Lansdowne and European Cooperation in the Caribbean: Guatemala and Venezuela, 1901-1902

During 1901–1903 Great Britain took part in two multilateral European coercions of Latin American states. At first glance, these seem to be rather curious undertakings for a nation supposedly "withdrawing" from the Western hemisphere in deference to the United States. Britain's prominent role in the coercions of Guatemala and Venezuela was not, however, the result of any hypocrisy in the British policy of cultivating Anglo-American friendship. This activity was rather an indication that the British Foreign Office did not yet fully realize that their nineteenth-century views regarding the protection of British interests in the Caribbean had become outmoded by their own policy of friendship with the United States. The joint European pressure on Guatemala never went beyond diplomatic notes and verbal threats and caused no repercussions from the United States. Britain's decision to join Germany in the Venezuelan intervention was a more fateful move because it eventually forced the British to ponder the implications of a Latin American "entente" with the United States.

The notoriety of the Anglo-German intervention in Venezuela has diverted historians' attention from the European coercion of Guatemala. This is unfortunate because understanding the Guatemalan episode helps our perspective of the British role in the Venezuelan intervention. The Guatemala episode gives clear evidence that Lansdowne and the Foreign Office still thought it possible in 1901–1902 to pursue a vigorous claims policy in the Caribbean without jeopardizing Britain's new relationship with the United States; even within the American "sphere of influence" cooperation with European nations had not as yet been ruled out.

Historians of Central America have found little good to record about the long presidency of Manuel Estrada Cabrera of Guatemala from 1898 to 1920. Even in an area in which dictatorships were the rule rather than the exception, Estrada Cabrera's government seems to have been particularly corrupt, cruel, and oppressive. His years in power were characterized by farcical elections, a ruthless use of the secret police and spies, and a worsening exploitation of the Indian majority of Guatemala. Coffee and banana exports increased during his presidency and many foreigners and wealthy Guatemalans liked the political stability he was able to maintain, but Estrada Cabrera's influence on the history of his country was generally deplorable.

To the British, however, the one fault of Estrada Cabrera that mattered was his refusal to cooperate with the bondholders. Germans and Americans controlled the coffee and banana export trade, but a large share of the external debt of Guatemala was held in Britain. After a long history of defaults, the external and internal debts of Guatemala were consolidated in 1895 into a new 4% debt of £1,600,000, the new bonds to be secured by a special coffee export tax. To the dismay of the bondholders, Estrada Cabrera violated the terms of the new arrangement by lowering the tax which had been fixed "irrevocably" for ten years and then used the revenues for other purposes. By the end of 1899 the debt was again in default on a principal of £1,482,800, and by mid-1901 the unpaid interest had raised the sum to £1,631,080. The Council of Foreign Bondholders estimated that £1,057,000 of the bonds were in British hands.[1] As there seemed to be little hope for a settlement without government support, on January 21, 1901, the Council asked the Foreign Office to instruct the British minister at Guatemala City to join the Belgian and German representatives there in vigorously pressing the claims of the bondholders.

The Foreign Office's response satisfied the Council. Lansdowne not only sounded out the Germans regarding joint action, but he eventually extended the invitation to Belgium, Italy and France as well.[2] On September 4, 1901, the five European nations warned Estrada Cabrera of "the urgent necessity" of satisfying the foreign bondholders "without further delay." Following the lead of the French and German representatives, the British minister to Central America, Ralph S. Paget, also reminded Guatemala of other outstanding claims awaiting settlement.[3]

Lansdowne seemingly had no misgivings about cooperating with other European powers in Central America. His Under Secretary of State in charge of the Foreign Office's American Department, Francis Villiers, was actually enthusiastic about it. Villiers welcomed the Belgian suggestion that certain postal charges owed by Guatemala be added to the demands. "I am all in favour of bringing as much general pressure as possible upon these C. American rogues," he advised Lansdowne. "We do not often get a chance."[4] When Guatemala and the Council of Foreign Bondholders signed an *ad referendum* agreement in March of 1902, Lansdowne and Villiers even took the unusual step of agreeing to an article requiring Guatemala to notify "the Governments of the Countries interested" that she accepted the arrangement "as constituting a binding engagement."[5] As Villiers argued, "I do not see that any financial obligation is necessarily incurred & on the other hand it is of real importance that the joint action—the first of the kind in C. or S. America —should be maintained & lead to a successful result."[6]

Although Estrada Cabrera paid the small postal claims and was forced to negotiate with the bondholders, he remained reluctant to settle the other foreign claims. The European representatives were anxious to continue the joint pressure, and in March of 1902 Britain, France, Germany, and Belgium demanded payment of their claims without further delay. When Estrada Cabrera did not answer, Lansdowne told the other powers that Britain was ready to consider suggestions from the representives in Guatemala for further joint action. Germany, Italy, and France all seemed willing to engage in a bit of gunboat diplomacy. Both the Italians and French were ready to participate in a naval demonstration if necessary, and the Germans were "quite disposed to join in Anglo-French coercive measures against Guatemala as far as they are actually able to do so there." Only the Belgian reply was weak. In fact, the British, who were still at the point of merely considering recommendations, were slightly embarrassed by the vigor of the replies. "It may come to a demonstration," Lansdowne noted, "but we have hardly arrived at that stage yet."[7]

Lansdowne was spared any further decisions, for in mid-April Estrada Cabrera's resistance finally collapsed. Convinced that it was "absolutely necessary to put a stop to any more shuffling," Paget and his German and French colleagues sent another note to the Guatemalan President on April 9th warning him that "an evasive answer . . . would surely entail grievous consequences." The note was well timed. HMS *Grafton* was due to arrive at San José within a a few days on a cruise, and the German cruiser *Vineta* was expected at Puerto Barrios about the same time. As Paget cabled the Foreign Office, the "mere presence of our ship of war on the Pacific side and German ship of war on Atlantic Coast should enable us to obtain full settlement." Estrada Cabrera sent a "satisfactory" answer to the joint note, but once the German ship had sailed he began stalling once again. On April 16th, after more warnings, Paget finally told the Guatemalan Minister for Foreign Affairs that "I would give him one hour to go and see the President and obtain answers respecting our claims and at the end of that time I would return with Admiral Bickford of the *Grafton* and, if necessary, get replies from the President in the Admiral's presence." When the Guatemalan Minister claimed he was unable to see the President, Paget and Bickford visited Estrada Cabrera and were able to get all but one of the British claims recognized.[8]

What Paget did not tell the Foreign Office in his reports was that Admiral Bickford and he had threatened to seize some customs houses. According to Bickford's account to the Admiralty, before leaving San José for Guatemala City he had ordered the captain of the *Grafton* to prepare landing parties for the occupation of the customs houses of San José and Champerico. He and Paget then decided to tell the Guatemalan Foreign Minister that if a favorable answer was not forthcoming, British forces would "land and occupy certain custom houses till the claims were satisfied." It was this threat repeated to Estrada Cabrera on the 16th that brought about his capitulation.[9] Although the Foreign Office had not authorized such strong and specific threats, there is nothing in the records to indicate that either Villiers or Lansdowne were disturbed by their minister's actions.

The entire incident had been a successful application of routine gunboat diplomacy. The stakes had been small—Paget reported that all of the foreign claims were finally settled for between £40,000 and £45,000—but the desired multilateral approach had succeeded. Germany, France and Italy had expressed their willingness to cooperate with Britain in a naval demonstration; although it had not reached that stage, the threats made by Paget and Bickford had led to a general settlement of the European claims. The external debt of Guatemala was still unsettled, but on the eve of the Venezuelan intervention Britain was still cooperating with the other European powers on behalf of the bondholders. When the Guatemalan Congress modified the March agreement with the Council of Foreign Bondholders and deleted the notification article, Villiers once again contacted the four cooperating powers. On November 11th another collective note was sent to Estrada Cabrera warning him that the reinsertion of the notification article was the only way to bring an end to the pending negotiations.

But what of the United States and the Monroe Doctrine? Were any attempts made to sound out the views of the State Department? There is no evidence in the Foreign Office records that the British made any overtures to the United States on the subject of Guatemala. In February of 1902, the American representative in Guatemala, Mr. Hunter, did report to Secretary of State John Hay that a joint note had been sent the previous September regarding the external debt, but Hunter's information came from the Guatemalans, not from the European Ministers at Guatemala City. Hunter informed Washington that the representatives "of the powers on this continent were neither asked to join in the note, nor were they consulted regarding it."[10]

Judging from his instructions to Hunter, the Secretary of State was not alarmed over the situation. Hay wanted to be kept informed, but he saw nothing in the joint note that called for any action or comment from the United States, "inasmuch as it is within the right of the creditor nations to require payment of debts due to their nationals." Alvey A. Adee, the perennial Second Assistant Secretary of State, was sufficiently aroused to write to Judge W. L. Penfield, the Department's Solicitor, that Hunter's reports were "an important correspondence, in view of our traditional jealousy of any concerted action of European powers to coerce an American State into payment of its debts." Penfield was obviously unimpressed, for he was the one who drafted the March 22nd reply to Hunter.[11] When the Germans asked the State Department on April 3rd if the United States wanted to join Germany and Britain in acknowledging the new arrangement that the Council of Foreign Bondholders was seeking with Guatemala, Hay again displayed little interest in the affair. He wanted equal treatment for American creditors in any adjustment of Guatemala's foreign debt, but the United States was "indisposed to join in any collective act which might bear the aspect of coercive pressure upon Guatemala."[12]

The State Department seemingly did not learn of the events of April, 1902, regarding the other claims until July when the American Chargé, James Bailey, reported that Guatemala had recently paid a number of foreign claims.

> Very reliable information discloses the fact that collective pressure was resorted to by the respective diplomatic representatives here of England, France, Germany, and Belgium in order to bring about the payment of said claims. It appears that they as a body notified this Government that if arrangements were not made to satisfy their respective creditors on a specific date a man-of-war would take possession of each of the principal ports of the Republic of Guatemala.[13]

Even though Bailey's "very reliable" informant exaggerated the scope of the joint European action, there were no repercussions from Washington. Did silence mean consent on the part of the Roosevelt administration? Was the way open for more multilateral European pressure against the states of Latin America? In his annual message of December, 1901, Roosevelt had told the world that the Monroe Doctrine was "in no wise intended as hostile to any nation in the Old World" and that the United States did "not guarantee any state against punishment if it misconducts itself, provided that punishment does not take the form of the acquisition of territory by any non-American power."[14] The Guatemalan coercion had not really tested this statement, for the European nations had not been forced to go beyond the use of threats. But the test was soon to come. By the fall of 1902 Great Britain and Germany were already coordinating their plans for Venezuela, and mere threats would not be enough to bring about the capitulation of Cipriano Castro.

Rumors and talk of possible European intervention in Venezuela in 1901 came as no surprise to those familiar with the situation in that unhappy and unstable republic. After seizing power in 1899, President Cipriano Castro was able to maintain his control over Venezuela for nine years, but, plagued by civil war and numerous intrigues, he was partially unwilling and partially unable to follow the usual canons of international law in his dealings with foreign powers. Venezuela's financial troubles and Castro's treatment of foreign residents and their property soon resulted in an impressive list of foreign grievances and claims.

By the summer of 1901, British relations with Venezuela were already deteriorating rapidly. Some of the controversies between the two countries had their origins in the long standing antipathy between Venezuela and the Government of Trinidad. In 1882 Venezuela had levied a 30% surtax on imports from Trinidad and other West Indian islands, a tax that the British government considered a violation of the British-Venezuelan commercial treaty of 1825. The tax not only hurt legitimate commerce between Trinidad and Venezuela but also stimulated a very lucrative smuggling trade. When Castro tried to get Trinidad to forbid the export of arms that might fall into the hands of his many rivals, neither the Governor of Trinidad nor the British Colonial Office was in any mood to take extraordinary measures to aid his regime.

Castro's attempts to stop smuggling and outside aid to his enemies led to a number of British shipping claims that were to play a large role in subsequent events. Beginning in January of 1901, Venezuela seized some small British owned vessels in Venezuelan waters and at Patos island on charges of smuggling and revolutionary activity. British subjects were also involved in the seizures of some Venezuelan owned ships. The value of the ships seized or destroyed by the Venezuelan gunboats was small, and in some cases Castro's charges were seemingly true, but the Venezuelan President refused to consider the British complaints. When the British charged that Venezuelan gunboats had violated British territorial waters by their operations at Patos, Castro countered by reviving an old Venezuelan claim to the island, thus interjecting a small territorial dispute into the mutual recriminations. A small island three miles off the coast of Venezuela and five miles from the nearest British island, Patos was uninhabited at the time. Venezuela had claimed ownership of the island for the first time in 1859 and during the 1880's had suggested arbitration. In 1887 the British refused to arbitrate on the grounds that British sovereignty there was not open to question. The issue then died out until revived by Castro in 1901.

In addition to the "specific outrages" of the ship seizures, there were the inevitable claims from British subjects and companies in Venezuela that had accumulated during the years of civil strife. The total claims from private individuals were small in value (about £2,000 in 1902), but the claims of some of the British controlled Venezuelan railroads against the government had reached more than £260,000. There was little prospect of any settlements. In January of 1901, Castro had created a Venezuelan claims commission, but the commission refused to consider claims originating before Castro's coming to power in 1899, and Venezuela proclaimed that the decisions of the commission were not subject to diplomatic protest. Britain, Germany and other foreign powers—including the United States—refused to recognize the commission and reserved their rights to intervene. Those foreigners and Venezuelans who did use the commission were unable to get payments even when they were successful in getting their claims accepted.

Venezuela was also one of the Latin American states in default in 1901 on its external debt. In 1881, after the usual pattern of arrangements and defaults, Venezuela's earlier loans were converted into a "New Consolidated Debt" of £2,750,000. In 1896 the Venezuelan debt was swelled by another sizable loan contracted by the *Disconto Gesellschaft* of Berlin. Most of the bonds of the external debt of 1881 were in the hands of British investors, while the bulk of the 1896 bonds were held in Germany. Thus the British Council of Foreign Bondholders and the German *Disconto Gesellschaft*[15] had common interests and common cause for alarm when after partial payments both debts went into complete default after August of 1901. As of August 15, 1902, the total principal and interest arrears of the Venezuelan debt was £5,262,077, £2,974,570 on the debt of 1881 and £2,287,507 on that of 1896.[16]

In addition to the debt default, Germany also had a sizable number of claims for personal injuries and property damage, and reports from Caracas in 1901 seemed to indicate that German patience was beginning to run out. According to William Haggard, the British Minister to Venezuela, Herr von Pilgrim Baltazzi, the German Chargé d'Affaires, was attempting to organize a concert of the powers to exert pressure on Castro. In July, when Pilgrim Baltazzi suggested that Haggard take the initiative, the British minister evaded the invitation on the grounds that British claims were "insignificant," but the following month Haggard pointed out to the Foreign Office that, if there were "no difficulties and jealousies" and "if all or some of the Powers interested" could "come to some agreement as to common action, it would seem that this might offer a favourable opportunity for us to settle once and for all" the claims and the other issues with Castro. Pilgrim Baltazzi told Haggard that he had also sounded out the American Chargé and had found him "very well disposed personally." Russell reported the talk of joint action to the State Department, but Hay replied that it was not the policy of the United States to act with other governments in claims protests.[17]

In September, both Pilgrim Baltazzi and the Dutch Chargé wanted Haggard to join them in telling their governments that foreign intervention was necessary. According to Haggard, the two envisioned "something of a permanent administrative nature which will go far beyond the occupation of one or more Customs Houses," some intervention "as has taken place in Egypt." Again Haggard evaded the request:

> I replied that, speaking purely academically, I did not consider that there was sufficient similarity between the interests of Great Britain here and those which she used to have in Egypt . . . and that under any circumstances, we could not blink the fact that no such action could possibly be taken by any Power or Powers without the concurrence or at least previous consultation with and agreement of the United States.[18]

Pilgrim Baltazzi and Chargé von Leyden admitted that they had not spoken with the new American minister, Herbert Bowen, who had arrived in Venezuela in August. When the two showed "an evident reluctance" to take Bowen into their confidence, Haggard "repeated and emphasized" his views on consultation with the United States. Although Haggard told the German and Dutch representatives that he did not "feel at liberty" to suggest such an intervention, he did tell the Foreign Office in October that his own "impression" was "that both foreign and native interests could be saved by the administration for a prolonged period of the Customs Houses by one or more of the foreign Powers."[19]

The Foreign Office had no desire for a Venezuelan condominium, and they rightly suspected that Pilgrim Baltazzi's views were "somewhat in advance" of his government's. But Haggard had also expressed the opinion that Germany would probably act alone to settle her claims if necessary, and he reported plans for a number of German ships to gather in Venezuelan waters, presumably for a naval demonstration. "Without being an alarmist," he wrote, "it is difficult to suppose that a Power which has never before—as far as I am aware—had more than a ship at a time here, can be collecting a fleet—for it is nothing else—without some object."[20]

The Foreign Office was sufficiently interested in Haggard's reports to sound out the German government, but Ambassador Lascelles at

Berlin was unable to get much definite information from Baron von Richthofen. The Germans seemed ready to settle their claims even though they had not yet decided what action to take if they failed. An Egyptian style intervention in Venezuela would be difficult to carry out, and for this kind of move an agreement with the United States would be necessary.

> For the moment, however, the German Government had no intention of taking any definite action. The fact of another German ship being sent to Venezuelan waters where German interests were now being represented by one small naval vessel, could not be considered as a naval demonstration and he hoped that a settlement of the claims might be obtained by ordinary diplomatic methods.[21]

Again in December there were signs that German coercion of Venezuela was imminent. On December 17th Richthofen told the British Chargé, George Buchanan, that Germany was going to present her claims to Venezuela "en bloc." When Buchanan asked him if Germany was prepared to enforce a settlement, Richthofen admitted that "strong measures" against Venezuela were "not improbable." Germany had already sounded out the American government and they had "no reason to fear that any steps which they might take" would "give umbrage" to the United States.[22]

There is no question then that Germany first conceived of the idea of using force against Venezuela, but which of the two countries first approached the other regarding the possibility of Anglo-German cooperation? Pilgrim Baltazzi's suggestions for joint European action in 1901 seem to have been his own rather than those of his government, and there is no indication that either side issued any invitation during Richthofen's talks with Lascelles and Buchanan. The first explicit reference by a member of either Foreign Office to possible cooperation is found in a reported conversation between Villiers and Baron von Eckardstein. According to the German Chargé d'Affaires, on January 2, 1902, Villiers told him Britain possibly would propose common action as soon as the situation in Venezuela became clearer.[23] There is no record of such a conversation in the Foreign

Office papers but, in light of Villiers' enthusiasm for the multilateral approach to Latin American "rogues," it is not improbable that some such statement was made. In any event, the Germans, by January of 1902, were convinced that the British Foreign Office was not adverse to the idea of cooperation in Venezuela. Were they correct?

Regardless of the accuracy of Eckardstein's report, there is little doubt that Britain was considering joint action against Venezuela. The day after the reported conversation between Villiers and the German Chargé, the British bondholders made their first appeal to the Foreign Office for aid. Spurred on by press reports of the intended German action, the Council of Foreign Bondholders asked Lansdowne to consider "whether, in the event of action being taken now or at a later period by the German Government on behalf of German bondholders, His Majesty's Government could not take steps to secure equal recognition for the claims of the holders of Venezuelan Bonds in this country."[24] The Council did not specifically ask for joint action with Germany, and the Foreign Office made no promise to help the bondholders, but with the two countries already cooperating in Guatemala it seems safe to conclude that the possibility was considered. The role of the bondholders should not be overemphasized, for subsequent events showed that the debt default was definitely secondary to the other grievances. For example a later Foreign Office memorandum of July 20, 1902, on the existing causes of complaint did not even list the Venezuelan default. On the other hand, Haggard did include the interest on the English debt in his list of claims that he sent to the Foreign Office on December 13, 1901, "in the event of your thinking it worth considering whether, if the Germans enforce their claims, we can do anything to benefit therefrom in any way."[25] Even if the Foreign Office was not considering action on behalf of the bondholders, they were thinking of it for other British claims. Although the passage was deleted in the final form, the draft of a Foreign Office letter of January 16th to the Colonial Office on Venezuela stated that Lansdowne was "awaiting a favorable opportunity for further action, which may possibly take the form of joint action with one or several of the Powers interested."[26]

On the other hand, it is also clear that the British Foreign Office was still undecided in January. Uncertain about German intentions, Lansdowne wanted more information. On January 14th, he instructed Lascelles to find out if any arrangement had been concluded between Germany and Venezuela, "as seems possible from the apparent suspension of any measures of compulsion." If no agreement had been reached, Lascelles was to ask "what steps" the Germans contemplated.[27] Certainly Villiers and Lansdowne did not believe that they had made any actual invitation to Berlin in January.[28]

One can only conclude that both countries "instigated" the joint Venezuelan intervention. Germany would make the first formal proposal in the summer of 1902, but by then the British had made enough inquiries to encourage Berlin to think that the proposal would be accepted. The delay in the German invitation was due to the Kaiser. After preparing the way with the United States the previous December, the German Foreign Office was ready to move in January but the Kaiser thought that the British position was "too vague" and he feared that an intervention at that time would jeopardize the success of Prince Henry's coming good will visit to the United States.[29]

The Germans, who did not answer Lansdowne's inquiry of January 14th, obviously did not intend to use force at the time. A number of German warships did gather at the port of La Guayra in February, but the "naval demonstration" was a failure. Pilgrim Baltazzi either knew or suspected the reason for the German delay, but he expressed to Haggard "his astonishment—not to say his disgust—at the action of his Government in, as he put it, leading him on to the very point of action and then letting him drop."[30] The British, Americans, and Dutch all followed the German lead in presenting their claims formally, but Castro ignored everyone.

Meanwhile, relations between Great Britain and Venezuela continued to deteriorate. With the question of joint action with Germany in abeyance, the worsening situation now forced the British to consider acting alone. In January, 1902, another British owned and registered ship was seized in Venezuelan waters. More pleas for protection from British corporations were coming in to the Foreign Office.[31] Particularly galling were the reported activities of the Venezuelan consul at Trinidad who was hindering the despatch of British vessels to Venezuela and collecting improper fees and charges. Venezuela did not even answer Haggard's complaints and, when Pilgrim Baltazzi made a similar protest, the Venezuelan government said it was aware of its consul's misconduct, but that he was kept at Trinidad because he was offensive to Great Britain.

Any attempts at negotiations between Britain and Venezuela reached a complete impasse in the spring of 1902 over the confusing career of the steamship *Ban Righ*. The *Ban Righ* left London under British registry in 1901, supposedly for service with the government of Colombia, but early in 1902 there were reports that she had taken aboard a revolutionary Venezuelan general and was engaged in a marauding expedition along the Venezuelan coast, apparently using different names and flying both the Colombian and British flags. On March 23rd she arrived at Trinidad in need of repairs, with Venezuelan gunboats in hot pursuit. The British decision to allow the ship to refit and depart for Colombian waters added fuel to the controversy.[32] Refusing to accept British explanations, the infuriated Castro charged that Great Britain was responsible for the *Ban Righ*'s activities since leaving London. Ostensibly because of this controversy, Castro now refused to discuss any of the disputes between Britain and his country.

The first suggestion for a specific reprisal against Venezuela came from Governor Maloney of Trinidad. On hearing that a Venezuelan gunboat had destroyed another British vessel, the *In Time*, in the Venezuelan harbor of Pedernales in May of 1902, Maloney wanted to seize a Venezuelan gunboat in retaliation and close all British ports to Castro's warships. However, the Foreign Office's legal advisers did not believe that the evidence was strong enough as yet to justify reprisals, and the mild decision was made merely to warn Venezuela that British ports might be closed unless they could disprove the reports of the destruction of the *In Time*. But the diplomatic deadlock continued. By the end of June Haggard calculated that since February a total of seventeen notes to Venezuela on a variety of subjects were both unanswered and unacknowledged. In his own words, his position at Caracas had become "somewhat absurd and almost useless."[33]

While the Foreign Office was still debating over retaliation against Castro in the summer of 1902, the French proved less reluctant to show force than either the British or the Germans. Angry over the intimidation of the French Consular Agent at Carupano and the imprisonment of some French merchants involved in a customs dispute, the French government decided on direct action. When a French cruiser, the *Suchet,* was unable to get immediate satisfaction from the local authorities at Carupano, the commanding officer trained his guns on a Venezuelan gunboat and refused to allow it to get underway. The local officials capitulated, released the French prisoners, and gave a public apology to the French consul. The French minister at Caracas refused to accept a Venezuelan protest, and when Castro's Foreign Minister asked him what foreign warships were doing in Venezuelan waters, he reportedly replied: "I do not know what the others are doing but Your Excellency will observe that the French Ship came here to do something."[34]

The *Suchet*'s show of force produced fast results without alarming the State Department at Washington. Bowen did attempt to arouse the State Department but he had little success. Washington agreed with Bowen that the *Suchet*'s detention of the Venezuelan gunboat before the Venezuelan government had refused satisfaction was "irregular and reprehensible," but they regarded the incident as closed "so far as we are concerned." "Should the case be reopened, or a similar one arise in future," Adee instructed Bowen, "your Legation may exert its discreet and friendly influence to bring about diplomatic adjustment before resort is had to force in the nature of reprisals."[35]

France's successful use of gunboat diplomacy was fresh in mind when news arrived in London in July of yet another Venezuelan seizure of a British ship. Not only had a Venezuelan gunboat captured the *Queen* on suspicion of gun-running, but the British ship had been intercepted on the high seas and confiscated. When as usual there was no reply to Haggard's protests, the Foreign Office's legal advisers were convinced that the time had come for reprisals. Accordingly, William E. Davidson argued:

> This is really going a little too far.
> I think we must seriously consider whether we ought not to seize a Venezuelan gunboat pending an explanation & ample apology from the Venezuelan Government.
> The French—in a case *comparatively* mild though sufficiently serious in itself—employed drastic measures with good effect—and we are in some danger of carrying the forbearance of a great power towards a petty Statelet unduly far, if we suffer this gladly.

His assistant Cecil J. B. Hurst agreed:

> It appears to be just what was lacking before, clear proof of an outrage that justifies, and, coupled with the other outrages, requires reprisals.

"We clearly cannot let this pass," Lansdowne ruled, and Villiers ordered his Chief Clerk in the American Department, Arthur Larcom, to prepare a memorandum listing the various causes of complaint against Venezuela.[36]

Thus the British government, by mid-July of 1902, was on the verge of unilateral retaliation against Castro, but at this point the Germans revived the question of cooperation. On July 23rd, just one week after the news of the seizure of the *Queen* reached London, the German ambassador, Count Metternich, told Lansdowne that Germany believed that the time was approaching when joint pressure on Venezuela would be necessary.

> He observed that a new Ministry was about to be formed, and he thought the opportunity might be a good one for making it clear to them that some form of coercion would, if necessary, be applied. What did I think of a pacific blockade of the Venezuelan ports during the export season?
> I told his Excellency that we should be quite ready to confer with the German Government with a view to joint action, but that I should

like to consider his proposal further before expressing an opinion as to its opportuneness in present circumstances.[37]

Before "proceeding to extremities," Lansdowne decided to send a final protest to Venezuela. He told Haggard to warn Castro "in unmistakable terms" that, unless explicit assurances were given that the ship seizures would cease and compensation given for those in the past, Great Britain would "take such steps as may be necessary" to get reparations for them as well as for the railway claims and the losses caused by the Venezuelan consul at Trinidad. Once again Castro was unimpressed. He ignored the British threat of action to enforce their claims and retorted with his own complaints over the *Ban Righ* and the Trinidad government's unfriendly attitude.[38] Lansdowne was now ready for serious consideration of "extremities."

When informed of the Venezuelan situation, the British Admiralty wasted little time giving the green light to intervention. On August 14th, the Admiralty assured the Foreign Office that a blockade of Venezuela was feasible if postponed until November when the unhealthy season along the coast was over. If Great Britain were to act with Germany, a blockade was the best method of coercion. Five days later Lansdowne informed Metternich of the Admiralty's opinion, and they agreed that the two countries should be ready to send ships at the proposed time.

Metternich's only specific suggestion for the type of coercion had been a blockade, but it was inevitable that other traditional means of force would be considered. One such possibility was an occupation of the customs houses, but, although this was discussed, it was not considered feasible. When Metternich later told Lansdowne that Germany was opposed to any plan to take the customs houses both for practical reasons and for fear it might lead to difficulties with the United States, the Foreign Secretary assured him that he had "never regarded the seizure of the Customs-houses as an advisable form of coercion."[39] During an earlier quarrel with Venezuela over the seizure of British ships in 1887, the British government had considered occupying the customs houses of La Guayra and Puerto Cabello, but they had rejected the idea because too many troops would be needed to capture the towns and the climate was too hot and unhealthy for a prolonged occupation. Admiral Douglas, the Commander-in-Chief of the North American Squadron in 1902, agreed with this earlier decision. Douglas favored either a blockade or a seizure of Venezuela's gunboats, and it was around these two alternatives that discussions were to center.[40]

On October 11th, Villiers suggested that the matter be brought before the Cabinet "before we become in any way committed with the Germans." Lansdowne's memorandum on the Cabinet meeting of October 21st indicates that his colleagues had some misgivings over a blockade, but the Foreign Secretary did not record any objections to the general idea of coercion or cooperation with Germany. Lansdowne wrote:

> Objections were raised to a belligerent blockade as likely to involve us in difficulties with other Powers, while a pacific blockade was regarded as probably insufficient. Of the other forms of coercion discussed in the memorandum the seizure of the Venezuelan gunboats was thought to be the best.
>
> We should tell the Admiralty that this step will probably be resorted to in the event of the Venezuelans remaining obdurate. . . .
>
> We should however, in the first instance, address a final warning to the Venezuelans, & I propose to inform the German Amb^r that we are about to do so, & that if it is disregarded we are prepared to join with them in measures of coercion.
>
> I should add that the particular measure which we have in view is the seizure of the gun boats.[41]

The British had now decided upon joint action, for no one expected anything but a negative answer to the second "final warning" to Castro.

The Cabinet seems to have spent little time worrying about the attitude of the United States. Lansdowne assured the Cabinet that Britain could "assume the acquiescence of the United States and I do not think we need do more than inform them when the time comes of our intention to act with Germany."[42] Although the Cabinet's preference for the seizure of the Venezuelan gunboats rather than a blockade did reflect qualms over possible trouble with other countries, Lansdowne's colleagues seemingly accepted his assurances regarding the United States.

It is possible that Prime Minister Balfour and the Cabinet, diverted by more pressing problems, did not realize the full implications of Lansdowne's Venezuelan policy.[43] But why were Lansdowne and the Foreign Office not more apprehensive about coercing a Latin American state, particularly one whose cause the United States had championed against Britain only a few years before? Mistakenly underestimating the dangers of public opinion in the United States, the Foreign Office was primarily interested in the probable reaction of the Roosevelt administration. Although Roosevelt in actual fact was worried about a possible German threat to the Monroe Doctrine in Venezuela,[44] the Foreign Office was convinced that neither the President nor Hay was unduly alarmed over the prospect of European intervention. There were certainly many signs indicating that the United States would remain passive. Roosevelt's message to Congress in December of 1901 and the American reply to the German soundings in the same month were of course the most soothing,[45] but the lack of any American response to the joint pressure on Guatemala and the *Suchet* incident must have been reassuring as well.

It is true that there were some early indications that Herbert Bowen, the American minister at Caracas, might prove troublesome. For example, in November of 1901, in reference to a rumor that the French intended to use force to settle their claims, Bowen warned the French Chargé that "if you meddle in matters out here, you will have to count with Uncle Sam." And in the same month he professed to see in the simultaneous presence of German, Italian and Austrian warships at La Guayra "a menace on the part of the Triple Alliance against the Monroe Doctrine." But Bowen's reported views were erratic. The previous month he had told Haggard that any action by the United States "to interfere with Germany or any other Power in securing her just claims here would be simply to assist and encourage robbery." And in December he startled the diplomatic corps with a

proposal for an international occupation of Caracas to prevent blood-
shed in the event of Castro's overthrow.[46]

Oddly enough, in light of his role in subsequent events, Bowen
may have actually encouraged the idea of European intervention. In
September, 1901, Bowen read to Haggard an extract from Bowen's
own book on international law in which he argued that the Monroe
Doctrine did not contain a single word to justify the belief "that it
was intended to relieve any American nation of its duty to meet all
its obligations to European Powers, or to prevent such Powers
from obtaining satisfaction from any wrong they may suffer or any
injury they may sustain in their intercourse with the American peo-
ples. ..." At the Foreign Office, Larcom found Bowen's views "interesting and unusual," and Villiers noted that Lord Pauncefote "has
many times told me that the U.S. do not object to claims etc. being
enforced. There was an attempt when we took Corinto [in Nicaragua
in 1895] to agitate on Monroe principles but it was a complete failure."[47] In 1902, Haggard's reports on Bowen became more disparag-
ing and suspicious, but they did nothing to modify the Foreign Office's assumptions about the all-important attitude of Roosevelt and
Hay.

Following the German approach in the summer of 1902, Lans-
downe at one point did suggest to Metternich that perhaps the
United States should be invited to take part in a naval demonstration.
The Germans were willing but doubtful:

> The German Gov^t were quite agreed in principle to inviting the
> cooperation of the United States, the more so as they knew that the
> U.S. Gov^t approved of our proposed action. But the interests of the
> United States in the enforcement of the claims are comparatively so
> small that the German Gov^t doubt their taking any effective part in
> the proceeding—and they believe that this explains the passive atti-
> tude which the United States has hitherto maintained.
>
> The German Gov^t would be glad to learn as soon as possible in what
> manner we could propose to invite the cooperation of the United
> States, and what our plans are as to the effective action on the part of
> the three Governments or of Great Britain and Germany, failing the
> United States.[48]

Lansdowne's suggestion was never carried out. Three days later, when Metternich mentioned that Berlin was ready to invite American cooperation if the British thought it desirable, Lansdowne "thought it would be sufficient if we were to give the United States Government notice of our intention without asking them to act with us in the matter. Such notice might, I thought, be given when the time drew nearer."[49] There are no indications in the documents as to why Lansdowne changed his mind regarding his own suggestion. In any event, the idea of American participation in the use of force was never revived by either side.

On November 8th, the day of the Kaiser's arrival in Britain on a twelve day visit, Villiers pointed out to Lansdowne that the Admiralty had suggested the end of that month for the proposed operations. Undaunted by the hostile reception given the German Emperor by the British press,[50] Lansdowne and Villiers plunged ahead. On November 11th, instructions went out from the Foreign Office telling Haggard to send a "last" warning to Castro, and ordering Herbert to brief Hay on the Venezuelan situation and to notify him that Britain "was compelled to consider what course it may be necessary to pursue in order to enforce their demands."[51]

That same evening Metternich told Lansdowne that Germany was ready to join Britain in a final warning to Venezuela, but in the ensuing discussion he made it clear that his government wanted a firmer commitment, one that would ensure an equally satisfactory settlement for both countries. Metternich suggested that Britain and Germany rank their claims. He admitted that there was a "sharp distinction" between their "first line" claims, but Germany wanted them "to stand or fall together."

> Each Government ought, therefore, to come to an understanding before it embarked upon a project of coercion that neither Government should be at liberty to recede except by mutual agreement; and before common action was initiated, we ought to come to a distinct agreement to this effect.

Lansdowne thought the request was "reasonable," but he first wanted to examine the question of the "pacific" blockade that the

Germans still wanted to use if the seizure of the gunboats was insufficient. As the Germans "evidently desired that once embarked we should travel with them to the end of the voyage," Lansdowne wrote to Buchanan, "it was reasonable that we should spare no pains to find out whether there were likely to be any obstacles in our course."[52]

Two days later, one possible obstacle was seemingly removed by an encouraging answer from the United States. Hay regretted "that European Powers should use force against Central and South American countries," but the United States "could not object to their taking steps to obtain redress for injuries suffered by their subjects, provided that no acquisition of territory was contemplated."[53] The way was now clear for the final commitment. On November 17th Lansdowne informed Count Bernstorff that Britain agreed that joint action should be carried through until both were satisfied. Now the die was cast. The British had entered into what Lansdowne considered "a hard & fast engagement."[54]

By the time the British claims were ranked in November, the British bondholders had entered the picture once again. On September 23rd the Council of Foreign Bondholders again appealed for government aid. Although the Council had asked for assistance as early as January, 1902, a settlement of the debt default had not been one of the British demands in the July note to Castro, but Villiers was now disposed to wipe the slate clean by including the bondholders' claims in the general settlement. Although the ever-cautious Foreign Office promised the bondholders only that the matter would receive careful consideration, on October 9th the Council sent the Foreign Office a "Bases of Arrangement" that had been drawn up by the Council and the *Disconto Gesellschaft*. Unwilling to get too deeply committed for future action on the bondholders' claims, the Foreign Office balked at the provision by which the British and German governments were to take formal note of the contract and Venezuela was to give a formal understanding to the two never to alienate the hypothecated revenues. The objectionable pledge was dropped, and the bondholders' claims were relegated to the lowest status when the Foreign Office ranked the British claims, but a settlement of Venezuela's external debt was now one of the official goals of the proposed intervention.

By the end of November, Britain's and Germany's plans were nearing completion. After much discussion, the two governments decided to exact immediate payment from Venezuela for their claims of the "first rank"—the British shipping claims and claims for personal injury and illegal imprisonment, and the German claims from the Venezuelan civil war of 1898–1900. The other classes were to be settled by a three member British-German-Venezuelan mixed commission. In order to ensure that the Venezuelans did not take advantage of the ranking of the claims, Lansdowne decided to demand first a general admission of liability from the Venezuelans for all categories of claims. Thus the British ultimatum was drafted to demand that Venezuela recognize in principle the justice of all "well-founded claims which have arisen in consequence of the late civil war and previous civil wars, and of the maltreatment or false imprisonment of British subjects, and also a settlement of the External Debt." Venezuela was to pay the shipping and maltreatment claims at once and accept the decisions of the proposed mixed commission as to the amount and security of the others.[55] Germany drew up a separate ultimatum but both were to be sent simultaneously to Castro on December 7th. If there was no answer in twenty-four hours, Haggard and Pilgrim Baltazzi would leave Caracas for the port of La Guayra, telling the Venezuelan government that their countries' interests were being left in the charge of the United States legation. (Both Britain and Germany took the extra precaution of requesting the United States to take charge of their interests if the need arose.) If there was no answer in another twenty-four hours, they would inform the naval commanders, who would then seize the Venezuelan gunboats.

What measures would follow if this failed to bring results? Since both Germany and Britain opposed any seizure of the customs houses, the much discussed blockade seemed to be the only feasible means of applying more pressure. "I cannot see why," Lansdowne wrote on November 29th, "if the seizure of the gunboats does no good, we should not go in for a blockade which we can enforce in whatever manner seems to us most convenient."[56] However, the nature of the probable blockade was still a matter of dispute. Hoping to avoid the trouble of getting the *Bundesrat*'s consent, the German

Foreign Office wanted a "pacific" blockade, one that would apply to neutral ships but would not lead to their confiscation. This is the type of blockade that the Germans had mentioned to the United States the previous year.[57] But despite German citations of "pacific" blockades used in the past by the British and France, Britain adamantly refused. The Foreign Office admitted that their views in the past had been perhaps more elastic, but the British government now believed that the only legal form of blockade was a "belligerent" one, although the severity of it could be mitigated by any means the two powers wished. Although they still hoped to avoid calling it "belligerent," the Germans agreed to the British conditions on December 6th. Thus by December 7th the two countries had decided that, if needed, a full blockade of the Venezuelan coast would follow the seizure of the gunboats; the details of phraseology were to be worked out when necessary.

In spite of attempts at secrecy, the fact, if not the details, of the imminent Anglo-German action soon leaked out to the press and to the other European Foreign Offices. Wondering how the British and the Germans could get any money out of Venezuela unless they seized the customs houses, the French were afraid that certain liens France had on the Venezuelan customs were in danger. Once assured that their rights would be respected, the French had no further objection; Belgium also had a lien on the Venezuelan customs and was similarly assured that her interests would not be prejudiced. According to France's Delcassé, "the Venezuelans were an extremely troublesome people, as well to France as to the other European countries, and required firm, and indeed severe, handling."[58]

A more serious complication arose in early December when the Italian government came forward with a proposal to take part in the joint action. The Italians were self-invited and the first British and German reactions were unfavorable. At Berlin the German Undersecretary of State reportedly "threw cold water on the idea of Italian participation." Not only were the Germans opposed on practical grounds, but they also feared that the Italian claims were not as well-founded as British and German claims, and that "the action of three Powers might create some feeling in the United States, more especially if the Venezuelans could appeal for sympathy on the ground that bad Italian, and therefore, perhaps bad British and German, claims were being forced upon them." The British Foreign Office was equally opposed. When first approached by the Italian ambassador, Villiers "told him as little as possible" and emphasized the long preparations that had been necessary and the lack of time for any changes. Within the Foreign Office, Larcom argued that Italy's claims "stand on a different basis to ours, and her cooperation would be the reverse of an assistance." Lansdowne agreed. They "could not allow other Powers to 'cut in' at this stage."[59]

However, Foreign Minister Prinetti continued to press the issue. Nervous about criticism in the Italian parliament over the lack of vigor in his defense of Italian interests in Venezuela, Prinetti did not want to miss an opportunity to collect Italy's claims in what seemed to be a safe operation. By linking the Venezuelan issue with a British request for the use of a port in Italian Somaliland for a punitive expedition into the interior, Prinetti was able to influence the British with more than the usual platitudes about Anglo-Italian friendship. Such an African campaign, he observed, would "be more favourably viewed by public opinion here if joint action with England were taken on the other side of the Atlantic."[60]

Lansdowne remained opposed to allowing Italy to take part in the seizure of the Venezuelan gunboats, but he did finally tell Prinetti that the British would gladly consider any suggestions he might have for Italian participation in "ulterior measures." Prinetti decided to inform the Italian parliament that the first phase of German and British action had to do with "offenses against the flag" which did not concern Italy and that Italy would join in pressing ordinary claims. The British Chargé at Rome now found Prinetti in "a calmer state of mind," but the Italian was still afraid that he had missed an opportunity to teach a lesson to "degenerate" Venezuela and to join with Britain and Germany "in establishing a precedent which might be invoked against any future attempts of insubordinate South American Republics to take shelter under the aegis of the Monroe Doctrine."[61]

All the preliminaries to intervention were now completed. There were a few dissenting voices. Chamberlain doubted that cooperation with Germany would be popular,[62] and in Washington the new British Ambassador, Sir Michael Herbert, was having qualms.[63] "I wish we were going to punish Venezuela without the aid of Germany," Herbert wrote Lansdowne on November 19th, "for I am not sure that joint action will be very palatable here." It was an accurate prophecy but one that had little effect on Lansdowne. It was "perhaps unlucky" that they were "harnassed" to the Germans, Lansdowne replied, "but it was quite inevitable."[64] In fact the Foreign Office had worked quite hard to make intervention "inevitable," and there is no reason to believe that they were not satisfied that the stage had been set for a successful coercion of Venezuela. An agreement to cooperate with the Germans had been struck and most of the details hammered out; the United States had been sounded out and notified; the Venezuelans had been warned, the French and Belgians reassured, and the Italians satisfied. All that remained was the expected refusal of Castro to accept the terms of the ultimatums, and then the two naval squadrons would move into action.

NOTES AND REFERENCES

1. C. of F. B., *Annual Report*, 1900–1901, pp. 179–84; Fremantle to Villiers, June 27, 1901. F. O. 15/344.

2. Germany suggested that France and Italy be invited to join.

3. Paget to Lansdowne, September 4, 1901. F. O. 15/344.

4. Villiers' minute on Phipps to Lansdowne, April 14, 1901. F. O. 15/344.

5. For the March 26th agreement, see C. of F. B., *Annual Report*, 1901–1902, pp. 176–78.

6. Villiers' memorandum of March 28, 1902. F. O. 15/352.

7. Lascelles to Lansdowne, April 6, 1902; Phipps to Lansdowne, April 6th; Monson to Lansdowne, April 7th; Currie to Lansdowne, April 3rd. F. O. 15/352.

8. Paget to Lansdowne, April 13 and April 17, 1902, and despatch of April 17th; Paget to Villiers, private, April 18th. F. O. 15/352.

9. Bickford to Admiralty, April 19, 1902. (Received F. O. May 17th). F. O. 15/352.

10. Hunter to Hay, February 26, 1902, United States Department of State, *Papers Relating to the Foreign Relations of the United States*, 1902, (Washington, 1903), pp. 569–77. Cited hereafter as U.S., *Foreign Relations*.

11. Hay to Hunter, March 22, 1902. U.S., *Foreign Relations*, 1902, p. 578. See Adee to Penfield, March 13, 1902. National Archives, Records of the Department of State, Despatches from United States Ministers to Central America, vol. 46, Guatemala and Honduras. Cited hereafter as State Department Despatches.

12. U.S., *Foreign Relations*, 1902, pp. 426–27, 578.

13. Hay to Bailey, July 3, 1902; Bailey to Hay, July 24, 1902. *Ibid.*, p. 579.

14. Annual message of December 3, 1901. *A Compilation of the Messages and Papers of the Presidents*, XV, 6662–63.

15. The German bondholders did not have a protective association as yet. The bankers issuing the bonds represented the interests of their clients when necessary.

16. C. of F. B., *Annual Report*, 1901–1902, pp. 439–44; C. of F. B. to F. O., September 23, 1902. F. O. 420/206.

17. Haggard to Lansdowne, July 26 and August 21, 1901. F. O. 80/435. See Russell to Hay, June 30, 1901, and reply of July 17th. U.S., *Foreign Relations*, 1901, pp. 550–51.

18. Haggard to Lansdowne, September 21, 1901. F. O. 80/427.

19. Haggard to Lansdowne, October 5, 1901. F. O. 80/427.

20. Haggard to Lansdowne, September 6, 1901. F. O. 80/427. See also Haggard's of September 15th. F. O. 80/435.

21. Lascelles to Lansdowne, October 25, 1901. F. O. 64/1522.

22. Buchanan to Lansdowne, December 17, 1901. F. O. 80/435. The German Ambassador at Washington talked personally with both Roosevelt and Hay about the Venezuelan problem, and, on December 11, 1901, the German Embassy sent the State Department a promemoria on the subject. Germany told the United States that they might be forced to blockade Venezuela or even temporarily occupy the customs houses, but they assured the Americans that "under no circumstances do we consider in our proceedings the acquisition or the permanent occupation of Venezuelan territory." In reply Hay merely quoted from Roosevelt's message to Congress of December 3rd and expressed the hope that Germany would live up to her assurances. See U.S., *Foreign Relations*, 1901, pp. 192–95. In light of the later uproar, the reaction of the American press to the German soundings was surprisingly friendly. See *The Literary Digest*, January 11, 1902, pp. 27–28.

23. *Die Grosse Politik der Europaischen Kabinette, 1871–1914* (Berlin, 1922–1927), XVII, footnote p. 242. Cited hereafter as *Die Grosse Politik*.

24. C. of F. B. to F. O., January 3, 1902. F. O. 80/443. On receipt of the Council's letter, Villiers noted that he expected a similar appeal from the British owned Venezuelan railways.

25. Haggard to Lansdowne, December 13, 1901 (received January 4th). F. O. 80/435.

26. Draft of F. O. to C. O., January 16, 1902. F. O. 80/443.

27. Lansdowne to Lascelles, January 14, 1902. F. O. 80/443.

28. After the unpopular blockade was over, the inevitable question came up in Parliament regarding the origin of the proposal for Anglo-German cooperation. After studying the January 14th despatch, Lansdowne asked for the earlier papers. Villiers sent them with the following explanation: "Mr. Haggard's despatches were sent to Berlin in order to obtain information of what the Germans intended to do. There is no trace of H. M. G. having made any suggestion that we should cooperate. On the contrary, Mr. Haggard . . . was approved for his language in declining to suggest intervention." Thus the Foreign Secretary told Parliament that the "first definite proposal for cooperation" came from Germany on July 23rd. Villiers made no mention of any conversation with Eckhardstein on January 2nd. See Mr. Norman's question of February 19, 1903, and Villiers' note to Lansdowne of February 19th in F. O. 80/482.

29. Bulow to the Kaiser, January 20, 1902. *German Diplomatic Documents, 1871–1914*, ed. Edgar T. S. Dugdale, III, 161. Cited hereafter as *German Diplomatic Documents*; and *Die Grosse Politik*, pp. 241–43.

30. Haggard to Lansdowne, April 4, 1902. F. O. 80/443. In February Pilgrim Baltazzi mentioned Prince Henry's visit to the U.S. as a possible reason for the delay. Larcom found that explanation "not convincing." See Haggard's despatch of 17 February and Larcom's minute. F. O. 80/443. Villiers later stated his belief that the delay had been due to the influence of German merchants who were afraid that their interests would suffer if coercive measures were taken against Castro. See Villiers' minute to Haggard's despatch of August 17, 1902. F. O. 80/444.

31. From December 1901 to March 1902 the Foreign Office received appeals from: LaGuayra and Caracas Railway Co. Lmt., Venezuelan Central Railway Co. Lmt.,

Bolivar Railway Co. Lmt., LaGuayra Harbour Corporation Lmt., Venezuelan Telephone and Electrical Appliances Co. Lmt., and the Atlas Trust, Lmt.

32. The *Ban Righ* was allowed to leave Trinidad after Colombia assured Britain that she was a public ship and would not be used for further irregular hostilities.

33. Haggard to Lansdowne, June 30, 1902. F. O. 420/206.

34. Haggard to Lansdowne, June 27, 1902. F. O. 80/443.

35. Adee to Bowen, August 21, 1902. National Archives, Records of the Department of State, Diplomatic Instructions, Venezuela, vol. 5. Cited hereafter as State Department Instructions.

36. Haggard to Lansdowne, despatch 132, June 30, 1902, (received F. O. July 16th); minutes of Davidson of July 17th and Hurst of July 18th; Villiers to Lansdowne of July 19th with Lansdowne's minute. F. O. 80/443.

37. Lansdowne to Buchanan, July 23, 1902. F. O. 420/206.

38. Lansdowne to Villiers, n.d., with Larcom memorandum of July 20, 1902. F. O. 80/443; Lansdowne to Haggard, July 29, 1902. F. O. 420/206. Haggard to Lansdowne, August 5, 1902, F. O. 80/444.

39. Lansdowne to Buchanan, 318, November 26, 1902. F. O. 420/206.

40. Admiralty to Foreign Office, August 14 and October 10, 1902. F. O. 420/206.

41. Villiers to Lansdowne, October 11, 1902. Lansdowne's memorandum on the Cabinet meeting, October 21, 1902. F. O. 80/445.

42. Lansdowne's memorandum dated October 17, 1902, presented to the Cabinet October 21st. F. O. 80/445.

43. According to Lord Hamilton, the Cabinet only accepted Lansdowne's Venezuelan policy because it was preoccupied with the Education Bill and that Lansdowne "was for once caught napping." Hamilton to Curzon, December 19 and 24, 1902. In George Monger, *The End of Isolation, British Foreign Policy, 1900–1907* (London, 1963), pp. 105–106.

44. See Beale, *op. cit.*, pp. 403–5, 416–17.

45. Before taking the matter to the Cabinet, Lansdowne asked Villiers: "Am I right in believing that the U.S. have publicly announced that they do not intend to raise objections?" In answer Villiers referred to the exchange of notes the previous December between Holleben and Hay published in the State Department's *Foreign Relations* papers for 1901. Villiers' memorandum to Lansdowne, October 18, 1902. F. O. 80/445.

46. Haggard to Lansdowne, October 9, November 23, November 25, and December 23, 1901. F. O. 80/427.

47. Haggard to Lansdowne, September 30, 1901, and minutes. Haggard showed the extract from Bowen's book *(International Law, A Simple Statement of its Principles)* to Pilgrim Baltazzi who found it "very interesting and important." Pilgrim Baltazzi asked Haggard for a copy of it to send to his Government, "as apparently

this view of the Monroe Doctrine was new to him." F. O. 80/427. Bowen believed that a talk he had with Pilgrim Baltazzi about his book led to the German approach to Washington in December of 1901. See Herbert W. Bowen, *Recollections Diplomatic and Undiplomatic* (New York, 1926), pp. 254–55.

48. Thomas H. Sanderson memorandum of August 16, 1902, and Lansdowne's minute. F. O. 80/444.

49. Lansdowne to Lascelles, August 19, 1902. F. O. 420/206.

50. C. S. Campbell, *op. cit.*, pp. 272–73. This visit later gave rise to the interpretation that the Balfour ministry had been "hypnotized" by the wily Kaiser. See the *Literary Digest*, December 27, 1902, pp. 879–80; and February 7, 1903, pp. 196–97.

51. Lansdowne to Haggard, November 11, 1902; Lansdowne to Herbert, November 11, 1902. F. O. 420/206.

52. Lansdowne to Buchanan, November 11, 1902. F. O. 420/206.

53. Herbert to Lansdowne, November 13, 1902. F. O. 420/206.

54. Lansdowne to Buchanan, November 17, 1902. See also Villiers' minute of November 13th with Lansdowne's comments. F. O. 80/445; and *Die Grosse Politik*, pp. 250–55.

55. Lansdowne to Haggard, 50, December 2, 1902. F. O. 420/206.

56. Lansdowne to Villiers, November 29, 1902. F. O. 80/446.

57. See the German Embassy's promemoria to the State Department of December 20, 1901. U.S., *Foreign Relations*, 1901, p. 196.

58. Monson to Lansdowne, December 3, 1902. F. O. 420/206.

59. Buchanan to Lansdowne, December 2, 1902, and minutes by Larcom, Villiers and Lansdowne. F. O. 80/447. Lansdowne to Buchanan, December 7, 1902. F. O. 420/206.

60. Rodd to Lansdowne, December 3, 1902. F. O. 420/206.

61. Lansdowne to Rodd, December 5, 1902; Rodd to Lansdowne, December 8th. F. O. 420/206.

62. As early as February of 1902 the Colonial Office wrote to Lansdowne "that it does not appear to Mr. Chamberlain that joint action with Germany, as suggested by Mr. Haggard, would at the present time be likely to lead to useful results." C. O. to F. O., February 19, 1902. F. O. 80/443. Chamberlain was in South Africa when the joint intervention took place, and, in January of 1903, he wrote to his son: "I warned Lansdowne before leaving that joint action with Germany would be unpopular and I very much regret that we did not go into the matter alone." Joseph Chamberlain to Austen Chamberlain, January 9, 1903. Quoted in Monger, *op. cit.*, p. 105.

63. Ambassador Pauncefote died in May of 1902 and Herbert did not arrive in Washington until early in October.

64. Herbert to Lansdowne, private, November 19, 1902; Lansdowne to Herbert, December 4, 1902. Lansdowne Papers, U.S., vol. 28.

CHAPTER II

The Venezuelan Intervention, 1902-1903

On the afternoon of December 7, 1902, Haggard and Pilgrim Baltazzi sent their ultimatums to President Castro, and, not receiving an answer within twenty-four hours, they left for La Guayra. After another day with no reply, Haggard boarded HMS *Retribution*, and the naval commanders immediately began seizing the Venezuelan gunboats, capturing three and disabling one at La Guayra on December 9. On the same day British ships seized another gunboat at Port of Spain, Trinidad, and in the following days the rest of the Venezuelan navy was taken by the British and German fleets.

The Venezuelans did not resist the seizures of their gunboats, but the early naval operations did lead to some incidents that would soon prove embarrassing to the British and German governments, the first being the destruction of the two gunboats captured by the Germans at La Guayra. As the two ships were unable to steam and would hamper his movements, the German commander, Commodore Scheder, wanted to destroy his prizes. When Haggard, Pilgrim Baltazzi, and Captain Lyon of HMS *Retribution* protested, Scheder relented and ordered the *Panther* to tow the gunboats to Curaçao. But when Scheder decided to send a landing party ashore in answer to an appeal from the frightened German consul, he ordered the prizes sunk in order to free the *Panther* to cover the landing party. Haggard believed the sinkings were regrettable and unnecessary, and Pilgrim Baltazzi "was as much vexed as any one."[1] The same night that the Germans rescued their consul, Captain Lyon landed an armed party to bring aboard the British vice-consul and others. On December 11 Lyon put ashore another party for the threatened personnel of the British owned La Guayra Harbour Corporation. The rescues were accomplished without violence, but the second landing had been carried out in a potentially dangerous situation.

The most criticized British action was their part in the bombardment of the Venezuelan forts at Puerto Cabello in retaliation for the seizure there of the British merchant ship *Topaze*. When HMS *Charybdis* and the German cruiser *Vineta* arrived at Puerto Cabello on December 13th, they found that the British crew had already been released, but the British commander, Commodore Montgomerie, was incensed to learn that the captain of the *Topaze* had been forced to haul down his flag. He demanded an apology for the insult to the British flag and assurances that British and German subjects would not be molested. When the Venezuelans did not answer within Montgomerie's time limit, the British and German cruisers bombarded the forts and sent in landing parties to destroy the Venezuelan guns ashore. No one was killed in the shelling and Venezuelan resistance was minimal.

Montgomerie's superiors were far from happy with this instance of Anglo-German cooperation. Admiral Douglas castigated the action as "premature and unnecessarily provocative," and there was some sentiment within the Admiralty for censuring Montgomerie. Montgomerie had not violated any instructions, but, as an Admiralty official told Villiers, the incident at Puerto Cabello was "more important from its political significance than from the naval discipline aspect."[2] Talk of censuring Montgomerie soon subsided, but the "political significance" of these events did not. They were immediately seized upon by British and American critics of the whole idea of Anglo-German cooperation and used as ammunition in their agitation against the Venezuelan adventure.

While the British and German fleets were disposing of Venezuela's gunboats, the home governments were preparing for the naval blockade, the planned second phase of the coercion. In London, on December 10th, a conference at the House of Lords decided that each power would blockade a separate section of the Venezuelan coast and issue its own instructions to the naval squadrons. On the following day, Lansdowne told Metternich that he saw no reason why the blockade should not start as soon as possible, and the Admiralty instructed Admiral Douglas to set it in motion as soon as the two squadrons were ready. The last technicality was cleared up on December 13 when Bernsdorff told Villiers that Berlin had decided to use a "belligerent" rather than a "pacific" blockade, being "desirous to remove all points of difference" between the two governments. The Germans were already beginning to feel the heat of British and American criticism, and the Kaiser was more than willing to follow Bulow's advice to accept "the British programme." Thus, when on December 18th the United States questioned the legality of a "pacific" blockade, Lansdowne was able to reply that Britain had always opposed the use of such a blockade and there was "now no difference of opinion" between Germany and Britain.[3] On December 20 Britain and Germany formally announced their blockade of the Venezuelan coast.

Meanwhile the dual intervention had become a tripartite one. Fulfilling his promise to the Italians that they would be allowed to cooperate in the second stage of the coercion, Lansdowne, on December 9th, told the Italian ambassador that his country was welcome to join. The Italians were quick to accept the invitation and within a few days they presented their demands to Venezuela and withdrew their representative from Caracas. The Germans had no objections, and, although Italian participation was to be minimal and the agreement much more informal, Great Britain and Germany had acquired a new partner.

In spite of the successful coordination of the plans for a blockade, it was obvious from the beginning that the British government was in for stormy weather. There was some immediate criticism in the British press, and, as early as December 8th, Liberal leaders in Parliament were raising questions over the Venezuelan venture. Most of the early queries were for information, but after some of the correspondence was laid before Parliament on the 12th, the questions became more pointed. On December 15th, a full-fledged debate broke out in which the government's critics denied the necessity of the intervention, criticized the tactics of the Foreign Office, deplored the agreement with Germany, and questioned the effects of the affair on relations with the United States.[4] The opposition was up in arms, and the Parliamentary attack was terminated only because the session ended on schedule December 18th. To Sir Henry Campbell-Bannerman, the Liberal leader, the joint intervention was "a blunder with the seed of war in it," and, along with other Conservative iniquities, it made a "nice Christmas pie."[5]

Nor was all going well at Caracas. Instead of capitulating immediately on British and German terms, Castro decided to call for arbitration. Lansdowne was now faced with a delicate situation, for Castro relayed his arbitration proposal to the European powers via the State Department at Washington. Lansdowne was at his country house when the request was delivered on December 13th, but when the Foreign Secretary returned to London two days later he hastened to consult Metternich, as well as Henry White, who was in charge of the American Embassy in the absence of Ambassador Choate.

Since Metternich had been told by Berlin to comment upon the Venezuelan proposal as if he were merely giving his personal opinion, Lansdowne was uncertain of Germany's official reaction, but Metternich's remarks indicated that the Germans had little desire to alter their course.

> Speaking, however, for himself, he observed that while we should, no doubt, all of us desire to meet such a proposal in a manner agreeable to the United States Government, there seemed to him to be considerable objections to encouraging the idea of arbitration. He observed, moreover, that the proposal was merely passed on to us, and not in anyway supported by the United States Government.

Metternich argued that some of the claims had already been carefully considered and were not arbitrable. The two governments had already agreed on a mixed commission for the rest, and it was open to question whether Venezuela would honor its obligations under arbitration. Lansdowne wrote to Buchanan:

> I told His Excellency that some of these objections had already oc-
> curred to me, and that I thought we might add to them the further
> argument that the Venezuelan proposal was a belated one, and that
> the Venezuelan Government should not have waited to make it until
> we had given them three distinct warnings, and been finally driven to
> resort to coercive measures.[6]

That same day Lansdowne told White that he had not yet been able
to consult the Cabinet about the arbitration proposal, but that it
would obviously require "very careful" examination.

> I also mentioned to Mr. White that I observed that the proposal was
> merely forwarded by the United States' Government, and not in any-
> way recommended for our acceptance.
> Mr. White said that this was no doubt the case.[7]

But White also took advantage of his talk with Lansdowne on the
15th to express his own "grave apprehension" that a continuation of
hostilities could lead to some "untoward incident" that might arouse
American public opinion. Indeed, the indefatigable White was busy
spreading dire warnings throughout his wide circle of acquaintances
in London. He wrote to Hay on December 15th, "I am expressing
privately to my friends in the Government grave fears, of course as
my personal opinion only, lest Great Britain will, if hostilities continue, be involved . . . in some action which will estrange if not
antagonize American public feeling."[8] That day White also met Balfour at the House of Commons and "very frankly" told the Prime
Minister of his "feelings of anxiety at the whole situation and my
earnest hope that he would not allow his government to be led by
Germany into doing something to exacerbate our public opinion."[9]

As the critical debate in Parliament took place on the evening of
the 15th, the Cabinet knew they were saddled with an unpopular
and possibly dangerous adventure. Despite the obvious drawbacks to
arbitration that had been voiced, they decided on December 16th to
suggest to the Germans a modification of their plans. The "first-line"
claims could not be arbitrated, but as Lansdowne told Metternich, it

"seemed to us . . . worthy of consideration whether we might not admit the principle of arbitration" for the other claims "and perhaps invite the United States to arbitrate upon them."[10]

While the worried British government was waiting to hear the German reaction to a limited arbitration, the Roosevelt administration came out openly in favor of arbitration. The day following the Cabinet meeting, White received instructions from Hay to urge upon the British government "the great desirability" of arbitration. White did so "urgently," but Lansdowne was unable to tell him of the decision of the Cabinet until the German answer arrived.[11] To add to their worries, on the same day the Foreign Office received the first of Herbert's warnings from Washington. The British Ambassador reported a "growing feeling of irritation" in Congress due to the sinking of the Venezuelan gunboats and the bombardment of Puerto Cabello. The administration was "undoubtedly apprehensive" over the designs of Germany. "From the point of view of the good feeling in America towards Great Britain, our friends here regret that we are co-operating with Germany, as an impression prevails in Washington that we are being made use of by her."[12]

The Germans already knew there was widespread hostility in Britain and the United States toward the joint action. On December 16th Metternich warned from London that the British government was, "in the long run, too weak to stick to its guns" and "that the sooner we can honorably withdraw from this business in concert with England, the better it will be." That same day Ambassador von Holleben in Washington recommended accepting arbitration for its effect on American opinion.[13] Whether during the early days of the Venezuelan crisis Roosevelt delivered some form of warning or ultimatum to the Germans to accept arbitration has been a matter of hot dispute between American diplomatic historians.[14] If Roosevelt did indulge in decisive secret diplomacy as he later claimed, the British government knew nothing of it. In any event, Germany once again followed the British lead. As Metternich told Lansdowne on December 18th, Germany was "prepared to accept at every point" the British suggestions. A resort to arbitration would have a "salutary effect" and "action should be taken upon the Venezuelan proposal at once, without waiting until Washington 'exchanged the role of post-office for one of a more active character.' " The Germans wanted to invite President Roosevelt to act as arbitrator, but if this were not possible, the matter would have to be intrusted to the Hague.[15]

The British Cabinet's acceptance of the principle of arbitration on the afternoon of the 18th was a matter of formality. Lansdowne told White that there would be reservations and "the measures of coercion now in progress" would continue, but he carefully pointed out that the British decision had really been made before White had carried out Hay's instructions on the 17th. As White reported the discussion to Hay, Lansdowne wanted him "to acquaint you privately for the President's information" that the Cabinet had accepted arbitration on the 16th, and that the British government "are the better pleased to find that they had of their own accord adopted a course which would find favor with the Government of the United States."[16]

The decision to arbitrate was not the only sign of British solicitude for American feelings during these critical days. During their conversation on the 15th, Lansdowne told White that Britain did not at present contemplate landing any armed forces in Venezuela and would make every effort to avoid it in the future. Lansdowne wanted to keep this secret from the Venezuelans, but at the Cabinet meeting of December 16th Balfour persuaded his colleagues to make a public statement. When asked in the House of Lords that day whether any further coercive measures were intended by the government, Lansdowne replied that a blockade was planned but that it was not intended "to land a British force, and still less to occupy Venezuelan territory." Balfour was even more explicit in the House of Commons the following day: "We have no intention, and have never had any intention, of landing troops in Venezuela or of occupying territory, even though that occupation might only be of a temporary nature." At the same time the Admiralty instructed the captains of the British squadron "not to land men, nor bombard forts, nor sink ships without authority from the Admiralty."[17] The ban on unauthorized bombardments and sinkings was not mentioned in the public statements, but White learned of these "stringent orders" and was told that permission "will not be granted save under circumstances at present unforeseen."[18]

And of course there was always the Monroe Doctrine. The Parliamentary debate of December 15th abounded with references to the great American dogma, and in his defense of the government Lord Cranborne, the Foreign Office's Parliamentary Undersecretary of State, rose to the occasion:

> It has been asked what view the United States takes of the situation. I can inform the House that the United States takes the very reasonable and sensible view of the situation that was to be expected from that country. They recognize that the insistence of England that the Venezuelan Government should meet its engagements and respect the rights of British subjects is in no way an infraction of the Monroe Doctrine, and they recognize that no nation in the world has been more anxious than England to assist them in maintaining that doctrine.[19]

After Great Britain and Germany accepted the principle of arbitration, it is little wonder that Roosevelt could write to ex-President Cleveland to congratulate him "on the rounding out of your policy."[20]

Obviously the Anglo-German operation had taken a turn not foreseen by its planners. But what exactly had they given up? Arbitration by either Roosevelt or the Hague was certainly riskier than the mixed British-German-Venezuelan commission originally envisioned, and although they had never planned to land troops to occupy Venezuelan territory, the British at least had publicly restricted themselves. But the extent of the capitulation can be overemphasized, for an analysis of the reservations or conditions that the coercing powers attached to their acceptance of arbitration shows that they were still intent on protecting the interests of their claimants.

For example, in the British answer of December 23rd to the arbitration proposal, the Foreign Office no longer demanded an admission of liability for all the claims, but there were still a number of significant conditions. Not only were the first class claims exempted from arbitration, but Venezuela had to admit that a liability existed in principle for all claims for injury to, or wrongful seizure of, property. In these cases the arbitrator would only decide whether the injury took place or if the seizure was unlawful and, if so, what compensation was due. The other claims could be arbitrated without reservations. In addition, the tribunal was to define the security for the claims and the means to be used in guaranteeing punctual payments. It is true that when Lansdowne gave the British conditions to White, he "intimated" that, if the United States wanted any alterations or modifications, Britain "would be happy to consider any such provided they did not involve any question of principle."[21] But it was still clear that the arbitration would be limited, and that both Germany and Britain were determined to maintain the blockade until their conditions were accepted.

Up to this point there had been no friction between the British and German governments, but they were surprised by the virulence of the anti-German feelings in Britain. Ironically, Lansdowne's own Venezuelan policy had greatly intensified the new British Germanophobia which he himself deplored. The Foreign Secretary found the uproar "furious and unreasoning." He wrote Herbert: "The violence of the anti-German feeling here has been extraordinary & has produced a profound impression on the German mind. It has however been allowed to go much too far." Much the same could have been said about opinion across the Atlantic, but here the British had the consolation of knowing that most of the odium was being directed at Germany and not Britain. "The explosion of feeling against Germany here is somewhat remarkable," Herbert reported. "I confess to regarding it with malevolent satisfaction, especially when I think of all the German efforts to discredit us and to flatter America during the past twelve months."[22]

Obviously the crux of the problem now was to find a fast solution to terminate the unpopular partnership with Germany. One of the reasons that Lansdowne preferred Roosevelt to the Hague was the prospect that arbitration by the American President would produce a faster settlement. When Roosevelt declined the offer to act as arbitrator, the disappointed Lansdowne was sure that if Roosevelt "had undertaken the job we might probably have got through with a minimum of pedantry and red tape." It was now probable, he wrote to Balfour, that Venezuela "will haggle over our conditions, and I should be rather afraid of the U.S. Govt. being too officious in its attempts to bring us together."[23]

This desire for a rapid solution weighed heavily in the British decision to deal with Bowen as a representative of Castro. When Castro recognized the European claims in principle on January 1, 1903, he also asked that Bowen go to Washington and arrange for either an immediate settlement or for the preliminaries to the Hague.[24] Once again Lansdowne was unsure of the American government's position. Did the Roosevelt administration desire this unorthodox procedure? Hay assured Herbert that Castro's selection of Bowen had not been prompted by the United States and that Roosevelt would refuse to allow Bowen to represent Venezuela if the European powers objected. If Bowen were accepted he would be "absolutely independent" of the U. S. government and would get no instructions from the State Department. In London, White also emphasized that Bowen's designation was not due to the "suggestion or wish" of his government. The United States thought that Bowen had been chosen apparently "in the interest of prompt and favourable action."[25]

Prompt and favorable action was precisely what Lansdowne wanted. In passing on the Venezuelan proposal to Balfour, the Foreign Secretary urged the advantages of negotiating with Bowen rather than using the slow and complicated machinery of the Hague. Lansdowne did not know whether Balfour thought that "at this stage, as in earlier ones," the United States was "assuming too conspicuous a part in the proceedings," but he himself did not think it wise "to exclude entirely the good offices of mutual friends." The Prime Minister assured Lansdowne that he did not resent the American connection.

> I have no objection whatever, as you seem to suppose, to Hay's action. I thought their original offer a little previous, as I feared it was open to the interpretation that they were forcing arbitration upon us. Whether this was so, or not, their subsequent action seems to be all that could be wished.[26]

Balfour was as anxious for a fast settlement as Lansdowne, but he was apprehensive over the reports from Caracas that Bowen was "anti-British and cantankerous." Was there "any danger of his being captured by the extreme American jingoes at Washington and asking for impossible terms?" Haggard had already warned that Bowen was "a mischievous man, and that it would be suicidal to allow him to have a voice in any settlement," and, just as the matter was being considered, a secret despatch arrived from Haggard in which he considerably expanded upon his theme. Bowen was described as an intriguer, working for his own ends by backing Venezuela and belittling Haggard himself. The British Minister was convinced that the defiant attitude of the Venezuelan government stemmed from Bowen's encouragement, and "it was really a matter of common knowledge in Caracas that he was trying to build up his own influence by doing his best to thwart us." Herbert in Washington was not opposed to negotiating with Bowen, who "would probably be more practical to deal with than a Venezuelan," but he was not hopeful of an immediate settlement and admitted that Bowen might play up to the "anti-foreign element" in the United States.[27]

Lansdowne, however, was able to convince himself that he could discount bad reports from Caracas because Haggard had quarrelled with Bowen in the past; even before Herbert's views arrived, the Foreign Secretary was busy trying to secure the necessary German concurrence. Once again the Germans cooperated, and on January 5th the news was relayed to Caracas. Three days later Castro accepted the British and German reservations, and Bowen confidentially promised that the claims would be guaranteed by the Venezuelan customs revenues. This was considered sufficient by the blockading powers, and Bowen was soon on his way to the United States aboard an American warship.

While Bowen was crossing the Caribbean, the Foreign Office was drafting detailed instructions for Herbert to follow in the coming negotiations. The British Ambassador first had to find out whether Bowen's instructions were "in strict accordance" with the British reservations laid down in December, and particularly whether he was authorized to settle the "first line" claims immediately, now

estimated by the Foreign Office at £5,500. The second rank claims
—about £600,000—could be paid in cash, but Britain would accept
a guarantee "based on security which must be adequate, and which
the Venezuelan Government must be bound not to alienate for any
other purpose." These claims, unlike the first rank, could be reviewed by a mixed commission. As for the third class claims, a new
arrangement had to be made with the bondholders, including "a
definition of the sources from which the necessary payments are to
be provided." If there was no direct settlement, Herbert was to
arrange preliminaries to refer all the claims, except the first rank, to
the Hague. If Bowen should raise the question of Patos Island or the
Ban Righ case, Herbert was to reply that he had no authority to
discuss them.[28] Nor did the blockading powers have any intention of
raising the blockade until their conditions were met. When on January 12th White carried out his orders to "suggest discreetly" that the
blockade be lifted, Lansdowne refused, holding out "no hopes" that
the pressure would be removed until a satisfactory settlement had
been attained.[29]

At this point Lansdowne was rather optimistic. As he wrote to
Herbert, he was sure that they had been wise not to discourage the
unconventional procedure of dealing with Bowen at Washington.
Even assuming Bowen "to be a bit of a rogue & an accomplice of
Castro," it was better than dealing with the Venezuelans. Venezuela
was in favor of an early settlement, and Bowen should be "keen to
come to terms" with Herbert. Lansdowne's only fear was the possibility that the American government might "exhibit too much interest in the proceedings, & anything like officiousness on their part, &,
still more, the appearance of dictation, w^d do endless harm here &
perhaps spoil the game altogether."[30]

Once the negotiations got underway at Washington, it seemed that
Lansdowne's optimism was well founded. The three blockading powers decided to hold separate negotiations with Bowen, and Herbert's
first meetings with the American seemed promising. Although Herbert found Bowen to be rather overbearing and "very adverse to
putting anything on paper," he was able to report on January 23rd
that he had Bowen's "written acceptance of our conditions without

reserve."[31] On the following day the news arrived in London that Bowen had accepted both the German and Italian conditions in principle. Even the change of German representatives at Washington seemed to bode well for the future. After dismissing Ambassador von Holleben in early January and leaving the German Chargé d' Affaires, Count von Quadt, to handle the early negotiations with Bowen, the Kaiser decided to send Baron Speck von Sternburg, a personal friend of Roosevelt, to Washington. On January 22nd Bernsdorff told the Foreign Office that Sternburg was on his way "with more detailed verbal instructions exactly in accordance" with those sent to Herbert, and again there were assurances that Berlin was "most desirous of acting on every point in agreement" with the British.[32]

The darkest cloud forming over the negotiations at this stage was caused by the German blockading squadron rather than the diplomats. While crossing the bar at Maracaibo on January 17th, the *Panther* was fired upon by Fort San Carlos, and four days later Commodore Scheder bombarded and destroyed the fort. The British fleet was not involved—Admiral Douglas had not been consulted and was quick to telegraph the Admiralty that he did not support Scheder's action—but the storm of protest aroused by Germany's new naval exploit did create a climate of opinion in the United States that worried the British diplomats. Herbert was "very nervous as to what was going to happen, for complications with Germany mean trouble with us," and, as he later wrote, the "friendly feeling towards us began to change after the unfortunate bombardment of Maracaibo." In London, while making one of his usual warnings about American opinion, White found Balfour "much annoyed and perturbed" over the German bombardment.[33]

The bombardment was proof positive of the dangers of prolonging the blockade, but unfortunately for the British the news from Washington soon indicated that the once promising negotiations were bogging down. Two troublesome issues now developed that threatened to wreck the entire proceedings: the Germans wanted immediate payment of all first rank claims, and both the Germans and the British refused to have their claims treated on the same basis as the claims of countries not taking part in the blockade.

From the very beginning the British and the Germans agreed on the principle of preferential treatment for the blockading powers. When Metternich expressed "some alarm" that Bowen was going to deal with the claims of other countries as well as their own, Lansdowne agreed that Britain and Germany "stood on an entirely different footing from the rest," and that it would be impossible for their ministers "to take part in a general discussion at which a number of other Powers would also be represented."[34] Unfortunately, nothing had been said about preferential treatment in the conditions accepted by Venezuela, and Bowen was in a position to argue, with some justice, that it was a new demand.

The problem came up during the negotiations in connection with the security offered by Bowen for the second class claims. Bowen proposed that thirty percent of the customs receipts from the ports of La Guayra and Puerto Cabello be turned over to Venezuela's creditors each month, and if Venezuela failed to do so, the creditor nations could administer the two customs houses until all claims were paid. Although Herbert was decidedly in favor of the plan, Lansdowne found it unacceptable because of Bowen's insistence that each of Venezuela's creditors receive a share of the thirty percent and his refusal to give priority payment to the blockading powers because of commitments he had made with Venezuela's other creditors. The most Bowen would agree to were shares proportionate to the size of each country's claims. This was not enough for Lansdowne, who refused to admit that any pledges by Bowen were binding on Britain. Lansdowne did not insist that all of the thirty percent go to the blockading powers, but he did want a separate arrangement by which Britain, Germany, and Italy would get a portion of the customs receipts adequate to pay off their claims in a suggested six year period.

The Foreign Secretary was already regretting the decision to negotiate with Bowen. On January 28th Lansdowne complained to Herbert via telegram:

> Bowen does not seem to be behaving very well. I should be glad to have privately your impression of him. If he will not meet us reasonably, we shall have to break off and fall back on the Hague. You should

let him understand plainly that public opinion here has to be reckoned with.

"I have been very careful to conceal my impression of him and one has to take American diplomatists as one finds them," Herbert cabled back, but his opinion of Bowen was "not good" since Bowen had "behaved badly" in communicating his version of the negotiations to the press and had tried to "sow discord" between von Quadt and Herbert. But despite his tribulations, Herbert was opposed to ending the negotiations because "the tension here is very great & I realize the danger of an explosion of public opinion if the blockade continues much longer."[35]

By the end of January there was a seeming deadlock over preferential treatment while Bowen remained "very obdurate." Not only should the question of preferential treatment have been raised at the beginning of negotiations, Bowen argued, but it was "unjust, unfair, and illegal" in regard to Venezuela's other creditors, and he said if "I recognize that brute force alone can be respected in the collection of claims I should encourage the said other nations to use force also." His only concession was to offer the blockading powers the customs revenues for one month if the demand for preferential treatment had been raised "simply as a point of honour."[36]

While the British and the Germans were in general agreement on the matter of priority, the dispute between Bowen and the Germans over payment of the German first-class claims became an acute embarrassment for the British. The German first-class claims had originated during the Venezuelan civil war of 1898–1900 and consisted of claims from German merchants and landlords against the government for the plundering of homes and lands, for extorting forced loans, and for appropriations of supplies without payment. These claims had been reviewed, and in some cases reduced, by the legal department of the German Foreign Office and were not considered arbitrable by the German government. Before intervention began, Lansdowne had particularly obligated the British to aid Germany in settling them. While Metternich had admitted a "sharp distinction" between the first rank claims of the two countries, they were "to stand or fall together."[37] After the intervention got underway Metternich soon forgot his "sharp distinction," but Britain's obligation to the Germans remained.

When the negotiations began in Washington, the British were still determined to exact a cash payment for their first class claims. Lansdowne flatly rejected Bowen's proposal to pay them out of the customs receipts as they were "of a different nature to any others, and, although trifling in amount, are of the first importance in principle." When Bowen agreed to an immediate payment of £5,500 to the British, the Foreign Office was under the impression that Germany would be content with accepting security for all their claims.[38] To their dismay the British discovered that Berlin had also requested immediate payment of the German first rank claims—now estimated at £66,000.

Balfour, who was now faced by strong pressure for an immediate settlement even within his own Cabinet, was particularly unhappy. He had known little about the nature of the German first rank claims, and during the Parliamentary debate in December his critics had charged that his government had foolishly bound itself to collect German debts. Unconvinced by Metternich's argument that "the only difference in the nature of the first-rank English or German claims is that the one refer to ill-treatment on sea, the other to ill-treatment on land," the Prime Minister equated the German first class claims with the British second class.[39] As he wrote to Lansdowne, the "new situation created by the last German demand is embarrassing." If the government prolonged the blockade by further negotiations, they ran the risk of dangerous complications. On the other hand, if they reversed their instructions to Herbert demanding immediate payment of the British first class claims, "our parliamentary position will be much endangered—and the statements that we have been acting throughout as Germany's catspaw will receive apparent confirmation." Balfour preferred the latter risk, but would "it be impossible to induce the Germans to be content with a cash equivalent in amount towards their (so called) first class claims equivalent in amount to that which we have demanded?" This would "save *their* face & *our* face" at an immediate cost of only £11,000 to Venezuela.[40]

Villiers hastened to Metternich with Balfour's request, and frankly noted that a German refusal would endanger the Cabinet and adversely affect Anglo-German relations. It looked as if everyone's face was saved when the Germans agreed to ask for only £5,500 in cash and to accept a first charge on the customs receipts for the balance of their first class claims. But at this point a gloomy report from Herbert told of Bowen's latest refusal to consider preferential treatment.

Disgusted by Bowen's behavior, Lansdowne and Balfour decided to invite Roosevelt to arbitrate once again. On January 30th, Lansdowne cabled Herbert that Britain could accept equal footing with the non-blockading powers only at the ruling of a competent tribunal of arbitration. Therefore he was to arrange the preliminaries for the Hague, unless Roosevelt would agree to decide the question of preferential treatment. On the same day, Lansdowne, Balfour and the First Lord of the Admiralty called White to Lansdowne House and explained their decision. In actual fact, the Foreign Office doubted that Roosevelt would accept, and they thought that the Germans might object to inviting him, but by now everyone was desperate.

Meanwhile the unhappy Herbert was attempting to salvage some settlement at Washington. In Henry Adams' words, "Herbert rushes —or rather shuffles, about—desperately trying to straighten things out, and worried half threadbare."[41] The British ambassador began bombarding London with suggestions and finally came up with an idea that appealed to the Foreign Office. Would it be possible to draw up protocols embodying all the points that had been accepted by Bowen? These could be signed at Washington and only the question of priority of payment would have to go to the Hague.[42] This seemed promising, and the idea of separate protocols could still be used if Roosevelt wanted to arbitrate.

Villiers complicated the situation by presenting his own plan, which Lansdowne liked even more. Villiers' scheme aimed at getting a complete settlement at Washington and was an elaboration of Lansdowne's idea for a separate agreement giving a part of the thirty percent to the blockading powers: if Britain, Germany, and Italy were given approximately two-thirds of the thirty percent returns of the two customs houses, their claims would be paid off in about six and one-half years. By an earlier protocol Venezuela had already pledged thirteen percent of its customs to a number of its creditors. According to Villiers, this sum plus the one-third of thirty percent remaining for the neutrals equalled the sum to be pledged to the blockading powers. Thus a two-thirds to one-third split would make both groups even. The neutrals could make their own arrangements to everyone's satisfaction. Lansdowne thought that Villiers' plan was better than using either Roosevelt or the Hague, and for his part Balfour was ready to try whatever might work. The Prime Minister wrote to Villiers:

> I have no objection to the compromise you suggest, *if we could produce an immediate settlement.*
>
> As you are aware I myself proposed to Lord Lansdowne that, after the first rank claims were settled, the powers might share alike in the available assets of Venezuela—it was Mr. Bowen's attitude that seemed to render this impossible—Your plan might afford the basis of a compromise. . . .[43]

Before exploring the idea of drawing up protocols and making a formal request to Roosevelt, Lansdowne decided to see if Bowen would be impressed by Villiers' scheme for dividing the revenues. It was an ill-fated maneuver. The Foreign Office was not overly surprised when Bowen rejected the Villiers' plan in favor of referring preferential treatment to the Hague, but the manner in which he acted infuriated the British. Breaking a promise to Herbert to consult with the non-blockading powers about the British plan, Bowen sent his refusal to the British ambassador by letter late in the evening of February 2nd. In spite of another promise to discontinue information to the press, Bowen gave his answer to the newspapers at the same time, and the outraged Herbert was faced with the morning newspapers all discussing Bowen's "ultimatum, as they are pleased to call it."[44]

Herbert found one sentence in the letter particularly offensive in which Bowen stated that "it will occasion great surprise and regret when it becomes generally known that Great Britain has ever proposed continuing her present alliance with Germany and Italy one moment longer than she must." But the whole letter was "couched in his usual style," and Bowen took full advantage of the British offer to make a play to the gallery:

> I cannot accept even in principle that preferential treatment can be rightly obtained by blockades and bombardments. It would be absolutely offensive to modern civilization to recognize that principle. . . . Furthermore, that proposition is objectionable because it would keep the allied Powers allied for a period of over six years. Venezuela cannot, I am sure, be expected to encourage the maintenance of alliances against her. On this side of the water we want peace, not alliances.[45]

On the morning of February 3rd, Herbert called on Bowen and accused him of a breach of diplomatic courtesy. If Bowen did not withdraw the offensive sentence and express regrets for publishing the letter, Herbert threatened to break off negotiations. Considering Herbert's great desire to keep the talks in progress, this threat reflected extreme anger, and the same day he complained to Roosevelt about Bowen's conduct. Bowen complied with Herbert's demands and the negotiations continued, but once again damage had been done. Bowen's statement that preferential treatment for six years meant a continuation of an anti-American alliance "has unquestionably produced an unfavourable effect here."[46]

The formal invitation of February 6th to Roosevelt to arbitrate the question of preferential treatment fared no better. The delay in sending the invitation to Roosevelt was due to the brief consideration given to a compromise plan worked out by Bowen and Sternburg by which the entire 30% of the revenues of the two customs houses would be turned over to the blockading powers for three months. Both London and Berlin turned down the new offer as inadequate and asked Roosevelt to arbitrate. On being assured that the blockade would end as soon as the protocols were signed referring the matter of priority to the Hague, Roosevelt immediately declined. An end to the intervention now depended on Bowen's acceptance of the Italian and German protocols.

Unfortunately for the nervous British statesmen, the haggling between Bowen and the Germans over the first class claims continued. At the beginning of the negotiations in January, Bowen had accepted Germany's condition that the German first class claims were to be exempted from arbitration, and Venezuela was "to either pay the said amount cash without any delay or, should this be impossible, to guarantee the speedy payment of them by warrants which are deemed sufficient" by the German government. But what constituted a guarantee of "speedy payment"? When Bowen agreed to pay both Germany and Italy £5,500 immediately, a sum equal to the payment of the British first class claims, the Germans still wanted a first charge on the customs receipts for the balance of their claims of the first rank.

Even the Italians were proving troublesome. Until now the Italians had docilely followed their partners and played little part either in the blockade or in the diplomatic decisions. When they had accepted the principle of arbitration and agreed to deal with Bowen, their only condition had been equal treatment with Britain and Germany for "analogous" claims. The British and Germans assumed that all of the Italian claims were "second class," but the Italians evidently felt that many of their claims were "analogous" to Germany's first-class claims. According to Herbert, the Italian ambassador at Washington was demanding equal treatment with Germany on priority for claims totaling £112,000 in addition to the promised £5,500. Herbert, who was opposed to supporting the German demand, was even more unhappy about the new hitch. Lansdowne too was in no mood for new complications. The Italians, he wrote Villiers, "must see that we are not bound to them as we are to the Germans." He immediately called for the Italian ambassador and pointed out that nothing had been said about any Italian first class claims during Britain's negotiations with Italy.

On the contrary, frequent mention had been made of the first-rank claims of Great Britain and Germany, and the Venezuelan Government had given assurances with regard to them. This new Italian demand would, I feared, complicate the situation still further, and I therefore earnestly expressed the hope that this demand would not be seriously maintained.[47]

Hopes for any settlement with Bowen seemed increasingly dim. Earlier in the month Herbert had charged Bowen with inspiring press reports that Sternburg and Herbert were adopting different policies and that Britain and Italy were the obstacles to a settlement. According to the Germans, Bowen had frankly told the Italian ambassador "that the main principle of his diplomacy was to create discord between Baron Speck von Sternburg and Sir M. Herbert."[48] Lansdowne and Balfour were haunted by the rapidly approaching opening of Parliament. Was anything to be gained from Bowen except more delay?

On February 7th Lansdowne suggested to Herbert that perhaps the time had come to break off negotiations with Bowen and deal with the Hague for all but first class claims. Herbert immediately dissented. The Germans and Italians had no one to blame but themselves, he argued, "inasmuch as they did not, as we did, make their conditions clear to Mr. Bowen at the outset." Since the British had obtained all their original demands except preferential treatment, they could reach an immediate settlement with Bowen "if we were alone." Thus, it would be "folly" for Britain to take the lead in ending the negotiations, and, if the British were "bound" to support the "unfair" German and Italian conditions, let the proposal to break off negotiations come from Germany. Herbert advised the Foreign Office to apply pressure on Germany and Italy to modify their protocols. A "great change" had taken place in American feelings towards Britain since late December, and "our good relations with this country will be seriously impaired if this Alliance with Germany continues much longer." "The time has almost come, in American opinion," he concluded, "for us to make the choice between the friendship of the United States and that of Germany."[49]

Herbert's blunt advice struck home and the negotiations continued, but Lansdowne was understandably loath to make the choice that "American opinion" demanded. He had already spoken to the Italians, but, as for the Germans, he wrote Villiers, "the moment

cannot have come for putting pressure on them as Herbert suggests."[50] Unfortunately for Lansdowne that moment was approaching. On the following day Metternich told him that Berlin had decided to refuse to sign the protocol or raise the blockade until there
was a satisfactory settlement of the first class claims. Germany
wanted Herbert to take the same line with Bowen. Lansdowne admitted that Germany had the right to expect satisfaction for its
claims, but he also explained "most frankly" the seriousness of the
situation.

> I was, however, bound to tell his Excellency that the situation which
> was being created by the unfortunate prolongation of these negotia-
> tions at Washington and the continuation of the blockade of the Vene-
> zuelan ports was most serious. We were warned by Sir M. Herbert as
> to the danger of an explosion of public feeling in the United States. In
> this country, too, the tension was becoming acute. I feared that the
> position of His Majesty's Government might become intolerable if,
> when Parliament met, it were found that although our own demands
> had been complied with, we had broken off negotiations on account
> of difficulties arising in consequence of the terms demanded by Ger-
> many for the payment of claims, the nature of which, it was well-
> known, differed materially from that of our own.

Metternich retorted that the British second class claims were
much larger than Germany's, that many of the German first class
claims were not "too different" from the British, and that, above all,
Germany's "whole action" against Venezuela had been based on its
first class claims. Admitting that Metternich's arguments had some
validity, Lansdowne countered with an offer to help Berlin save face.
Britain would continue to uphold the non-arbitral nature of the German first class claims and, in addition, would agree that in any settlement arrived at these claims would get precedence over all British
claims other than those covered by the £5,500.[51]
While Berlin was considering his offer, Lansdowne decided the
time had come for more pressure on Britain's other partner. After
Lansdowne's first complaint, Rome had assured him that Italy had

presented no first class claims and did not intend doing so. Bowen "spontaneously" offered a payment of £5,500, and, as the reported £112,000 represented all of Italy's claims, it was obvious that there was some misunderstanding. Lansdowne was not satisfied and frankly warned the Italian ambassador that the British government viewed Italy's pressure for identical treatment with Germany "with serious concern." The Ambassador was to tell Rome that Britain "could not possibly support the Italian Government in making such a demand."[52]

Two days later the welcome news arrived that Italy had ordered her representative in Washington to propose conciliatory terms, but the ending of the blockade still depended on the Germans, and Berlin's reply to Lansdowne's offer of February 9th regarding German first class claims was not encouraging. Germany was also pressuring Italy to give up her "first class" claims, and, if she did, Berlin still thought that Bowen would give way to the German demand. They were "extremely gratified" at Lansdowne's loyalty and thanked him for his offer.

> They felt, however, that it was one which it would be difficult for them to accept. The prompt settlement of their first-rank claims was with them a point of honour. If those claims were to be satisfied merely by the postponement of the British and Italian claims, the sacrifice would be ours, not that of the Venezuelan Government. The German Government feared that if such an arrangement were to be made it would be severely criticized, and would lead to unfavourable comments both in this country and in Germany.[53]

Germany had not responded to what Lansdowne told White had been a "hint" to Metternich that Britain might be forced to sign her protocol alone.[54]

At Washington on February 10, Herbert had "one more go" at Bowen, using his "only weapon," the fact that Bowen did not want to rely on the Hague for the whole settlement any more than the British did. "By dint of alternately flattering him and threatening him with the Hague," Herbert was able to get a new concession from the American negotiator. If Italy would follow Britain in waiving priority to the German first class claims, Bowen was now willing to offer £5,500 to each of the three blockading powers and pay one-half of the balance of the German first class within thirty days. Both Herbert and Sternburg thought it was a fair compromise, and the Italian representative agreed to stop insisting on identical treatment with Germany when Bowen conceded that those Italian claims which were similar to Germany's first class would not be subject to arbitral revision. Herbert reported the offer as one-half within three months, but Metternich told Lansdowne it was 30 days.[55]

What did Berlin think of this newest compromise? The German government, Metternich told Lansdowne, welcomed the admission that they were entitled to preferential treatment, but they did not think that one-half was sufficient. The balance did not have to be paid with "equal promptitude," but they did want to put further pressure on Bowen for "a later security" for it. Lansdowne had reached the point of complete exasperation:

> In reply, I stated that, although I did not contest the validity of the German claims of the first-rank, I could not assume the responsibility of giving encouragement to an attempt by which, if successful, still better terms would be obtained by them. Under the proposed arrangement, Germany would receive a payment of more than £36,000 immediately, which was equivalent to about 11s in the £, and would also obtain priority for the remainder, with our consent. I could not understand in what way the point of honour came into consideration, and I thought that this arrangement might certainly be held to comply with the conditions laid down in the German note of the 23rd of December, 1902.

Lansdowne bluntly warned Metternich that Berlin "would take a serious responsibility" if they declined the offer. It would be "impossible" for Britain to support Sternburg in trying to better the terms or "to associate ourselves" with Germany in a demand which would only prolong the negotiations.[56]

Germany probably would have given way rather than risk losing

British support. Metternich had already warned Berlin of the danger that Balfour's Conservative government might fall in the face of the growing British dislike of Germany combined with "the American fetish."[57] But fortunately for both London and Berlin the news now arrived that Bowen and Sternburg had worked out a new arrangement. In effect, Bowen had backed down and the Germans had attained their "point of honour," for in addition to the £5,500 the balance of the German first class claims were to be paid in five monthly installments from the general treasury of Venezuela. The last obstacle had been hurdled by the weary negotiators. The protocols were signed on February 13th. Britain and Germany lifted the blockade on February 14th and 16th respectively. The coercion of Venezuela was at an end.

If one were to evaluate the Venezuelan expedition solely in terms of its original purpose as a claims collecting expedition, it had been a success. The first class claims were exempted from arbitration and paid promptly according to the terms agreed upon with Bowen. Despite the misgivings felt by many in the Foreign Office regarding arbitration, the Hague Tribunal, in February of 1904, upheld the three blockading powers on the question of priority of payments for the second class claims. These claims, after adjudication by mixed commissions in Caracas, were paid by 1907, while Venezuela's other claimants waited until 1912 before all claims were extinguished.[58]

The British bondholders were unhappy with their third-class status, but they too were remembered in the final settlement. Their claims were not included in the arbitration, but the protocols of 1903 did specify that Venezuela would make a fresh arrangement of the external debt including "a definition of the sources" of payment. Still stinging from criticism in Parliament for aiding the bondholders by force, the Foreign Office refused to help the Council of Foreign Bondholders to get this promise carried out, but even here the intervention eventually led to the desired "clean slate" when in June of 1905 the Council and the *Disconto Gesellschaft* finally negotiated a new arrangement consolidating the Venezuelan debt and converting the bonds of 1881 and 1896 into new ones.[59] Venezuela made the payments punctually and left the list of defaulting Latin American states.

Such an evaluation, of course, would be completely superficial, and no one knew this better than the British statesmen involved. There was no feeling of victory at the signing of the protocols, only a profound relief that a dangerous incident had been brought to a close. "These negotiations will leave a bad taste in my mouth for the rest of my life," Herbert wrote from Washington.[60] It was a reaction that could be heartily appreciated at the Foreign Office.

What had gone wrong? In the first place, it had not been a particularly skillful diplomatic operation. Even if one grants that the Foreign Office could not have foreseen the intensity of feelings that would erupt at home and in the United States, the fact remains that little thought was given to this eventuality. Even Ambassador Herbert knew little of the early negotiations with Germany, something that Lansdowne later admitted "was quite wrong."[61] The British statesmen had been naive in calculating upon the supposed "acquiescence" of official Washington.

It is also clear that not enough attention was paid to the types of claims that were linked together in the bargain with Germany. The idea of formally ranking the claims had come from Berlin, and the Foreign Office had made no objections to the German "first class" ranking. When the character and size of these claims later became an embarrassment, the Foreign Office had no one to blame but themselves. In addition, the question of preferential treatment should have been settled earlier. Germany and Britain knew of the existence of sizeable claims against Venezuela by nations not taking part in the coercion, and it should not have been too difficult to foresee that they would try to take advantage of the intervention. "You can spank Venezuela if you like. She deserves it; but don't take too long about it," an American Congressman told Herbert during the early days of the incident.[62] Britain and Germany had taken "too long" in their spanking, owing partly to their own lack of foresight.

Also, it had probably been a blunder to impose a complete and formal blockade on December 20th, after the decision for arbitration had been made. Given Castro's past record, it was an understandable decision, but, particularly after the United States threw its influence behind such a solution, it is difficult to see how Castro would have been able to evade his obligations. In any event, after Venezuela had accepted their reservations on January 8th, it would have been prudent to lift the blockade. As seen by the effects of the bombardment of Maricaibo, the dangers of its continuance far outweighed the benefits of its continuing pressure.

Much of the British resentment over the length of the negotiations centered upon Bowen, who Lansdowne believed could have settled "the whole business in 48 hours if he had wished to do so and run straight."[63] The British could never quite become accustomed to American lawyer-diplomats with their legal briefs for their clients and their diplomacy by press release. In Washington, Herbert tried to conceal his impressions of Bowen but there was little restraint in his private communications. "Bowen is all Haggard has described him as, and more," Herbert complained. "He is a blustering, insolent, untrustworthy cad."

> I cannot figure myself for not refusing at first to allow Bowen to come here. However, at that time I suppose I could not have been expected to realize how Bowen would really act here. From the beginning of the negotiations he has held all the trump cards and has worked public opinion in America by means of the press in a manner which could not fail to handicap the three representatives. Both the Germans and I have had to think of the relations between our respective countries with the United States, and Bowen has been sharp enough to realize the fact. . . .
>
> Bowen has naturally become a most popular man here and the picture of the brave American defending poor Venezuela from the greed and avarice of the three Powers appeals strongly to the average American. He has done me personally a good deal of harm in the eyes of the American public by the lies he has started about me. . . . This I do not care about, but what I do mind is the manner in which he has influenced public opinion in America, which is always fickle and quick to move against England.[64]

There was of course a much deeper significance to the Venezuelan episode than faulty preparation and mistakes in tactics. Despite the superficial success of the joint cooperation with Germany, it had been a dismal failure in the broad context of Anglo-German relations.

On the morning of February 18th, the Kaiser paid an unannounced visit to Ambassador Lascelles, and "had nothing but satisfaction to express." He was glad that the blockade was over and wanted to thank Lansdowne and the British government for the "loyal manner" in which they had acted towards Germany during the negotiations.

> He fully understood the difficulties which the hostility which public opinion in England had entertained against common action of the two governments had caused your Lordship, and he was all the more grateful for the determined manner in which your Lordship had acted throughout. He trusted also that people would now understand that it was possible for the two Governments to act together in questions in which their interests made it advisable that they should do so without incurring the terrible consequences which had been threatened by the English press.[65]

Undoubtedly the Kaiser was merely putting the best face possible on a bad situation, but if he actually believed his conclusion he was being diplomatically obtuse. In any event, the British government knew better, and Lord Hamilton's remark that the Venezuelan intervention "conclusively disposes of any idea of our being able to form or make any alliance" with Germany in the future was much closer to the mark.[66]

It was not that the Germans had been faithless or uncooperative, for they had deferred to the British from the beginning, particularly as soon as the unpopularity of the joint undertaking was evident. There had been irritation over the bombardment in January and over the matter of the first-class claims, but Lansdowne never blamed the Germans as much as he did Bowen for the prolonged negotiations. "The Germans have on the whole behaved well," he wrote Herbert after the signing of the protocols, "although they have been fussy & fond of raising unnecessary points, but they have almost invariably given way to us." And two years later he still expressed his opinion to Balfour that "the Germans upon the whole ran straight so far as we were concerned."[67]

The basic flaw in the whole operation was that the Germans were an unpopular partner, not only at home, but across the Atlantic as well. To those primarily interested in American friendship, the moral of the story was quite clear, and perhaps there was some consolation to be drawn from the whole affair. Herbert told Lansdowne that he would be "amazed at the language" used "by men in the highest positions at Washington" regarding Germany, and perceptively pointed out:

> This anti-German spirit cannot fail in the long run to be of benefit to Anglo-American relations. It must be remembered that, up to the time of the Spanish war, the United States, since they became a nation, have had only one enemy worthy of the name—Great Britain. Spain has been disposed of, and is forgotten. Germany is now gradually taking Great Britain's place in the American mind as the "natural foe," and the more general this feeling becomes, the more will the American people be instinctively drawn towards the people of Great Britain with whom they have so much in common. But it is obvious that this theory will not hold good if Great Britain is in any way associated with Germany in the future.[68]

Of more immediate concern at the time was the possible effect that the affair might have on present Anglo-American relations. In answer to their critics, Balfour and his government spokesmen denied that they had done anything to endanger American friendship, but here too they also knew better. A few days after the Kaiser's talk with Lascelles, Roosevelt made a few pointed comments to Herbert. The President spoke against Germany's actions in the Venezuelan affair "with considerable warmth," but "he stated, at the same time with some asperity, 'she would never have dared to behave as she has if England had not been acting with her.'" Herbert consoled Lansdowne with the hope that the Venezuelan incident would "soon be forgotten in this country where public opinion is so fickle and moves so illogically and so rapidly," but he had no doubts that "from the point of view of continued friendly relations between Great Britain and the United States, the Venezuelan negotiations were not brought to a close a day too soon."[69]

What did all of this mean specifically for Britain's Latin American policy? For one thing it meant "accepting" the great American dogma, the Monroe Doctrine. Lord Cranborne's statement of December was followed by others in Parliament during the postmortem of the Venezuelan incident that occurred in the new session. And none of these spokesmen was more emphatic than Balfour himself speaking at Liverpool on February 14. The Prime Minister was fully aware that public opinion in the United States was sensitive about the Monroe Doctrine.

> But the Monroe Doctrine has no enemies in this country that I know of. (Cheers.) We welcome any increase of the influence of the United States of America upon the great Western Hemisphere. (Hear, hear.) We desire no colonization, we desire no alteration in the balance of power, we desire no acquisition of territory. (Hear, hear.) We have not the slightest intention of interfering with the mode of government of any portion of that continent. (Cheers.) The Monroe Doctrine, therefore, is really not in the question at all. (Hear, hear.)

The Prime Minister knew better in this instance too. For he immediately followed up his bow to the doctrine with an invitation to the United States.

> I go further, and I say that, so far as I am concerned, I believe it would be a great gain to civilization if the United States of America were more actively to interest themselves in making arrangements by which these constantly recurring difficulties between European Powers and certain States in South America could be avoided. They are difficulties which are constantly occurring, but they cannot be avoided. . . . As long as the canons of international relations which prevail between the great European Powers and the United States of America are not followed in South America these things will occur, and the United States of America can perform no greater task in the cause of civilization than by doing their best to see that international law is observed, and by upholding all that the European Powers and the

United States have recognized as the admitted principles of international comity.[70]

Or as he put it more succinctly in a letter to Andrew Carnegie in December of 1902: "These South American Republics are a great trouble, and I wish the U. S. A. would take them in hand!"[71]

Balfour's hope was a logical one to flow out of the events of 1902–1903, and, as the future would show, the idea that the United States had responsibilities to the European powers under the Monroe Doctrine was already taking form in the mind of Theodore Roosevelt.[72] But British "acceptance" of the Monroe Doctrine, and wishes that the United States would take Latin America "in hand" did not solve the Foreign Office's problem of determining how far they could go in the future in helping settle British claims.

Was it still possible to consider armed intervention in Latin America? As far as the Roosevelt administration was concerned, it seemed that European intervention was still permissible, in theory at least, even in cases of bondholders' claims. Luis M. Drago, the Foreign Minister of Argentina, got nothing more than a noncommittal reply when he tried during the Venezuelan blockade to get the United States to accept his "doctrine" that "the public debt cannot occasion armed intervention or even the actual occupation of the territory of American nations by a European power." The United States favored arbitration in such cases, but without "expressing assent or dissent" to the Drago Doctrine, Hay again used Roosevelt's statements to Congress of 1901 and 1902 on the Monroe Doctrine as the position of the United States.[73] Was Roosevelt's policy unchanged?

And what of American public opinion? Many Americans obviously thought that any European intervention was a violation of the Monroe Doctrine. Lansdowne believed that the trouble over Venezuela had arisen from "ill informed popular feeling" rather than the conduct of the American government,[74] but even if the Foreign Secretary was correct who was to say that American opinion would be any better informed if a similar situation arose? If the United States did not take Latin America in hand, was the Foreign Office to do nothing in the defense of British interests? And if the

United States did exert more influence on the troublesome republics, would this always benefit those interests?

One thing at least was certain in the aftermath of the Venezuelan intervention: the British bondholders would have little chance of getting strong support from the Foreign Office. This became clear immediately in the case of the defaulted Guatemalan debt. As late as November 1902 Britain, Germany, France, Italy and Belgium were still applying pressure to Guatemala for an acceptable arrangement of the external debt, but by the spring of 1903 no one had any illusions that Estrada Cabrera would give way as he had to European claims in 1902. The European representatives at Guatemala City were still under instructions to follow the British minister's lead, but the Foreign Office no longer had any intention of taking the lead in Guatemala or elsewhere. Lansdowne wrote to Villiers in March:

> In the interests of the Bondholders themselves any active intervention on their behalf at this moment would be most undesirable. It is useless to conceal from ourselves the fact that the recent agitation as to our action in Venezuela will greatly strengthen the position of those fraudulent countries who have been led to suppose that public opinion in this country & in America will secure them immunity.[75]

Thus in Guatemala the hoped for multilateral approach to Central America came to an inglorious end, a casualty of the "war" with Venezuela.

NOTES AND REFERENCES

1. Haggard to Lansdowne, December 14, 1902. F. O. 420/212.

2. Douglas to Admiralty, December 19, 1902, in Admiralty to F. O., January 8, 1903. F. O. 420/212; Villiers' memorandum of January 8th. F. O. 80/479.

3. Lansdowne to Buchanan, December 13, 1902, F. O. 420/206; Bulow to Kaiser, December 12th, *German Diplomatic Documents*, pp. 162–64; White to Lansdowne, December 13th; Lansdowne to Herbert, no. 244, December 17th. F. O. 420/206.

4. For the debate of December 15th, see Great Britain, *The Parliamentary Debates*, vol. 116, pp. 1245–87.

5. Quoted in J. A. Spender, *The Life of the Right Hon. Sir Henry Campbell-Bannerman* (London: 1923), II, 84–85.

6. Lansdowne to Buchanan, December 15, 1902. F. O. 420/206; *Die Grosse Politik*, pp. 260–64.

7. Lansdowne to Herbert, December 15, 1902. F. O. 420/206.

8. White to Hay, December 15, 1902, and despatch 1001 of December 17th. State Department Despatches, Great Britain, vol. 206.

9. White to Hay, December 17, 1902; quoted in Allan Nevins, *Henry White, Thirty Years of American Diplomacy* (New York, 1930), p. 310. Nevins has misdated this letter December 13th. See Campbell, *op. cit.*, pp. 280–81. This conversation therefore took place on the 15th rather than December 8th as often cited.

10. Lansdowne to Buchanan, December 16, 1902. F. O. 420/206. Metternich to the Foreign Office, December 16th. *Die Grosse Politik*, pp. 265–66.

11. Lansdowne to Herbert, 245, December 17, 1902. F. O. 420/206. White to Hay, December 17th. State Department Despatches, Great Britain, vol. 206.

12. Herbert to Lansdowne, 60, December 16, 1902. F. O. 420/206.

13. *Die Grosse Politik*, pp. 264–66.

14. For two opposed analyses, see Perkins, *op. cit.*, pp. 377–90; Beale, *op. cit.*, pp. 395–431. For Roosevelt's use of the press to publicize his diplomatic and naval moves, see Paul S. Holbo, "Perilous Obscurity: Public Diplomacy and the Press in the Venezuelan Crisis, 1902–1903," *The Historian*, XXXII (1970), pp. 482–98.

15. Memorandum from Metternich of December 18, 1902; Lansdowne to Lascelles, December 18th. F. O. 420/206.

16. Lansdowne to Herbert, December 18, 1902. F. O. 420/206. White to Hay, December 18, 1902. State Department Despatches, Great Britain, vol. 206. For Germany's similar declarations, see U.S., *Foreign Relations*, 1903, pp. 423–24.

17. *The Parliamentary Debates*, vol. 116, pp. 1289–90, 1489; Admiralty to Douglas, December 16, 1902, in Admiralty to F. O., January 24, 1903. F. O. 420/212.

18. White to Hay, December 16, 1902. State Department Despatches, Great Britain, vol. 206.

19. *The Parliamentary Debates*, vol. 116, pp. 1262–63.

20. Roosevelt to Cleveland, December 26, 1902. E. E. Morison (ed.), *The Letters of Theodore Roosevelt* (Cambridge, Mass., 1951), III, 398.

21. White to Hay, December 24, 1902. State Department Despatches, Great Britain, vol. 206.

22. Herbert to Lansdowne, private, December 19, 1902; Lansdowne to Herbert, December 27, 1902, and January 2, 1903. Lansdowne Papers, U.S., vol. 28.

23. Lansdowne to Herbert, December 27, 1902. Lansdowne Papers, U.S., vol. 28. Lansdowne to Balfour, January 1, 1903. Arthur J. Balfour Papers (The British Museum, London), 49728. Cited hereafter as the Balfour Papers.

24. On December 19th the Foreign Office heard by way of Washington that Castro had empowered Bowen to enter into negotiations. As Roosevelt had not as yet refused to act as arbitrator, the British quickly rejected the idea. When Roosevelt did decline, the Foreign Office assumed that the matter would go to the Hague.

25. Herbert to Lansdowne, 67, December 31, 1902; Lansdowne to Herbert, January 1, 1903. F. O. 420/212.

26. Lansdowne to Balfour, January 1, 1903; and Balfour to Lansdowne, January 2nd. Balfour Papers, 49728.

27. Balfour to Lansdowne, January 2, 1903, Balfour Papers, 49728; Haggard to Lansdowne, 87, December 17, 1902, F. O. 420/206, and despatch 240 of December 18, 1902 (arrived Jan. 2), F. O. 420/212; Herbert to Lansdowne, private, January 3, 1903, Lansdowne Papers, U.S., vol. 28.

28. Lansdowne to Herbert, 15 and 17, January 13, 1903. F. O. 420/212.

29. Lansdowne to Herbert, 14, January 12, 1903. F. O. 420/212.

30. Lansdowne to Herbert, January 13, 1903. Lansdowne Papers, U.S., vol. 28.

31. Herbert to Lansdowne, 13, January 23, 1903, F. O. 420/212; Herbert to Lansdowne, private, January 30th. Lansdowne Papers, U.S., vol. 28.

32. Lansdowne to Lascelles, January 22, 1903. F. O. 420/212.

33. Herbert to Lansdowne, January 30, 1903, and February 10th, Lansdowne Papers, U.S., vol. 28. White to Hay, January 24th, State Department Despatches, Great Britain, vol. 206.

34. Lansdowne to Lascelles, January 15, 1903. F. O. 420/212.

35. Foreign Office to Herbert, private, January 28, 1903; Herbert to Lansdowne, private, January 28, 1903. Lansdowne Papers, U.S., vol. 28.

36. Herbert to Lansdowne, 31, January 29, 1903. F. O. 420/212.

37. Lansdowne to Buchanan, November 11, 1902. F. O. 420/206.

38. Lansdowne to Herbert, 11, January 24, 1903. F. O. 420/212. In their ultimatum before the intervention, the British had demanded an immediate payment equal to that paid to Germany. By the time the negotiations started with Bowen, the

Foreign Office was only demanding the estimated £5,500 for their first class claims.

39. Metternich to Balfour, December 17, 1902. Balfour Papers, 49747.

40. Balfour to Lansdowne, January 27, 1902. F. O. 80/480.

41. Quoted in Beale, *op. cit.*, p. 424.

42. Bowen suggested using the Hague on the matter of priority to Sternburg on February 1st, but Herbert was unaware of this move when he made his similar proposal to the Foreign Office on the same day.

43. Balfour to Villiers, January 31, 1903. F. O. 80/481.

44. Herbert to Lansdowne, 45, February 3, 1903. F. O. 420/213.

45. Herbert to Lansdowne, despatch 35A of February 3, 1903. F. O. 420/213.

46. Herbert to Lansdowne, private, February 4th. F. O. 80/481.

47. Lansdowne to Bertie, February 7, 1903. F. O. 420/213. Lansdowne to Villiers, February 8, 1903. Lansdowne's note to Villiers is misdated 1902 and filed in F. O. 80/443.

48. Lansdowne to Lascelles, 48A, February 6, 1903. F. O. 420/213.

49. Herbert to Lansdowne, 58 and 58A of February 7, 1903. F. O. 420/213.

50. Lansdowne to Villiers, February 8, 1903. F. O. 80/443.

51. Lansdowne to Herbert, 47, February 9, 1903; and to Lascelles, 51, February 9th. F. O. 420/213.

52. Lansdowne to Herbert, 45, February 8, 1903, and 46 of February 9th. F. O. 420/213.

53. Lansdowne to Lascelles, 54, February 10, 1903. F. O. 420/213.

54. White to Hay, February 10, 1903. State Department Despatches, Great Britain, vol. 206.

55. Herbert to Lansdowne, 67 and 68, February 10, 1903. F. O. 420/213; Herbert to Lansdowne, private, February 10th. Lansdowne Papers, U.S., vol. 28.

56. Lansdowne to Herbert, 57, February 11, 1903; and 58A to Lascelles of February 11th. F. O. 420/213.

57. Metternich to Bulow, private, February 4, 1903, *German Diplomatic Documents*, pp. 164–65.

58. For a listing of the amounts claimed and the amounts paid under the protocols of 1903 to both the blockading and non-blockading powers, see Council of Foreign Bondholders, *Annual Report*, 1912, p. 391. On the proportion of award to claim for the second class claims, Britain received 63.7%, Germany 28.35%, Italy 7.46%. Of all the powers, the lowest percentage of award to claim was the United States at 2.78%. Venezuela also paid claims to Belgium, France, Holland, Mexico, Spain, Sweden, and Norway.

59. For the debt settlement, see the Council of Foreign Bondholders' *Annual Report* for 1905. For the Foreign Office's refusal to aid the bondholders following the signing of the protocol of 1903, see the pertinent documents in F. O. 80/476, and Platt, *op. cit.*, 24–27.

60. Herbert to Lansdowne, private, February 13, 1903. Lansdowne Papers, U.S., vol. 28.

61. Lansdowne to Herbert, December 27, 1902. On January 2, 1903, Lansdowne again wrote: "I am very sorry that you were not kept fully informed as to the course of the negotiations here, & I have given instructions that the Office is to be more careful for the future." Lansdowne Papers, U.S., vol. 28.

62. Herbert to Lansdowne, private, December 19, 1902. Lansdowne Papers, U.S., vol. 28.

63. Lansdowne to Herbert, February 20, 1903. Lansdowne Papers, U.S., vol. 28.

64. Herbert to Lansdowne, private, January 30, 1903, and private of February 10th. Lansdowne Papers, U.S., vol 28. According to Hay, both he and Roosevelt were also unfavorably impressed by Bowen's handling of the negotiations. Hay told Herbert that the only advice he gave to Bowen was to "behave better." Herbert to Lansdowne, February 9th. F. O. 420/213.

65. Lascelles to Lansdowne, February 20, 1903. See also his telegram of February 18th. F. O. 420/213.

66. Hamilton to Curzon, December 31, 1902. Quoted in Monger, *op. cit.*, p. 107.

67. Lansdowne to Herbert, February 20, 1903. Lansdowne Papers, U.S., vol. 28; Lansdowne to Balfour, January 18, 1905. Quoted in Monger, *op. cit.*, p. 179.

68. Herbert to Lansdowne, February 25, 1903 (received March 9th). F. O. 420/214.

69. Herbert to Lansdowne, February 25, 1903. (Received March 9). F. O. 420/214.

70. The London *Times*, February 14, 1903.

71. Balfour to Carnegie, December 18, 1902. Balfour Papers, 49742.

72. At the time of the Venezuelan intervention Roosevelt was not yet willing to involve his government in any guarantees, but he was reportedly interested in the possibility of Americans financing Venezuela's claims. Indeed, even before the intervention got underway the State Department and White tried to help Issac Seligman arrange Venezuela's finances. The Foreign Office was seemingly unaware of this, but as early as December 31st Herbert reported that some New York syndicates were ready to pay the claims in the event of an award, and the subject of American financing came up a number of times during and after the negotiations in Washington. In the end, however, nothing came of these early attempts at "dollar diplomacy."

73. U.S., *Foreign Relations*, 1903, pp. 1–6.

74. Lansdowne to Herbert, February 20, 1903. Lansdowne Papers, U.S., vol. 28.

75. Lansdowne's minute to Villiers' memorandum of March 3, 1903. F. O. 15/366.

CHAPTER III

Cuba and the Open Door

A most disturbing question raised by the Foreign Office's policy of accepting American political predominance in the Caribbean was the possible effects this policy might have on British commercial interests. As long as the "open door" was maintained, the British government professed to have no objections to American ambitions in the area, but from the very outset there were fears that the United States would use its political domination to destroy economic competition. Such fears in British commercial and shipping circles reached their peak in connection with Cuba, the United States' first Caribbean protectorate. American-Cuban reciprocity and the unsuccessful attempt by the British to negotiate a satisfactory commercial treaty with Cuba caused many in Great Britain to worry about the future of the "open door" in Latin America.

Although reforms which the United States introduced into Cuba did much to revivify the island during the American military occupation following the Spanish-American War, many in both countries were convinced that the real solution to Cuba's economic problems could be found only in some form of reciprocity with the United States. Even before the Cuban war for independence the island's economy had become attuned to the export of sugar to the United States, and post-war Cuba was having difficulties competing in the world sugar market. Faced with continuing depression and serious unemployment, many Cubans were willing to give preferential tariff treatment to American imports in return for reciprocal advantages in the United States for Cuban sugar. American arguments in favor of this arrangement reflected the usual blend of humanitarianism, economic self-interest and the political desire, as Theodore Roosevelt put it, "to foster our supremacy in the lands and waters south of us. . . ."[1] The fight for reciprocity, however, was not destined to be an easy one. A number of influential Cuban political leaders were far from enchanted at the prospect of American "supremacy," and in the United States there were powerful economic groups opposed to reciprocity as well as those who hoped to gain by it.[2]

The movement for American-Cuban reciprocity also spelled trouble for the British Foreign Office. British commercial interests in Cuba were far larger than in such countries as Guatemala and Venezuela. Although the United States had supplanted Spain as the chief exporter to Cuba after 1898, Britain still maintained third place in the competition for the Cuban market. Cuba was Britain's best customer in the entire region of the Caribbean, ranking even ahead of Mexico. In 1900 Cuba imported approximately £2,000,000 of British goods, principally textiles and Indian rice. In addition, British shippers were making considerable profits, not only in the rice trade via Liverpool and in general cargoes, but in the sugar trade between Cuba and the United States as well. The merchants, manufacturers and shipping companies interested in maintaining this Cuban trade formed a vocal and important pressure group that was not reluctant to appeal for government aid.

From 1898 to 1905, Great Britain's representative in Cuba was Lionel Carden, an able and energetic diplomat who was to become the most outspoken advocate of vigorously defending British interests in the Caribbean and Central America against the expansion of American influence. A veteran of many years' service in Cuba and Mexico, Carden was named Consul General to Cuba in December of 1898 and became the first British minister to the new republic when the American occupation of the island ended in May, 1902. Carden was alert to the potential dangers of American policies to British commercial interests, and during the years of his stay in Cuba the Foreign Office became familiar with his dire warnings from Havana.

Carden became apprehensive long before the Cuban-American reciprocity treaty was negotiated. As early as January of 1901, he warned the Foreign Office that the "very existence" of British trade with Cuba was threatened if tariff advantages to American imports were added to such natural advantages as geographical proximity and lower freight rates. According to Carden, Britain's only hope was to influence the Cubans themselves. He was convinced that Cubans were mistaken in their enthusiasm for reciprocity. The principal benefits would go to the American consumer, and Cuba would be forced to use direct taxation to replace the resulting loss in customs revenues.

> These arguments I have not failed to urge on several of the leading Cuban delegates, who are already opposed on political grounds to too intimate a connection with the United States, and it is to be hoped that their efforts may have the effect of neutralising the action of the planters and their sympathizers.[3]

Carden's superiors in London were more worried about present relations with the United States than about the future of British trade with Cuba. "I think Mr. Carden ought to be careful how he puts his finger into this pie," Under Secretary of State Sir Thomas Sanderson advised. The American authorities "might get very angry if they thought he was intriguing against their policy." Lansdowne was equally cautious. He instructed Carden to watch the situation closely and to report new developments, but the British consul was to "be very careful in giving advice on this subject to prominent people in Cuba," and especially to "avoid any appearance of putting forward views on political subjects which might not be acceptable to the U. S. Authorities."[4]

Carden was not the only one worried about American plans for Cuba. By the spring of 1901 British Chambers of Commerce, fearful that a Cuban protectorate would mean imposition of the United States' tariff on the island, were already beginning to send memorials to the Foreign Office. When three memorials from Birmingham, Sheffield and Wolverhampton were passed on to the British ambassador in Washington, Pauncefote warned that any inquiry to the American government would be ill-timed. There was no danger of the American tariff being applied to Cuba. It was "highly probable" that the United States would try to get preferential commercial advantages, but Pauncefote could not see that this gave the British any "legitimate ground for protest or remonstrance."[5]

If his counterpart in Washington had no desire to touch the subject, Carden was by no means content to play the part of a passive observer. While in London in the summer of 1901, Carden, at Villiers' request, drew up a confidential memorandum on the future commercial relations of Britain with Cuba. Now that the Platt Amendment had defined Cuba's political relationship with the United States, Carden thought the time had come for Britain to determine the type of commercial treaty she wanted, and to ascertain "so far as may be possible the views of the leading Cuban politicians on the subject, so that when the moment for action arrives we may not find ourselves forestalled by other countries." Carden still hoped that reciprocity would be blocked in the American Congress, but even if it passed he thought the Cubans might be persuaded to minimize the preference to the United States by reducing their customs rates. In any event, "a timely demonstration of friendly interest in and consideration for the new Republic" would certainly help in any future negotiations.

Once again the benefits to British commerce had to be weighed against the danger of ruffling American feelings. Lord Cranborne realized that the United States "might be annoyed," but he was "inclined to think that if Mr. Carden is a good man he should be trusted to act confidentially." Lansdowne was still cautious, but convinced himself that Carden could safely sound out "the views of the leading Cubans," as long as the inquiries were made "unofficially and in the most tactful manner possible in order to avoid giving offense to the United States Government."[6]

What type of commercial treaty did the British want? Both the Commercial Department of the Foreign Office and the Board of Trade were opposed to offering any tariff advantages to Cuba as an inducement. As usual the British hoped for a treaty unconditionally giving both countries most-favored-nation treatment in all respects. Obviously Carden was being given a most delicate task, and the Foreign Office was treading on dangerous grounds in asking him to prepare the way in Cuba for an unconditional most-favored-nation treaty with Britain "without giving offense" to an American administration pledged to Cuban reciprocity.

The United States could have most-favored-nation treaties and at the same time negotiate reciprocity treaties with individual countries embodying special concessions because of her traditional "conditional" interpretation of most-favored-nation clauses. According to the American view, a third country with most-favored-nation status was not entitled to any special advantages that one country gave to another unless the third power gave the same or equivalent concessions. The conflict between the British "unconditional" and the American "conditional" interpretations of most-favored-nation treatment was a long-standing one.[7]

Carden realized that there was little chance of exerting influence at Havana without taking an anti-American stance. In October of 1901 the Foreign Office sent him a draft treaty and authorized him to open negotiations as soon as the new republic was established, but the British consul was chafing under the Foreign Office's restrictions on his activities. On January 15, 1902, the same day that hearings began in the American House of Representatives on a reciprocity bill, Carden wrote a personal letter to Villiers asking for advice. Without opposition, reciprocity seemed just around the corner, but if he tried to influence any of the Cuban leaders except those with whom he was on "terms of some intimacy," his action "could scarcely fail to become known to some extent to the American authorities and would certainly not be to their liking. . . ." He was supposed to avoid stating political views which might antagonize the United States, but "the political and commercial sides of the Cuban question are so interwoven that it is impossible to say where one ends and the other begins."

Under the circumstances do you not think that the importance of the issue to us, and its urgency, would warrant a relaxation of these instructions, even at the risk of its not being altogether acceptable to the U. S. authorities? I do not wish to pretend that I can do impossibilities, but there are so many and such cogent arguments which might be used to show how disadvantageous reciprocity with the U. S. would prove to Cuba, that, if I felt myself authorized to make the attempt, I think I might be able to persuade some of the leading men to use their influence against the hasty conclusion of any Treaty of a permanent character, with a reasonable prospect of success.

Lansdowne's misgivings over American susceptibilities were too strong. Lord Cranborne was willing to tell Carden "to be cautious and to trust him to feel his way in the direction he suggests," but Lansdowne was unwilling to run the risk. "It will be safer," the Foreign Secretary decided, "to tell him that we are not prepared to relax our instructions."[8]

Although the Foreign Office rejected Carden's suggestions, more complaints and petitions regarding Cuba forced Lansdowne to make a gesture in defense of British interests. Lansdowne flatly refused to consider the suggestions of the Liverpool Chamber of Commerce that Britain join Germany and France in a joint protest to the United States. With any confidential efforts at Havana also ruled out, a direct unilateral approach to the United States by Pauncefote seemed the only alternative. Cranborne had "very little hope" of any results, but something had to be done "in deference to this commercial pressure."[9]

The commercial pressure that had moved the Foreign Office was centered in Liverpool. In mid-February of 1902, twenty-one Liverpool firms engaged in export and shipping with Cuba petitioned the Liverpool Chamber of Commerce for aid. The Liverpool Chamber in turn circulated a resolution to all of the principal Chambers in the United Kingdom and asked Lansdowne for an interview, since most of the delegates of the Association of Chambers of Commerce were to be in London for the organization's spring meeting. Lansdowne tried to avoid a meeting, but the opponents of American-Cuban reciprocity were determined to air their grievances personally. On March 11th, the Foreign Secretary met with representatives from the Chambers of Liverpool, London, Manchester, Birmingham, Wolverhampton, Bury, Bradford, Glascow, Belfast, and a delegate from the central association.

The Vice President of the Liverpool Chamber of Commerce sounded the keynote in his opening address:

> Cuba, of course, can do what she thinks best, but the deputation desires that the "open door" should be maintained. Mr. Cox referred to what His Majesty's Government had done to maintain the open door in the Far East; he said the United States' citizens had the benefit of this policy, and surely this could be urged by His Majesty's Government in endeavouring to maintain the open door in Cuba. Mr. Choate [the American Ambassador] only a few days ago made a speech in favour of the best relations between the two countries. He had said "if you want to have a friend you must be a friend"—this should be acted on at Washington.

Sir Vincent Barrington of the London Chamber caustically remarked that the "philanthropic purposes" of the United States in the war with Spain had turned out to be "philanthropy" plus "a twenty-five percent differential tariff" against Europe. Other speakers again urged some form of joint European action. Nor were the fears confined to Cuba. With Puerto Rico gone and Cuba on the way, the Belfast delegate feared "that by some amplification of the Monroe Doctrine British trade would be ousted, not only from Cuba, but from all Central and South America as well."

Lansdowne's answer to the delegation was not encouraging. He told them of the draft treaty sent to Carden and the instructions to Pauncefote, and asked them to draw up a memorandum of their views which he would send to Washington. What else could the government do? The United States had not made any "pledges" that were "definite enough" to hinder reciprocity with Cuba. A "formal remonstrance" at the moment would be "unsuitable" and would probably irritate the Americans.[10]

The Foreign Office was correct in believing that protest to the State Department would be futile. On March 10th Pauncefote had sent Hay extracts from the Liverpool and Manchester memorials, along with a note expressing the hope that the Secretary of State would consider the Chambers' complaints "and that the President may see his way to take some action to protect the long established British trade with Cuba against the peril with which it is threatened." The State Department merely acknowledged the note with the terse reply that the matter would receive "due consideration."[11]

The Foreign Office remained reluctant to see the subject of Cuba come into the open. Not only had Lansdowne refused to allow the press to attend his meeting with the delegates from the Chambers of Commerce, but Cranborne unofficially told Charles MacArthur, MP from Liverpool, that the Foreign Office was anxious to avoid questions in Parliament, or any public discussion of the matter, for fear that British pressure would only reconcile the conflicting interests in the United States. But for all the Foreign Office's desire to evade the subject, agitation persisted, the flow of petitions from many British companies continued, and many Chambers of Commerce endorsed the Liverpool Chamber's request for the "strongest possible representations" to the American government. In June the Foreign Office finally relented and told Arthur Raikes, the British Chargé d'Affaires, to send the Liverpool Chamber's memorandum on the meeting with Lansdowne to the State Department and ask for a favorable consideration of it. The only result was more silence from official Washington. The State Department did not even bother to answer Raike's note.[12]

With the end of the American occupation of Cuba approaching, Carden was again getting restive in Havana. Should he wait until the United States secured a commercial treaty, or was he to open negotiations with the new Cuban government as soon as it came into power in May? With the usual warning to use caution, Lansdowne told Carden to proceed at his discretion, and, as Carden later reported, he "lost no opportunity" in telling the Cuban Secretary of State that Britain was ready to conclude a commercial treaty. Carden realized that Tomás Estrada Palma, the first President of Cuba, belonged to that faction of Cuban politicians most friendly to the United States, but the British minister was undaunted. In August he pointed out to Estrada Palma the many supposed disadvantages to Cuba that would result from reciprocity with the United States and warned him of the dangers of alienating friendly nations and discouraging the investment of European capital in his country. Estrada Palma professed to be "much impressed" by Carden's arguments, but he feared that Cuba was too deeply committed to the United States to turn back. However, he did tell Carden to send the British draft treaty to the Cuban State Department and promised to talk with him again on the matter.[13]

Meanwhile the situation in both Washington and Havana was looking more favorable for the opponents of reciprocity. Roosevelt's program ran into stiff opposition in Congress, and when the legislature adjourned in July of 1902 an administration reciprocity bill was still buried in the Senate committee. Roosevelt immediately turned to treaty negotiations with the now "independent" republic, but the terms of the proposed treaty disappointed the Cubans. The twenty percent reduction of the American tariff on Cuba's goods was considered too low, and Cuba was being asked to give higher reductions— from twenty-five to forty percent—on some categories of American products.[14] Even Estrada Palma was now showing some signs of independence.

Was there any way for the British to take advantage of the situation? The ever-alert Carden thought that a great opportunity was at hand. After the American Congress adjourned in July without lowering the tariff on Cuban sugar, Carden reported that the Cuban Government was seeking an £800,000 loan to aid its planters. Estrada Palma had received American proposals to furnish the necessary funds, but he "would prefer England, and has asked me for help." This opened up great vistas to Carden. As he cabled home:

> Venture to strongly urge that government influence be exerted in furtherance of proposal of President as affording a means of preventing the conclusion of a reciprocal Treaty with the United States; this might be effected by stipulation that no part of import duties shall be alienated during subsistance of contract. Suggest that merchants who petitioned your Lordship re reciprocity be invited to raise funds required.

Exceptional opportunity to secure commanding financial influence here.

This was dangerous terrain. The Platt Amendment did not forbid Cuba to contract foreign loans, but it did contain a provision restricting debts beyond her normal ability to pay, and the United States was obviously intent on controlling her protégé's financial commitments. As usual, Lansdowne drew back from any overt attempt to frustrate American designs. He was willing to let it be known privately in London that Estrada Palma wanted to make enquiries, but that was as far as the Foreign Secretary would go. The British government could not assist the Cubans "in any official or formal manner," and any arrangement making the Cuban customs revenues inalienable was out of the question. Nor would Lansdowne recommend any financial houses "who undertake such business" when Carden tried to get some specific suggestions.[15] Evidently this was too vague and unofficial for Estrada Palma, and the Cuban attempt to offset American dominance by English capital was not followed up through the Foreign Office.[16]

Although they had dashed cold water on another of Carden's ideas, the Foreign Office's position towards American-Cuban reciprocity was ambivalent. Torn between the desire to placate the United States and the need to assuage commercial interests at home, their orders to Carden had been rather contradictory. They had repeatedly told him not to offend the United States, but his reports had made it clear that he was doing his best to convince the Cubans to reject the American plan. He received no reprimands. Indeed the Foreign Office itself specifically instructed Carden, on October 8, 1902, to discuss Roosevelt's proposed reciprocity bill with Estrada Palma and draw his attention "to the far-reaching nature of these provisions which we regard with serious misgiving in this country."[17]

It is difficult to see how the most tactful diplomat, much less one as zealous as Carden, could have avoided giving offense to the United States. In fact, Herbert Squiers, the American minister at Havana, had been suspiciously watching Carden's activity, and in mid-October he reported to the State Department that the British minister was attempting to prevent Cuban acceptance of the American treaty. According to Squiers, Carden had promised Cuba the "material and moral support" of Great Britain, and that Germany would join Britain in support of Cuba if she rejected the American treaty. Hay thought the reported intrigue "almost incredible," but he ordered Ambassador Choate in London to find out "discreetly whether there is any truth in the story." Lansdowne assured Choate that Squiers' report was due to a "gross exaggeration" of something Carden had said, but he promised that an enquiry would be made.[18]

It was an embarrassing situation for the Foreign Office. On October 20th, Squiers' charges were sent to Carden along with a warning to be especially careful at the moment not to raise any American suspicions. At the same time, the Foreign Office covered its own tracks with a private telegram from Villiers ordering Carden not to carry out his instructions of October 8th regarding the reciprocity bill. The following day, Lansdowne again assured Choate that the report on Carden was due to "misunderstanding or misrepresentation," and that the British minister had "been constantly instructed to be most careful to avoid in the course of commercial negotiations with the Cuban Government any conduct which might bear the appearance of an attempt to thwart policy" of the United States.[19]

Carden immediately cabled back to London in his own defense. Following Lansdowne's instructions, he had repeatedly urged Estrada Palma and his Secretary of State to conclude a most-favored-nation treaty with Britain, "and in so far as this might conflict with the U. S. policy which is directed towards exclusion of British trade there is some truth in the report."

> Need scarcely say there is no foundation whatever in statement that I offered Cuba moral or material support of Great Britain nor have I ever alluded in conversation with President or S. of S. for Foreign Affairs even remotely to Germany or German interests here. I can only characterize statement as a deliberate invention which I cannot believe came from any authoritative source. The arguments which I have used in regard to treaty have been based on exclusively commercial grounds and inadvisability of excluding British trade from Cuba.[20]

The Foreign Office was relieved that Carden's "straight-forward" reply satisfactorily disposed of the story of British and German support to Cuba, but the problem still remained of explaining Carden's very real activities to negotiate a British treaty. Lansdowne was forced to admit to Choate that he had sent a draft most-favored-nation treaty to Cuba for discussion, but he played down its importance. Nothing had resulted because of Cuba's negotiations with the United States. The Foreign Secretary was "anxious to remove all misunderstanding, and will be glad at all times to give fullest information as to British action in Cuba."[21]

As the American government was seemingly satisfied by the British explanations, Lansdowne realized that he had been fortunate. When Sir Michael Herbert, the new British Ambassador at Washington, voiced his uneasiness over newspaper comments on Carden's "supposed unfriendly attitude" towards the United States, Lansdowne was able to reassure him that all was well. "Between ourselves," the Foreign Secretary admitted, "I have no doubt that Carden was a little over zealous; we moderated his energy but perhaps not quite sufficiently. Luckily we have been able to turn the tables by showing that the evidence on which the American complaint was based was quite apocryphal."[22] There were no more despatches from Havana recounting further arguments by Carden against reciprocity before the American-Cuban treaty was signed on December 11th, 1902.

Although Carden had been silenced, the Foreign Office was still faced with pressure at home. The American-Cuban treaty contained all the benefits the United States had demanded but still had to face the perils of ratification. The commercial interests in Britain still hoped the Foreign Office could exert some influence in their behalf. On December 15th Charles MacArthur of Liverpool finally raised in Parliament the unwelcome question Lansdowne had so long avoided: had the government taken any steps to protect British interests in Cuba, and, if so, with what results? Cranborne could only reply that representations had been made at Washington that were as yet unanswered.[23]

Once again the Foreign Office felt obligated to go through the motions of approaching the American government. Realizing that any protest to the United States would be an exercise in futility, Lansdowne told Herbert that he did not want another written communication to the State Department, but it was necessary "for Parliamentary purposes" to get an answer to the notes sent by Pauncefote in March and Raikes in June.

> You might add as if from yourself, that the Bill would appear to be destructive of all trade with Cuba other than that of the U. S., and to be quite contrary to the policy of the "open door" so strenuously advocated by the U. S., and that it will create much irritation here. A considerably worded reply is therefore most desirable.[24]

Hay promised Herbert that he would answer the earlier notes, but he held out no hope that the response would be satisfactory. The Secretary of State was not exaggerating. In his formal reply of December 20th he merely refuted the assumption made by the Liverpool Chamber of Commerce that the reciprocity treaty was based on provisions the United States had put in the Cuban Constitution to carry out the Platt Amendment. The treaty, Hay concluded, "is based solely upon the prerogative of independent nations to enter into such compacts for their mutual benefit." So much for complaints to the United States. "Mr. Hay warned us the reply w^d be unsatisfactory, & it certainly is," Campbell noted. "But as it is quite certain we s^d gain nothing by further representations, it is no use irritating the Americans by further discussions."[25]

Embroiled at the time in the Venezuelan imbroglio, the Foreign Office undoubtedly would have preferred to forget the entire Cuban issue, but the commercial pressure refused to subside. In January of 1903, the Liverpool Chamber of Commerce asked Lansdowne to meet another delegation. Lansdowne told them of Hay's reply to the earlier notes and again tried to avoid a meeting, but when the Chamber proved insistent the interview was finally set for January 22nd. This second delegation received by Lansdowne was a large one, representing thirteen Chambers of Commerce and backed up by a number of Members of Parliament. The thirteen Chambers were:

Liverpool, London, Manchester, Glascow, Nottingham, Sheffield, Wolverhampton, Blackburn, Oldham, Dublin, Bradford, Edinburgh, and Belfast. There were actually two meetings, one on January 22 with forty representatives including twelve Members of Parliament, and one on January 23 at Lansdowne House with nineteen delegates from five of the Chambers. The proceedings were again kept out of the press.

As might be expected after the charges against Carden and Hay's reply of December 20th, the delegation achieved nothing but another airing of British resentment. The aim of the group, as stated by Sir Alfred Jones, the President of the Liverpool Chamber, was to urge the British government to "use their utmost influence" both in Washington and Havana against ratification of the American treaty. Other delegates went into great detail explaining the dangers to British shippers, textile manufacturers, the rice trade, and the Burma rice growers. The Glascow representative solemnly reminded the Foreign Office that the "Munro [sic] Policy spreads over Mexico, Central America, and all South America." Alfred Bigland, the Chairman of the Liverpool General Brokers Association, thought that Britain should warn the United States that she could not guarantee neutrality in any future American wars if the loss of large markets was "the price of our neutrality." According to Bigland, the Monroe Doctrine had been helpful in preserving peace, but that the time had come for a new "doctrine" to supplement it.

> Although it appears hopeless to succeed in preventing the ratification of this Treaty, we are very hopeful that you will make use of this opportunity and precedent to bring forward a new Doctrine (we might call it the "Lansdowne Doctrine") with regard to International rights to maintain the most favoured nation Treaty clause.

Bigland wanted nothing less than an international agreement by which "all neutral markets in the World that are neutral today" would be preserved. Each country could levy tariffs as they saw fit, but none could give "preferential rights of trading" to others. This would end the international jealousy caused by the anxiety of "various Governments" to obtain new markets, and keep open markets "in which they have at present an open door."

Lansdowne was having enough trouble at the time with one doctrine and was in no mood to lend his name to another. His answer to the delegation was even less encouraging than his reply to the earlier one. The Foreign Secretary could see no effective way to prevent ratification of the American-Cuban treaty. Representations had achieved nothing, and Cuba had every right to enter into such a treaty. What was left? No British Cabinet had ever considered retaliation to be good policy, and, although the idea of an international agreement "might be a good one," he could hardly commit himself to such "a new departure" in international law.[26]

After Cuba's acceptance of the reciprocity treaty with the United States, the British could do little but wait for the outcome of the fight for ratification. At the insistence of the Board of Trade, the Foreign Office did send a protest to the United States arguing that the Cuban reciprocity treaty conflicted with the most-favored-nation clause in the Anglo-American commercial treaty of 1815. The protest, however, was only for the record, and, when the State Department refused to comment because the treaty was still before Congress, the Foreign Office decided to drop the matter.[27] Carden tried valiantly at Havana to keep the negotiations going for an Anglo-Cuban commercial treaty, but by the summer of 1903 they were suspended. It was not until the American treaty finally cleared its last hurdle in the American Congress and went into effect in December of 1903 that Cuba was presumably in a position to make whatever commercial arrangements she could with other nations. Thus in 1904 the sporadic negotiations for a British treaty began once again.

Why were the British still interested in a Cuban treaty? As early as January of 1903 Carden had analyzed the probable effect of the reciprocity treaty on British trade and had concluded that the situation was not as bad as he had anticipated. The concessions to American imports were not likely to hurt either the textile or rice trades which made up about three-fourths of the British imports. What then was there to worry about? Carden was fearful that Cuba would raise her customs duties, thus increasing the preferential position of the

United States. Carden's fears were not baseless, for in January of 1904 the Cuban Congress did pass a surtax law that led to an increase in the Cuban tariff of twenty-five or thirty percent on most of the rates. Seemingly the surtax did little to damage British exports to Cuba, but the desire to maintain freedom of action for possible retaliation in the future against Cuban imports into Britain led the Board of Trade to suggest that the whole subject of custom rates be eliminated from a new draft treaty being drawn up by the Foreign Office.

In July, 1904, the Foreign Office told Carden to begin negotiations on the basis suggested by the Board of Trade, but the British minister still hoped to get some protection against future raises of the Cuban tariff. Carden first tried a plan by which Britain would accept a most-favored-nation clause that exempted the special treaty reductions given to the United States if Cuba would promise in return to maintain the existing rates on certain specified classes of British imports. The Cubans balked at giving such a promise and definitely rejected the idea in December of 1904.

Carden now had an alternative suggestion. Britain and Cuba would give each other most-favored-nation treatment, and Britain would not invoke the treaty to share in the special reductions of the American-Cuban treaty. But if either Britain or Cuba increased their tariff on foreign goods to the disadvantage of the other, the prejudiced country reserved the right to terminate either the most-favored-nation clause or the entire treaty with six months notice. Thus Cuba would retain her right to make new arrangements with the United States, but Britain would be able to renounce the treaty on short notice. The new most-favored-nation clause certainly seemed innocuous enough and was carefully phrased not to give offense to the United States. Carden was convinced that Cuba was on the verge of accepting, but in March, 1905 the Cuban Secretary of State, Juan O'Farrill, advised Estrada Palma not to sign the treaty unless modifications were made, particularly in the most-favored-nation clause allowing Cuba complete freedom to make new reciprocity agreements with the United States.

Since the Board of Trade was anxious to get most-favored-nation treatment from Cuba for British shipping, Britain reverted to the idea of excluding customs rates entirely from the treaty, and Carden's dogged negotiations continued. His talks with the Cuban Secretary of State were not too encouraging, for O'Farrill seemingly wanted to leave his country free to make special concessions to the United States in all particulars, but the situation brightened when Cuba once more modified its position and O'Farrill decided that it would be enough if Cuba were left "quite free" regarding import duties. Thus in the treaty as finally signed on May 4, 1905, Carden was successful in getting most-favored-nation privileges for British shipping. The British had no protection against an increase in the customs, but in this case O'Farrill hinted that some understanding might be possible after the Presidential elections in the fall.[28]

In 1905 the British were also encouraged by the defeat in the Cuban Congress of a bill to raise the duty on imported rice. Prodded by another "important deputation" representing the Liverpool rice merchants and shippers, Lansdowne found enough courage to tell the Cubans injuries to British trade would result if the bill passed.[29] As the American State Department was at the same time responding to the pleas of the Rice Association of America and American shipping interests to put pressure on the Cubans in favor of the proposal,[30] the rejection of the rice bill by the Cuban Senate in August of 1905 was a distinct defeat for American policy.

Unfortunately for the British, it soon became obvious that the signs of independence shown by the Cuban Senate over the rice bill were absent in its deliberations on the British commercial treaty. The treaty was soon bogged down in the Foreign Relations Committee, and the decision on ratification was postponed until after the Presidential elections. What was the problem? The Senate was not really opposed to the treaty, the Cuban minister in London told Villiers, but it had acted as a matter of party politics. The majority of the senators were only interested in obstructing government business. According to O'Farrill, the delay was due to the Chairman of the Senate Foreign Relations Committee, but Carden did not find much evidence that O'Farrill was "pushing him," and the Cuban government did not seem unhappy over the postponement.

There was another reason for the delay that the Cuban govern-

ment avoided mentioning officially to the British. Carden had suspected that the United States was exerting influence against a British
treaty in March of 1905, and in July he reported that he had heard
"on good authority" that his old opponent Squiers had protested
against ratification of the present one.[31] Carden's suspicions were
justified and his information about Squiers was correct. The American State Department was determined to block any Anglo-Cuban
treaty that would in any way vitiate further Cuban concessions to the
United States. As Squiers was told in March of 1905, "any agreement
with Great Britain that directly or indirectly renders ineffective our
advantages under reciprocity treaty, that grants Great Britain most
favoured nation treatment or any commercial concessions whatever
in the Cuban market will be most unsatisfactory to the United
States."[32] This undoubtedly was the reason why Estrada Palma and
O'Farrill in March refused to sign the commercial treaty that Carden
thought was about to be accepted.

Nor was the United States willing to accept the modified treaty
that was signed in May. Both the Department of Commerce and the
Treasury Department agreed with Squiers that a number of stipula-
tions in the treaty could cause "embarrassments" for the United
States in the future. The State Department wanted an additional
article inserted in the treaty that would exempt "any special advantages" that Cuba had given the United States in the past or which
might be given in the future.[33] In his instructions to Squiers in June,
Francis Loomis, the Assistant Secretary of State, made it very clear
that the Roosevelt administration was deadly serious about the
change.

> You will state to the Cuban Government that if it expects this Gov-
> ernment to continue its policy of commercial advantage for Cuba, the
> Government of the United States must request the Government of
> Cuba to insert the clause sent you. . . .
> The President directs me to say that the United States makes this
> urgent request not only in its own interests but far more in the inter-
> ests of Cuba's future.
> If Cuba fails to grant this request she alone will be responsible for

any trouble that may arise in the future with respect to the commercial
relations between the two countries.

Two days later, Loomis bluntly told Squiers to "insist" upon the
insertion of the additional article. When the harassed Cuban President promised that he would try to have the treaty modified, he
received the State Department's ominous observation that it was
"glad to be spared the necessity of giving consideration at this time
to the possible eventual denouncement of its reciprocity treaty with
Cuba."[34] It is little wonder that Carden found Estrada Palma and
O'Farrill reluctant to push the British treaty in the Cuban Senate in
the summer of 1905.

American opposition to the British treaty became evident in October with reports in both the American and British press. Carden, in
London at the time on leave, suggested that the British Ambassador
at Washington, Sir Henry Durand, urge the American government
to drop its opposition. Reluctant as usual, Lansdowne vetoed the
idea, arguing "the less we do to accentuate the difference—if
there be one—the better." Lansdowne even refused to have
the treaty published for fear it would add fuel to the press campaign.[35]

But Carden had no doubts that there was a difference between the
British and American governments, and once again he urged the
Foreign Secretary to adopt a more vigorous policy. Britain had already failed to get a Cuban promise on the customs duties, and now
it seemed obvious to Carden that the United States was even opposing most-favored-nation treatment for British shipping. He did not
think that most Cubans wanted to injure British interests, but
even the best disposed Cuban government could not hold out long
against American pressure "without the exertion of some counter
pressure" by Great Britain. The problem was not restricted to
Cuba.

It must, moreover, be borne in mind that the principle involved by
the United States' attitude towards our Treaty will not be limited in

its application to Cuba. The policy inaugurated by Monroe has already been extended to imply a right of intervention in the internal politics of all the States of the American Continent, and there is a movement now on foot, of which the present situation is the outcome, to claim that this entitles the United States to preferential rights in the trade of those countries.

Carden was unimpressed by the argument that the American-Cuban relationship was unique. The United States could always discover "exceptional grounds" for other cases in the future, and "a more or less tacit acquiescence" by Great Britain in America's present attitude towards Cuba would make it more difficult for the British "to make a stand at any future time when our commercial interests in some other country are similarly threatened." It was true that the "force of circumstances" might eventually give the United States the bulk of Latin American trade, but efforts by the British to retain their commerce could lengthen the time re quired.

Cuba must be regarded as an outpost of the position which the United States are laying themselves out to capture, and the result of their present attempt cannot but have an important influence in determining their future action. But, if we are to expect the Cuban Government to loyally sustain the Treaty they have concluded with us, there must be no doubt in their minds as to our readiness to support them in the exercise of their unquestionable right to do so as an independent State.[36]

Carden painted a dark enough picture, but the Foreign Office still doubted that a more active British policy was feasible. When the Foreign Office did make a mild approach to the United States, it was seemingly a reaction to more pressure from Liverpool rather than a response to the urgings of their minister in Havana. On November 9th, the reluctant Lansdowne met his fourth delegation regarding Cuba, and it was probably in anticipation of their complaints that he had told Durand a few days earlier of Carden's suggestion for a "friendly" representation to the American government and had asked the ambassador if he thought such a step would be useful.

The new deputation represented the Liverpool Chamber of Commerce, the Chamber of Shipping of the United Kingdom, and shipowners' associations of Liverpool, the North of England, Glascow, London, Hartlepool, and the Clyde. According to the delegates, the pending treaty with Cuba was just the thing to prevent "further aggression" by the United States. "We know the policy of America very well," complained the President of the Liverpool Chamber, "She never gives anything away, and she will take all she can get." What they were afraid the grasping Americans would take next was the Cuban shipping trade, in particular the British share of the sugar cargoes to the United States—estimated at from one-third to two-fifths of the crop exported to the United States. The proposed treaty was a "matter of life and death," and, according to one delegate, if it was not ratified "it will be the beginning of a very long and a very severe fight" for "what is done with Cuba today America will seek to do with the Spanish American countries tomorrow. . . ." A severe fight with the United States was the last thing that Lansdowne wanted, but he did promise the delegates that everything possible would be done to secure the desired ratification.[37]

When Durand talked to Elihu Root the following day, the new Secretary of State was rather vague about the American objections to the treaty, but Durand's report was encouraging enough to convince Lansdowne that it was "safe" to allow his ambassador to discuss the objections "in a friendly manner" with Root and to express the British hope that the United States would not find it necessary to oppose ratification.[38] Root's next conversation with Durand was more specific but hardly enlightening. As Durand cabled home:

> Opposition to Treaty comes from American shipping interest. They apprehend that its effects will be to prevent their obtaining special concessions in nature of preferential port dues and the like.
>
> They have been told to present their case which at present is indefinite.[39]

There had certainly been nothing indefinite about the State Department's threats to Estrada Palma in June, but the Foreign Office drew the erroneous conclusion from Root's words that the American government had not yet opposed their treaty. In any event, any hopes that the British might have had in Root were misplaced. An outspoken advocate of the Cuban reciprocity treaty, Root was one of those Americans who was unhappy with its results. As early as October of 1905, he had started negotiations with the Cuban Minister in Washington for a revision of the reciprocity treaty along lines more favorable to the United States. These talks were seemingly unknown to the British, but Root's plans for Cuba were a greater danger to British trade than those of his predecessor.

Estrada Palma was reelected President in December of 1905, but the British treaty continued to languish in committee. O'Farrill claimed that his party was still pledged to the treaty and that prospects were good for a fast ratification when the new Congress met in April of 1906. He even denied that there was any American opposition to the treaty. He assured Carden that the American government "had really never expressed any opinion about it at all, and on the contrary had disavowed to the Cuban Minister in Washington any responsibility for the attitude which Mr. Squiers had seen fit to assume and for the representations he had made in their name on the subject." According to O'Farrill, the removal of Squiers from his post in Havana the previous November "was largely due" to his unauthorized action against the British treaty.[40]

It is not clear what motives O'Farrill and Estrada Palma had in playing the British along in the fall of 1905 and the spring of 1906. Squiers was a tactless diplomat, and the manner in which he had made his protests in 1905 had irritated the Cubans, but his removal by Roosevelt could hardly have been due to the fact that he had opposed the British treaty.[41] Was it a matter of Cuban pride? Or was the Cuban government trying to bluff the United States now that the elections were over? Root certainly had not changed the American position. When the American Chargé d'Affaires, Jacob Sleeper, reported a statement by O'Farrill in December of 1905 that the United States had no objection to ratification of the British treaty, Root reminded Sleeper that the American attitude was still the same as it had been in the instructions to Squiers in June of 1905.[42] Or perhaps Squiers' successor as minister to Havana, Edwin Morgan, was correct in his belief that the Cubans possibly wanted to keep the treaty in committee indefinitely as a threat to the United States.[43] In any event, the British treaty, as signed, was doomed, and had been doomed since the summer of 1905.

On May 30th, the Cuban Senate did finally ratify the British treaty, but only after adding two amendments to the most-favored-nation clause. The first exempted the coastal trade and the fishing industry from most-favored-nation treatment, and the second completely undercut the British position by leaving Cuba free to make reciprocity arrangements on all matters rather than on customs duties alone:

> The two High Contracting parties shall in no case have the right to invoke the most favoured nation clause mentioned in this Treaty with respect to reciprocal or compensatory concessions which either of them may in future grant to a third Power.

O'Farrill still hoped the British would accept the treaty, arguing that the amendments to the most-favored-nation clause did not make "any essential alternation in its purport." The second amendment was only "an interpretation of the clause in a restrictive sense, as is done in some countries of America, which is based on scientific principles, and is well worthy of attention." As his government would never give preferential maritime concessions to any country, there was no threat to British shipping. Cuba wanted complete freedom only for tariff reciprocity, and was "most firmly resolved to deal with all nations on a basis of absolute equality as regards all the other matters agreed upon in the other Articles of the Treaty." The Foreign Office was not impressed. They cared little about the fishing and coastal trade stipulation, but the "restrictive" interpretation of the most-favored-nation clause favored by "some countries of America" was another matter.

They are asking us . . . to accept a declaration to the effect that we accept the American interpretation of the m. f. n. clause. We cannot do this on general grounds, notwithstanding the assurances they offer that in the present instance our rights would not be impaired.[44]

Because the Conservatives were defeated in the Parliamentary elections in December of 1905, Lansdowne was no longer at the Foreign Office during the last stage of the Cuban treaty negotiations. When the inevitable question arose over a possible complaint to the United States about ratification, the new Foreign Secretary, Sir Edward Grey, could not understand the American government's concern in the matter. "That U. S. subjects are pulling the strings, I understand, but on what ground could we base a representation to the U. S. Govt.?"[45] Grey was unaware that some of those strings extended directly into the State Department at Washington.

What role had the American administration played in the latest changes that made the treaty unacceptable to the British? As seen by his note to Sleeper in December, Root had not changed the policy of the United States towards the treaty in the slightest. By the spring of 1906, special advantages for American shipping had definitely become part of Root's plan for revision of his country's own treaty with Cuba. When Morgan warned that "a direct recurrence to the same arguments" used by Squiers in the spring of 1905 would only "increase an irritation which has already been evidenced" by Estrada Palma and O'Farrill,[46] Root merely opposed the British treaty in a less belligerent way. As he explained to Morgan:

I have already shown to Mr. Quesada [the Cuban Minister at Washington] a draft of a treaty of commerce which I am preparing to submit within a few days, providing for reciprocal tariff advantages to goods carried in Cuban and American ships, and which I think Cuba should certainly keep herself free to consider. The terms of the pending English treaty seem to interfere with this. Of course, Cuba may . . . determine not to make such a treaty with us, but it would seem unwise for her now, by making the English treaty, to cut herself off from the possibility of making such a treaty with us, if she determines that it is for her advantage.[47]

Root did not insist on the use of the article sent to Squiers in June of 1905, but the meaning was essentially the same. The wording of the clause finally accepted by the Cuban Senate was approved by Root and even amended to include "compensatory" as well as "reciprocal" concessions. The Americans had exactly what they desired, and, as Root told Morgan early in May, if the clause "thus amended be inserted we shall not be disposed to press further our objections to the proposed treaty with Great Britain."[48] American intervention in Cuba in 1906 ended Root's negotiations for more American advantages and nothing came of his proposed new treaty of commerce, but the United States had effectively emasculated the British treaty.

While the Foreign Office was waiting for news of the action of the Cuban Senate, the Liverpool Chamber of Commerce was now plaguing the new Foreign Secretary in the same way they had often bothered his predecessor. Grey, like Lansdowne, at first tried to avoid any interview, but British commercial pressure knew no party lines, and, after the unwelcome news of the Cuban amendments arrived, Grey consented to meet privately with another delegation from a number of Chambers of Commerce and shipping organizations. The arguments used by this last of the delegations in favor of the open door in Cuba were much the same as those heard by Lansdowne in the past.[49] Their aim, in the words of Austin Taylor, MP from Liverpool, was to ask the government to use "the resources of civilisation" at Washington and Havana in behalf of the British treaty.

Grey was no more anxious than Lansdowne had been to antagonize the United States. Still believing that the American Government had played no direct part in the Cuban amendments to the British treaty, Grey rejected the idea of another approach to Washington. He promised the delegation that the government would try to get another and more satisfactory treaty from Cuba, and made some vague references to bringing pressure to bear on the Cubans if they were unwilling to discuss the matter, but whatever type of pressure Grey had in mind was never to be applied. The negotiations with Cuba were never resumed. By the time the Board of Trade advised the Foreign Office that the amended treaty was unacceptable, Cuba was in the throes of the revolution of 1906, which resulted in the intervention of the United States and the second American occupation of the island.

The attempt to maintain the "open door" in Cuba and the long unsuccessful negotiations for a commercial treaty show clearly the difficulties that the expansion of American influence in the Caribbean could pose for the British government. It is equally clear that throughout the negotiations the Foreign Office had often been reluctant to act at all, much less in the vigorous manner advocated by Carden. What was done resulted only from constant prodding by British commercial interests, and the characteristic attitudes of the Foreign Office were fatalism as to the inevitability of American commercial inroads on British interests and fear that any real defense of those interests would lead to trouble with the United States. The representations made to the United States were half-hearted and often only for the record, and, judging by the unsatisfactory answers, this was obviously realized across the Atlantic. The only lapse in this policy were the rather contradictory instructions given to Carden in 1902, but the British minister himself served as a lightning rod to absorb the charges of "anti-Americanism" rather than the policy makers at home.

The Foreign Office had been fortunate in a number of ways. The edge was taken off the complaints of British merchants and shippers when they saw that the American reciprocity treaty was not actually damaging existing British trade with Cuba. Some categories of British exports to Cuba were hurt, but the total value of British trade with the island was actually higher than it had ever been. In 1904, the first year of Cuban reciprocity with the United States, British exports were more than £500,000 higher than in 1903; and in 1907,

1912 and 1913, they topped £3,000,000 per year.[50] Prior to the American occupation of Cuba in 1906, agitation in Britain had continued, but rising sales even in the absence of a British commercial treaty certainly took much of the urgency out of the negotiations.

Then too, despite the dire warnings from Carden and others over the relationship of the Monroe Doctrine and trade, the Foreign Office could use the unique relations of Cuba and the United States as a justification for excepting Cuba from its general policy of maintaining the open door in Latin America. Although Roosevelt used other means to create protectorates in Panama and the Dominican Republic, the economic device of reciprocity was not repeated, and he did not push for any general policy of Latin American reciprocity. Indeed, judging from the bitter fight waged by the opponents of Cuban reciprocity, it is highly improbable that any such policy would have succeeded if he had desired it. By the fall of 1906 Root had even given up his efforts to widen the agreement with Cuba, and, as he wrote in October, he was unable to get "any encouragement to believe that any reciprocity treaty with anybody will receive any consideration from the Senate. There appears to be an abandonment of the whole doctrine."[51] Fortunately for the British, American enthusiasm for Latin American reciprocity had waned by the beginning of the era of the "big stick."

Of course the British merchants, manufacturers and shippers did not have our advantage of hindsight. The spectre of German economic rivalry was not the only one haunting British commercial circles in the pre-World War I era. The awful prophecies of a "total annihilation" of Britain's Latin American trade that arose out of the Cuban situation can only be understood in the context of the very real fear that many Englishmen had of American economic competition throughout the world. It would take more to down these fears than the statistics on Cuban trade.

Even when it became obvious that Cuban-American reciprocity had not destroyed British trade, men like Carden merely transferred their fears from the present to the future. Who was to say what the United States would do next? Carden and many of the representatives who met with Lansdowne and Grey were sure that they saw a connection between the Monroe Doctrine and American economic policies in Cuba; and while the urgency of their complaints declined, their apprehensions for the future remained. Carden, in particular, would remember his frustrating Cuban experiences in his new post as Minister to Central America[52] when the time came to sound the tocsin against "dollar diplomacy."

NOTES AND REFERENCES

1. Quoted in Russell H. Fitzgibbon, *Cuba and the United States, 1900–1935* (Menasha, Wisc., 1935), p. 207.

2. For American economic policy during the period of the occupation, see David F. Healy, *The United States in Cuba, 1898–1902* (Madison, 1963), pp. 189–206.

3. Carden to Lansdowne, January 16, 1901. F. O. 108/9.

4. Bergne to Carden, February 7, 1901. F. O. 108/9.

5. Pauncefote to Lansdowne, April 1, 1901. F. O. 108/9.

6. Carden to Villiers, August 10, 1901, and minutes by Cranborne and Lansdowne; Lansdowne to Carden, August 17. F. O. 108/9.

7. See U. S. Tariff Commission, *Reciprocity and Commercial Treaties* (Washington, 1919), pp. 18–20, 39–48, 389–456.

8. Carden to Villiers, January 15, 1902, and minutes by Cranborne and Lansdowne. F. O. 108/9.

9. Liverpool Chamber of Commerce, February 17, 1902, and minutes by Cranborne and Lansdowne. Lansdowne to Pauncefote, February 28th. F. O. 108/9.

10. "Note on reception by Lord Lansdowne of deputation from Chambers of Commerce to call attention to Cuban Trade," March 11, 1902.

11. Pauncefote to Hay, March 10, 1902; Hill to Pauncefote, March 14th. F. O. 108/9.

12. Lansdowne to Raikes, June 6th. F. O. 108/9. Ambassador Pauncefote died in Washington on May 24. Arthur Raikes was in charge of the legation until October 6 when Sir Michael Herbert arrived.

13. Carden to Lansdowne, August 14, 1902. F. O. 108/9.

14. See David F. Healy, *The United States in Cuba, 1898–1902* (Madison, 1963), pp. 198–203. In the treaty as finally signed in December of 1902, American exports to Cuba were grouped in four classes of preference (20%, 25%, 30% and 40%). See U. S. Tariff Commission, *op. cit.*, p. 321. The percentage of tariff reductions on American goods that most affected British interests were: 40% on rice, 30% on cotton goods, and 40% on woolens.

15. Carden to Lansdowne, July 11, 1902, and July 14th; Lansdowne to Carden, July 13th, and F. O. to Carden, private, July 17th. F. O. 108/1.

16. During the period of the Platt Amendment restrictions, all of Cuba's external loans were floated in the United States. See Russell H. Fitzgibbon, *Cuba and the United States, 1900–1935* (Menasha, Wisconsin, 1935), pp. 228–29.

17. Foreign Office to Carden, October 8, 1902. F. O. 108/9.

18. Hay to Squiers, October 16, 1902; Hay to Choate, October 16th. State Department Instructions, Cuba, Vol. 1, and Great Britain, Vol. 34. Choate to Hay, October 17th, and despatch 963 of October 28th. State Department Despatches, Great Britain, Vol. 205. Lansdowne to Herbert, October 17th. F. O. 5/2484.

19. Lansdowne to Carden, October 20, 1902; Villiers to Carden, private, October 20th. F. O. 108/1. Choate to Hay, October 22, 1902. State Department Despatches, Great Britain, Vol. 205.

20. Carden to Lansdowne, October 22, 1902. F. O. 108/1.

21. Choate to Hay, October 25, 1902. State Department Despatches, Great Britain, Vol. 205. See also Lansdowne to Herbert, October 30th and November 19th in F. O. 5/2484, and Carden to Lansdowne, November 13th in F. O. 108/1.

22. Herbert to Lansdowne, private, November 19, 1902; Lansdowne to Herbert, December 4, 1902. Lansdowne Papers, U. S., Vol. 28.

23. *The Parliamentary Debates*, vol. 116, p. 1214.

24. Lansdowne to Herbert, December 17, 1902. F. O. 108/9.

25. Herbert to Lansdowne, December 23, 1902, and Campbell's minute. F. O. 108/9.

26. The proceedings of the meeting of January 23 were compiled by the secretary of the Liverpool Chamber. See Liverpool Chamber of Commerce to Lansdowne, February 4, 1903, and reply of February 13. F. O. 108/10.

27. See Lansdowne to Herbert, May 16, 1903, and replies of June 4 and June 17. F. O. 108/10.

28. Carden to Lansdowne, April 16, 21, 22, 27, and May 3 and 4, 1905. One argument used by Carden to modify O'Farrill's original position was the fact that in December of 1903 Cuba had given Italy most-favored-nation treatment in all respects except the reduction of duties on goods of other American states. For the text of the Italian treaty, see U. S. *Foreign Relations*, 1904, pp. 230–36.

29. Lansdowne to Carden, January 24, 1905. F. O. 108/12. Almost all of Cuba's rice imports were Indian rice, most of it coming by way of Great Britain. Louisiana and Carolina rice was much more expensive.

30. See the instructions of 1905 to Squiers in State Department Instructions, Cuba, Vol. 1.

31. Carden to Lansdowne, July 12, 1905. F. O. 108/12.

32. Adee to the legation, March 20, 1905, quoted in Fitzgibbon, *op. cit.*, p. 109.

33. The wording of the article was suggested by the Commerce Department. See Loomis to Squiers, telegram of June 6, 1905, and despatch of June 7th. State Department Instructions, Cuba, Vol. 1.

34. Loomis to Squiers, June 12, 14, 19, 21, 1905. Peirce to Squiers of June 28th. State Department Instructions, Cuba, vol. 1.

35. Durand to Lansdowne, October 12 and 17, 1905, and minutes by Law, Gorst, and Lansdowne. F. O. 108/12. For some comment in the American press, see the *Literary Digest*, October 21, 1905, p. 568.

36. Carden to Lansdowne, private, October 23, 1905. F. O. 108/12.

37. Proceedings of November 9, 1905. F. O. 108/12.

38. Durand to Lansdowne, November 10, 1905; Lansdowne to Durand, November 13th, and minutes. F. O. 108/12. Root took office as Secretary of State in July of 1905.

39. Durand to Lansdowne, November 16, 1905. F. O. 108/12.

40. Carden to Grey, January 20, February 15 and 28, 1906. F. O. 368/13.

41. Squiers was removed following a statement to the Havana press regarding the Isle of Pines controversy. Fitzgibbon, *op. cit.*, p. 110. For the rumors in the press following his resignation, see the *Literary Digest*, December 16, 1905, pp. 908–9.

42. Root to Sleeper, February 12, 1906. State Department Instructions, Cuba, vol. 1.

43. Morgan to Root, April 12, 1906, quoted in Fitzgibbon, *op. cit.*, p. 109.

44. Griffith to Grey, May 24, May 31, and June 11, 1906, and minutes; O'Farrill to Griffith, June 25th (received F. O. July 13th) and F. O. minute.

45. Grey's minute on de Salis memorandum (21335). F. O. 368/13.

46. Morgan to Root, April 12, 1906, quoted in Fitzgibbon, *op. cit.*, p. 109.

47. Root to Morgan, April 23, 1906, State Department Instructions, Cuba, vol. 1.

48. Root to Morgan, May 2, 1906, State Department Instructions, Cuba, Vol. 1. The proposed American-Cuban treaty submitted to Quesada on May 8th raised the American preferentials on a number of products, particularly cotton and rice, and it would have confined the tariff concessions to goods carried on Cuban or American ships. See Philip C. Jessup, *Elihu Root* (New York, 1938), I, 527–29.

49. See notes taken at interview of June 21, 1906. F. O. 368/13.

50. *Parliamentary Papers,* Cd 2626 (1905) lxxx, and Cd 4784 (1909) lxxxiii, and Cd 7585 (1914) lxxxiii.

51. Root to General James Wilson, October 24, 1906, quoted in Jessup, *op. cit.*, I, 529.

52. Carden was appointed Minister to Central America in December 1905, and he left for Guatemala in 1906 before the Cuban Senate voted on the British treaty.

CHAPTER IV

In the Shadow of the Big Stick

British diplomatic and naval activity in the Caribbean reached low ebb during the years following the Venezuelan crisis. With the settlement of the potentially dangerous Alaskan boundary dispute by arbitration in 1903, Anglo-American relations were unprecedentedly cordial and free from serious controversies, and the British government was more than ever determined to avoid even the appearance of opposition to the United States within the American sphere of influence. The change to a Liberal ministry in December of 1905 brought no change in this policy. Indeed, the Liberal spokesmen had been quick to berate the Conservatives in 1902–1903 for jeopardizing Anglo-American friendship by their adventure with Germany in Venezuela. As feelings hardened and naval rivalry with Germany intensified, the British felt that friendship with the United States was becoming more important with each passing year.

Favorable relations with the United States did little to mitigate British fears of antagonizing the Americans by any display of independence in Latin America. Cordial relations with the United States was a new experience, and while most of the British statesmen viewed the future of Anglo-American relations hopefully, it was an optimism tempered with caution. The American uproar over the Venezuelan episode confirmed their deep-rooted apprehensions over what they considered to be the illogical and mercurial nature of American public opinion. The administration at Washington seemed friendly enough, but Theodore Roosevelt aroused uneasiness as well as admiration from the British statesmen. "He must be a strange being," Lansdowne wrote to Ambassador Durand in 1905, "but he is to me an attractive personality, altho I should be sorry to have to deal with him if he happened to be in the wrong mood."[1] With the "Rough Rider" wielding the "big stick" in the Caribbean, the British had extra cause for caution in the area.

Even when the Foreign Office did try to maintain a degree of British influence and prestige in Latin American waters by "showing the flag," they ran into the formidable opposition of Sir John Fisher, the dynamic naval reformer who was First Sea Lord from 1904 to 1910. To Admiral Fisher, an extreme Germanophobe, all other considerations paled before the threat of the German navy. His determination to concentrate British sea power, particularly in home waters, led to a drastic reduction of the number of British ships in other parts of the world. As for the Western hemisphere, Fisher was in favor of a complete naval withdrawal, and his redistribution scheme resulted in the dismantling of what was left of British sea power in American waters. Under the new system there were to be annual cruises in the West Indies and along the coast of South America by a training squadron based in England, but when the squadron was absent British interests in the Caribbean were to be protected by a flagship in the West Indies and a single cruiser stationed at Bermuda.[2]

The Foreign Office had no quarrel with the Admiralty over the basic strategic considerations behind the fleet reorganization. The statesmen themselves had made this redistribution possible, not only in the Western hemisphere by the rapprochement with the United States, but in the Far East and the Mediterranean as well by the Anglo-Japanese alliance of 1902 and the new "Entente Cordiale" with France. What did bother both the Foreign Office and the Colonial Office were the drastic limits to which Fisher went in his scrapping and withdrawal of gunboats and small craft that had been used to bolster British prestige. The small vessels were a "fearful waste of men and money," Fisher wrote in 1902. "Burn them all at once and damn the Consuls and Foreign Office!"[3] When Fisher withdrew all gunboats from around the world except for a few in China and along the West coast of Africa, he aroused some heated opposition from those in the British government unwilling to lose the instruments of "gunboat diplomacy."

Frightened on the one hand by an aggressive American President who was obviously determined to dominate the Caribbean and, on the other, by a strong-willed admiral who was intent on removing as far as possible any temptation to resort to the use of naval vessels, the Foreign Office was particularly quiescent during these years. The policy of maintaining Anglo-American friendship made a vigorous defense of British interests in the Caribbean improbable; Roosevelt and Fisher made it impossible.

The most momentous manifestation of Roosevelt's desire to turn the Caribbean into an American sea was his expansion of the meaning of the Monroe Doctrine. By using the doctrine to justify his policy in Santo Domingo, Roosevelt found himself enunciating a "corollary" by which the United States, in theory at least, was accepting vast responsibilities, not only in the Caribbean, but in the entire Western hemisphere. The argument that the United States had a duty under the Monroe Doctrine to exercise an international police power in Latin America was stated by Roosevelt a number of times in 1904 and 1905.[4] It is true that there were qualifications to Roosevelt's "corollary." It was to apply to "flagrant cases" of "chronic wrong-doing, or impotence which results in a general loosening of the ties of civilized society,"[5] and as Roosevelt carefully pointed out in his annual message to Congress of 1905, a "tort against a foreign nation, such as an outrage against a citizen of that nation . . ., does not force us to interfere to prevent punishment of the tort, save to see that the punishment does not assume the form of territorial occupation in any shape."[6] On the other hand, foreign investors and bondholders (who tended to think of all cases as "flagrant") could hardly help but be drawn to such statements as Roosevelt's warning of 1904 that a Latin American state need not fear American intervention if it knew "how to act with reasonable efficiency and decency in social and political matters" and "keeps order and pays its obligations."[7] And if "an outrage" against a foreigner did not obligate the United States to intervene, presumably a violation of a "contractual obligation" might. As Roosevelt put it in December of 1905:

Our own government has always refused to enforce such contractual obligations on behalf of its citizens by an appeal to arms. It is much to be wished that all foreign governments would take the same view. But they do not; and in consequence we are liable at any time to be brought face to face with disagreeable alternatives. On the one hand, this country would certainly decline to go to war to prevent a foreign government from collecting a just debt; on the other hand, it is very inadvisable to permit any foreign power to take possession, even temporarily, of the custom houses of an American Republic in order to enforce the payment of its obligations; for such temporary occupation might turn into a permanent occupation. The only escape from these alternatives may at any time be that we must ourselves undertake to bring about some arrangement by which so much as possible of a just obligation shall be paid.[8]

As there were other means of coercion that would not involve even the temporary occupation of a customs house, Roosevelt's argument may not have been logical, but his meaning seems clear.[9] Under certain circumstances the United States would have to collect Europe's bills in order to avoid European intervention in the New World.

Was the Roosevelt "corollary" then one of the reasons for the Foreign Office's passive policy in Latin America? Did the British no longer have to worry about collecting their debts? Did the "corollary" end the constant pressure on the Foreign Office from the British bondholders? Fear of the United States may have contributed to the settlement of the Venezuelan debt in 1905, but the Roosevelt administration intervened only once in the Caribbean to carry out the "corollary," and, although a debt settlement was reached in Santo Domingo, it was one the Council of Foreign Bondholders was later to call "about the most glaring and inexcusable instance of injustice" that they had seen since their establishment.[10] At first glance, such a reaction seems strange, and it can only be understood by an analysis of the British role in the genesis of the Roosevelt "corollary" itself.

Britain of course had an indirect influence on the enunciation of the corollary by her part in the coercion of Venezuela. The joint action with Germany and Italy may have been a foreign policy blunder, but it was successful as a claims collecting expedition, and the subsequent decision by the Hague giving priority of payment to the blockading powers was deeply disturbing to the American administration. In addition, the uproar in the United States led many in Great Britain to revive the argument already voiced at times in the nineteenth century that the United States had responsibilities to Europe under the Monroe Doctrine. There is no evidence that the British government entered the Venezuelan adventure with any intention of maneuvering the United States into accepting the role of Latin American policeman. Lansdowne and Villiers had been quite willing to enforce British demands in Guatemala as well as Venezuela in 1901–1902. But once American displeasure was manifested during the coercion, such arguments in the press and in Parliament were inevitable because of Britain's policy of friendship with the United States.

The British government, taking the position that the entire Venezuelan episode had nothing to do with the Monroe Doctrine, could hardly argue that the United States should intervene in such cases to uphold it, but official British spokesmen could and did suggest the desirability of the United States playing the role of Latin American policeman in order to avoid such incidents in the future. Whether Roosevelt needed such invitations from the British is open to question, but the Venezuelan blockade was certainly in mind the following year when the corollary was formulated. As Roosevelt wrote to Elihu Root in June of 1904:

> If we are willing to let Germany or England act as the policeman of the Caribbean, then we can afford not to interfere when gross wrongdoing occurs. But if we intend to say "Hands off" to the powers of Europe, then sooner or later we must keep order ourselves.[11]

On the other hand, Great Britain was not one of those nations whose possible intervention in Santo Domingo worried Roosevelt and led to his expansion of the Monroe Doctrine. British trade and investments in Santo Domingo were not extensive and a greater share of the Dominican external debt was held in France and Belgium than in Britain. The Foreign Office did exert some pressure on behalf of the British bondholders in 1901 and 1902, but in this instance the British government found themselves acting in conjunction with the State Department because of the ties between the British bondholders and the "San Domingo Improvement Company" of New York. After the Venezuelan difficulties the bondholders had little hope for any strong government backing, but since the Council of Foreign Bondholders was still following a policy of staying under the protective wings of the American company in 1904, the Foreign Office was even free from any agitation for them to take part in the crucial international pressure on Santo Domingo that led to the "corollary."[12]

The peculiar tie between the interests of British bondholders and the San Domingo Improvement Company had its origins in the tangled problems of Dominican finances in the late nineteenth century. The history of the Dominican external debt in the nineteenth century was particularly unsavory even by the standards of the day.[13] The first loan that was floated in London in 1869 was followed by the usual defaults and conversions, with the only benefits being derived by foreign financiers and speculators and corrupt Dominican politicians. In connection with a bond issue in 1888, a Dutch firm received the right to collect the payments directly from the customs receipts. When the Dutch company ran into financial difficulties, their rights were purchased by the San Domingo Improvement Company. The misnamed Improvement Company and its subsidiaries—the San Domingo Finance Corporation, the Central Railroad of Santo Domingo, and the National Bank of Santo Domingo—thus came into effectual control of Dominican finances.

After new bonds were floated in 1893 and 1895, the company negotiated a new consolidation of the external debt in 1897. Two types of bonds were issued: those bearing 2¾% interest—the so-called "Brussels bonds" that ended up primarily in Belgium and France—and the 4% "Dominican Unified Bonds." The bulk of both categories of bonds—£2,986,750 of the total issue of £4,236,750—were used for the conversion of older securities. Although the

Dominican government perhaps received as little as $450,000 from the transactions, a Belgian syndicate purchased over £500,000 of the remaining 2¾% bonds at 24%, and the Improvement Company took up £277,980 of the 4% bonds at 32% of face value.[14] Within a few years a considerable number of the total 4% bonds outstanding were held in England, perhaps over £500,000 worth by 1902.[15]

Santo Domingo's default in 1899 on an external debt of £3,885,350 inaugurated a long series of complicated negotiations between the government, the Improvement Company, and the foreign bondholders, a situation that was further confused by frequent internal upheavals within the country.[16] After taking the collection of the customs out of the hands of the Improvement Company, the Dominican government, in March of 1901, reached an agreement with the Company to protect their interests in return for certain concessions. Santo Domingo then offered the foreign bondholders a new arrangement by which the outstanding bonds would be retired at 50% of their face value. Although the Belgian and French bondholders accepted the new offer, the Council of Foreign Bondholders was afraid that the security was insufficient and decided that it would be wiser to merge the interests of the British bondholders with those of the Improvement Company. The Dominican Minister for Foreign Affairs and the Company agreed to extend their arrangement of March to include the interests of the British bondholders. But when the Dominican Congress accepted the arrangement with the French and Belgian bondholders and rejected the agreement with the despised Improvement Company, the Council of Foreign Bondholders, on December 20, 1901, appealed to the Foreign Office for aid.

The British government, which had not hesitated to help British bondholders in Guatemala and Venezuela in 1901–2, certainly had no objections to acting in concert with the United States in Santo Domingo. After learning that the State Department had instructed the American minister to exert his good offices in behalf of the Improvement Company, Lansdowne ordered Consul General Cohen, the British representative for Haiti and Santo Domingo, to do the same.[17] There was never any question of strong diplomatic action by the British, since the entire maneuver by the Council was an attempt to get the all-important backing of the United States for the British bondholders. When Cohen reported that the Dominican government wanted to know the amount of the British claims, Sir C. W. Fremantle, the Vice-President of the Council, told Villiers that the bondholders definitely did not want to be dealt with separately from the Company.

> I add a line to our official letter about San [sic] Domingo just to say that we hope that Mr. Cohen's request to be informed as to the amount of the claims of the British Bondholders does not mean that an attempt is being made to detach & separate these claims from those represented by the Improvement Company, which are being, as we understand, strongly supported by the United States Government. . . .
>
> It is quite possible that Mr. Cohen may not be greatly impressed with the Improvement Company, but we believe that the interests of the British holders of San [sic] Domingo bonds will be best protected by keeping under the skirts of the Company & not by negotiating separately on their own account.
>
> We rather hope therefore that the F. O. will be able to continue (as we understand they had already done) to instruct Mr. Cohen to back up the action of his American Colleague.[18]

The Council's strategy seemingly worked. The Dominicans agreed to pay the Improvement Company $4,500,000 for all its rights and interests, and, when the negotiations broke down over the manner of payment, the American minister exerted more pressure. The result was a protocol, signed between the United States and Santo Domingo on January 31, 1903, referring the terms of payment to an arbitral board chosen by the presidents of the two countries. One of the interests to be relinquished by the Company was all of the Dominican bonds "of which they may be the holders, the amount of which shall not exceed £850,000 . . . and shall be no less than £825,000." With the exception of £24,000 of 2¾% bonds, these were to be of the 4% class, and a list of the bonds was to be submitted to the arbitrators.

After more prodding from the United States, the arbitration got underway, and the award was announced on July 14, 1904. The

$4,500,000 was to be paid in monthly installments to a financial agent appointed by the United States. The customs revenues of Puerto Plata and three other northern ports were assigned as security, and, in the event of default, the agent was authorized to take over collections at Puerto Plata and the other ports if the revenues there proved insufficient. The value of the bonds to be delivered by the Company was now set at £830,654, to be retired at fifty percent of their face value.[19] The Council of Foreign Bondholders had been very successful in keeping "under the skirts" of the Improvement Company. The fact that most of these bonds were held in Britain was neither mentioned in the protocol of 1903 nor in the award of 1904. The British had seemingly secured the same fifty percent settlement as the French and Belgian bondholders with much better security.

The arbitrative award of 1904 led to the establishment of American control of the customs. Being in no position to carry out any of its financial arrangements, the Dominican government failed to make the first monthly payment to the Improvement Company, and the financial agent took over the administration of the customs house at Puerto Plata in October of 1904. When Santo Domingo was unable to meet its obligations to its many other creditors, they too became insistent on a settlement, and it was this European pressure that caused Roosevelt to act to head off any foreign intervention or control. The result was the treaty of February, 1905, between the United States and Santo Domingo. By this agreement the United States undertook to adjust all the debts and claims of the small republic, and to collect all of the customs, turning over forty-five percent of the receipts to the Dominican government and using the remainder to pay her creditors. When the American Senate failed to act on the treaty, Roosevelt put the same arrangement into effect by means of a *modus vivendi* by which an American "General Receiver and Collector" was appointed, and the money set aside for debt payment was deposited in a New York bank pending investigation of the claims.[20]

How did the British react to Roosevelt's new use of the Monroe Doctrine? As might be expected in light of their homilies in the past on American responsibilities, the British press was generally favorable to the corollary. Speaking for those with specific interests in Latin America, the *South American Journal* found Roosevelt's statements "interesting and important" and hoped that he would take strong measures in Venezuela as well. British investors in Latin America had "everything to gain and nothing to lose from President Roosevelt's declared policy of applying the Monroe Doctrine in what may be called a broad and equitable spirit." Still, some of the press did not miss the significance of the opposition in the Senate. As the London *Outlook* pointed out, until Roosevelt won over the Senate "the immensely vital question of whether the Monroe Doctrine implies duties as well as confers privileges has still to be answered."[21]

At Washington, Ambassador Durand realized the possible significance of Roosevelt's utterances, but he too was equally impressed by the opposition to the corollary. After the Senate adjournment in March he reported:

> It is possible that this question may become one of exceptional importance. It has given rise to much discussion regarding the future attitude of the United States in the matter of the Monroe Doctrine, and also regarding the constitutional powers of the President and Senate. At present I think the balance of public opinion inclines to the view that the President has been wrong on both points—that he has shown a tendency to ignore the constitutional rights of the Senate, and that his interpretation of the Monroe Doctrine would impose upon the United States new and undesirable obligations. But the American public is curiously ignorant of everything connected with the conduct of foreign affairs, and it is by no means certain that the Senate is any better informed. It remains to be seen whether that body will find itself able to carry its views into practical effect.[22]

If Roosevelt's statements caused any great excitement at the Foreign Office, it did not find its way into the records.[23] When the British minister at Caracas mentioned the possibility that Venezuela might be forced into an arrangement like that in Santo Domingo, Larcom noted that the Dominican settlement "would probably be largely to the advantage of British interests, and a similar arrangement in Venezuela might almost be contemplated without regret, provided due respect were shown for the 'chose jugee' in the matter of preferential treatment of our claims." But Villiers thought U. S. action in Venezuela was improbable, and there are no indications that the Foreign Office expected any general application of the corollary.[24] They were probably gratified that the American arrangement reflected the idea that the Monroe Doctrine implied American duties as well as rights, but they were well aware that there was a difference in American politics between the statement of a policy by the executive and its acceptance by the legislature. There was certainly no opposition in London to the creation of a new U. S. protectorate in the Caribbean, particularly when British interests were seemingly protected. When Durand informed the Foreign Office of the *modus vivendi,* the Chief Clerk of the American Department merely said the arrangement seemed "a good one for all parties."[25]

Probably no one in Britain was studying the Roosevelt corollary with more interest than British bondholders. British holders of Dominican bonds were not the only ones rejoicing, for as the Council of Foreign Bondholders noted in their annual report for 1904–1905, Roosevelt's statements about the Monroe Doctrine had caused "a very remarkable appreciation in the market value of Spanish-American Securities" during the past year.[26] By the following year, the Council was ready to define the "two cardinal points" of the Monroe Doctrine "as expanded into what may perhaps now be more properly called the Roosevelt Doctrine."

(1) That while they cannot oppose the European Powers from obtaining redress for wrongs inflicted on their subjects by the Latin-American Republics, the United States claim that their consent must be obtained before any coercive action is taken, and (2) that as the interference of the European Powers in Latin America is liable to give rise to complications and endanger friendly relations, it is the duty of the United States to see that the Latin-American Republics give no cause for such interference, "by behaving with decency in industrial and political matters and paying their obligations."[27]

The Council obviously had high hopes for point two of the "Roosevelt Doctrine," but from the start there were also some serious doubts as to the President's intentions of living up to his "duty." In their report for 1904–1905, the Council was already complaining that the attitude of the United States regarding Panama, Santo Domingo and Guatemala "cannot, however, be regarded as affording the English Bondholders much cause for congratulations."[28] The Council's inclusion of Guatemala referred to their continuing troubles with Estrada Cabrera, but what were the problems in Panama and Santo Domingo?

In the case of Panama, the Council had already attempted to take Roosevelt at his word. Colombia defaulted on her external debt in 1900, and the Council had hoped that some of the money offered Colombia by the United States for canal rights would be used to liquidate the bondholders' claims. But when Panama seceded from Colombia in 1903 and became an American protectorate, the Council tried to induce the new republic to assume a proportion of the Colombian debt. When Panama refused to deal with the matter on the grounds that Colombia had not recognized her, the Council, in December of 1904, asked Roosevelt to arbitrate. When Hay said that the President would be unable to do so, the Council invoked the corollary:

> Unless some sort of pressure is applied we feel that any settlement of the matter may be indefinitely postponed, and in justice to the Bondholders the Council venture to request that Your Excellency's Government will withhold any further payments to the Government of Panama until a settlement has been arrived at.
>
> In spite of the fact that the President of the United States is not able, at any rate at the present time, to accede to the request of the Colombian Bondholders as regards arbitration, the Council still venture to hope that, as it is in the interest of Panama itself to come to an honorable arrangement, that they may rely on his powerful assistance in expediting this desirable object, in accordance with the policy foreshadowed in his recent message to Congress.

Hay's answer was terse. Since the Council was not an American citizen, they could not claim the assistance of the American government "in the collection of Bonds against Foreign Governments." The State Department could take no action in their behalf.[29]

What type of "Roosevelt doctrine" was this? As the President of the Council argued in a letter to Hay, Roosevelt had intervened in Santo Domingo, again reaffirming the principle of American responsibility in another message to Congress.

> We had therefore, we submit, good reason to hope that the President would be prepared to assist the holders of Colombian Bonds, whose claims are at least as good as those of the Santo Domingo Bondholders, and who, we venture to think, have a right to especial consideration in view of the prejudice which they have suffered in consequence of the secession of Panama from Colombia.[30]

The Council's pleas were in vain. Colombia resumed the service of her external debt in 1905, but the new agreement of that year was negotiated by the Council without the help of either the Foreign Office or the State Department.

Obviously the Roosevelt administration had no intention of intervening throughout Latin America for the aid of European bondholders. But what complaints did the Council have over the American attitude in Santo Domingo, the one country in which the United States had intervened to settle claims? The Council first became apprehensive over the *modus vivendi* announced by Roosevelt, which in effect set aside the arbitral award of 1904 to the Improvement Company by its provision that the customs revenues earmarked for claims settlements were to be deposited temporarily in a New York bank. As a result of the protocol of 1903 and the award of 1904, British investors had purchased more of the Dominican bonds included under the award and the *modus vivendi* had caused "a heavy depreciation" in their value.[31] When Hugh O'Beirne of the British Embassy requested assurance from the State Department for British bondholders that the United States did not intend to disregard the rights of the Improvement Company, the answer was far from reassuring. Roosevelt was "unable at present to recognize any special rights and privileges" of the Improvement Company over any other creditors of Santo Domingo. If these benefits were "eventually accorded," it would be after the Senate acted on the proposed treaty.[32]

Despite the Council's expressed "bewilderment" at the State Department's answer, it was obvious that the bondholders' tactics of alliance with the Improvement Company were beginning to boomerang. When O'Beirne made his request, Roosevelt had already decided to undercut the company's privileged position. Jacob H. Hollander, Roosevelt's special agent in the investigation of the claims against Santo Domingo, was instructed to include the company's claims with the rest of the Dominican debt. When Hollander completed his detailed study of the Dominican debt documenting the unsavory nature of the past transactions, the Council's ties with the Improvement Company became a liability rather than an asset for the British bondholders. In October of 1905, Root frankly told Ambassador Durand that the money owed the Company was "on the same footing as other debts" admitted by Santo Domingo, "and that all claims connected with these debts must be examined on their merits."[33]

The general debt settlement worked out by Hollander and the Dominican Finance Minister in 1906 aroused more cries of pain from British bondholders. The British had only lost their privileged position by the suspension of the arbitral award of 1904, but now they actually found themselves in a worse position than the French and Belgian bondholders. Because of Senate opposition to the idea of making the United States responsible for settling the Dominican debt by treaty, Roosevelt decided to try aiding Santo Domingo to make the necessary arrangements before a new treaty was drawn up on the customs receivership. While Dominican representatives negotiated a $20,000,000 loan from Kuhn, Loeb and Company of New York, Hollander helped the Dominicans draw up a general plan by which the various claims were scaled down from 10% to 90%. The French and Belgian bondholders were offered a settlement based on the agreement they had accepted in 1901 by which they would receive 50% face value for their bonds. However, the claim of the San Domingo Improvement Company was reduced to 90% of the $4,500,000 upon which the arbitral award was based. Thus the British bondholders, who were to receive 50% of the value of the bonds by the award, were faced with a similar reduction that would make their bonds worth less than those of France and Belgium. When the Council of Foreign Bondholders complained of discrimination, Hollander refused to deal with them as a separate claimant.

Attempting to help the bondholders, Grey soon found that the American position was unyielding. Assistant Secretary of State Robert Bacon denied that there was any discrimination. As he explained to Esme Howard, the Councillor of the British Embassy, the British claims "formed an inseparable part" of the Improvement Company's. The British bondholders were not separate creditors "but form, as it were, part of the shareholders" of the company. The United States "had pressed for the best terms possible" for the company, and if there was more delay in accepting the arrangement, the claim might be further reduced if examined on its merits. If the British bondholders wanted to get the 10% difference, they should talk to the Improvement Company rather than the Dominican government. In a letter to Howard, Hollander took the same line. It was up to the Improvement Company to determine how the proceeds of the claim were distributed. Under the award of 1904, the bonds listed were to be delivered by the company to the Dominican government, and if the company no longer owned the bonds, they were still in a different class from the independent French and Belgian securities.[34]

The indignant Council of Foreign Bondholders was infuriated at the American explanations. They hotly denied being "shareholders" of the company as their relationship had been solely concerned with the bonds of the external debt and not with any other interests of the company. According to the Council, the American government and Hollander knew that all of the bonds specified in the award were not owned by the Improvement Company because the Council had given detailed information at the time on the British holdings and had never pretended that the Company owned them.[35] The Council admitted that the bonds were to be delivered to Santo Domingo by the company, but only on the terms stipulated by the award, and the award itself had been suspended by the United States. The Improvement Company had not only accepted the new arrangement without the approval of the Council, but had refused to compensate the bondholders for the 10% reduction. The Council found themselves being "pushed from pillar to post," the Company blaming the American government and the American government telling them to deal with the Company.[36]

Grey should have realized from Howard's reports that there was not the slightest chance that the State Department would try to pursuade Santo Domingo to make any concessions to British bondholders and risk upsetting Roosevelt's settlement. But after the Senate's consent to Roosevelt's new treaty early in 1907, Grey told Bryce to take the case to Secretary of State Root himself. Root was no more helpful than his subordinate had been. He "seemed indisposed to express an opinion either way" as to what might be done later, but there could be no interference while the treaty was still awaiting Santo Domingo's ratification. Transcending any mere financial considerations, the treaty was a vital part of the administration's Caribbean policy:

> It was the policy of the United States now that their interest in the Panama Canal had made them more concerned with the petty States in and around the Caribbean Sea to do all they could to secure peace and as much good government as possible in those communities, which they were far from wishing to incorporate, but whose prosperity and tranquility they must desire.[37]

In May of 1907 Santo Domingo ratified the treaty with the United States providing for American control of her customs, but the loan contract with New York bankers was modified by the Dominican Congress. Because the financial "panic" of 1907 was underway, the bankers withdrew their offered loan and forced Hollander and the Dominicans to work out a new arrangement for paying the claims. Instead of full payment in cash, Santo Domingo's creditors were now offered 20% in cash from the money that had been accumulating in the National City Bank of New York under the *modus vivendi,* and the balance in new 5% Dominican bonds to be taken at 98½% of face value. The sums to be paid were the same as those agreed upon in 1906, and in the ensuing negotiations the Improvement Company failed to get better terms. Once again the Belgian and French bondholders were consulted and the Council of Foreign Bondholders was ignored.

Agreeing with the Council's complaint that British bondholders should have had the same right as the French and Belgians to consider the new proposal, Grey made one last attempt to help them secure "fair treatment." It was futile. When Bryce talked to Root early in 1908, the Secretary of State "listened with attention but in replying gave me to understand that the United States Government would continue unwilling to intervene in the matter, nor do I see any prospect that this attitude will be changed."[38] The Foreign Office decided that nothing more could be done. The Council continued to press for some assistance but the cause was hopeless.

Although the Council issued "Certificates of Claim" against the Dominican government, the British bondholders could do nothing but deliver the securities under the terms agreed to by the Improvement Company. As the Council claimed with some justice, the award of 1904 was dead and buried, but the British bondholders were "chained to its corpse."[39] What was the final monetary result of the attempt to get American influence by staying "under the skirts" of the Improvement Company? According to the Council, for each £100 of bonds held by the French and Belgian investors, $293.50 in cash and new bonds was received, while the British holders of the same amount received only $233.50 for 4% bonds and $160.55 for 2¾% bonds.[40] To the disinterested observer, the British may still have received more than was just for the old bonds, but to the Council the United States was off to a bad start in living up to its "responsibilities" under the "Roosevelt Doctrine."

During the very years that the British bondholders were becoming painfully aware of the fact that the Roosevelt corollary was not going to be a panacea for their Latin American problems, the British Admiralty was coming under increasing fire within the British government because of Fisher's curtailment of Britain's traditional role of international policeman. While the bondholders were accusing the government of not doing enough to protect British interests in Latin America, the Admiralty was convinced that the Foreign Office and the Colonial Office wanted to do too much. The diplomats had no intention of alienating the United States, but they did resent the Admiralty's reluctance to cooperate in doing what little could be done safely to maintain a degree of British prestige in the Western hemisphere. This difference of opinion became evident during the last year of the Balfour ministry in connection with the *Agnes Donahoe* incident with Uruguay when the Foreign Office made it clear that they had not ruled out the possibility of using force in cases of maltreatment of British subjects.

In November 1904, Uruguay seized a small Canadian fishing vessel, the *Agnes Donahoe*, on the charge of illegal sealing and interned the captain and crew pending trial. The crew was later released but the captain remained in detention aboard ship. The British minister at Montevideo was convinced the captain would not receive justice in the Uruguayan courts, and the Foreign Office, under pressure from Canada and the Colonial Office, felt obliged to protest. The case was eventually settled peacefully with a reduction of the captain's sentence and a payment of $25,000 by Uruguay to the owners of the *Agnes Donahoe*, but during the months in 1905 when the outcome was still uncertain both the Foreign Office and the Colonial Office had tried to make preparations for a possible show of force. The opposition to coercion came from the Admiralty, not the diplomats. As Fisher later wrote, for a time "the Admiralty was practically in revolt" against the government, and when he "was had up before the Cabinet" the "only sensible men were the Prime Minister and the Lord Chancellor."[41]

Nor did the United States voice any objections to the possible British coercion of a Latin American state in 1905. As might be expected after the Venezuelan uproar, Lansdowne hastened to sound out the State Department as soon as he thought the case might cause serious trouble. Acting Secretary of State Francis Loomis promised Durand that the American representative at Uruguay would give unofficial support to the British and added, "laughing," that his government was "tired of impertinent pranks of the South American republics and that we might be sure they would regard with complacence any action taken by us to bring Uruguay to reason."[42] But would the American public take the same view? The British were still apprehensive. The United States was invited to take part in any arbitration that might result, and Balfour ruled out any land operations against Uruguay, suggesting instead a seizure of some Uruguayan seal rookeries as a reprisal which would cause no injuries to non-combatants and "would not touch the Monroe Doctrine."[43] When informed about the possibility of a temporary British seizure of the rookeries, Loomis again betrayed little interest in the affair. According to Durand, the Acting Secretary of State seemed to regard the matter "with indifference." "Why don't you give them a licking?" Loomis advised the worried British Ambassador. "We should not be sorry to see them get it."[44] Uruguay was far from the Caribbean, and one can only wonder if Loomis would have been as indifferent to the British taking "any action" to give a "licking" to a Latin American state closer to home.[45] The American minister at Montevideo did use his influence to expedite the peaceful settlement of the dispute, but the fact remains that it was Fisher, not Roosevelt, who objected to the use of force.

The inter-departmental bickering over "gunboat diplomacy" did not end with the change from a Conservative to a Liberal government; in fact the quarrel reached its height in 1906 and 1907 when a number of incidents combined to put Fisher on the defensive. In 1906 the Admiralty's critics within the government and the press became more vocal over the absence of British ships during the Cuban revolution, a mutiny in the British protectorate of Zanzibar and an earthquake in Chile. When American ships reached the scene of the Jamaican earthquake disaster in January of 1907 ahead of the British vessels and landed relief parties, there were loud cries of indignation, and even some friends of Fisher's reforms began to wonder if he had gone too far. As Brassey's *Naval Annual* commented:

In reviewing the squadrons we now keep in commission on extra-European waters, it is well to consider whether the policy of concentration has not, in certain cases, been carried beyond the limits of safety for the widespread interests and commerce of the British Empire. Having regard to the withdrawal of white troops from the West Indies (in spite of the protests of the inhabitants), it is regrettable that United States warships should have been the first to reach Kingston after the earthquake, and that it was United States and not British sailors and marines who were landed. Again, though we have frequently urged in these pages the withdrawal of the numerous useless sloops and gunboats which we used to maintain in commission on foreign stations, we cannot afford to leave our commerce in any quarter of the globe at the mercy of any small cruiser or armed merchant-man.[46]

Lord Esher, a member of the Committee of Imperial Defense, summed up the feelings of many within the government by observing that "the practical needs of this scattered Empire, especially from the point of view—sentimental, if you please,—of Palmerston's 'Civis Romanus,' have been somewhat overlooked."[47] Although the Admiralty in 1906 believed that the "battle" within the British government over the navy's police duties "has been fought and won,"[48] Fisher was forced to give way a bit the following year. After riots in 1907 in St. Lucia, a British possession in the Windward Islands, an additional cruiser was sent to the West Indies.

In reply to his critics, Fisher denied that the Admiralty had ever resisted "any reasonable requirement" of the Foreign and Colonial Offices. Was he correct regarding the requirements of the Foreign Office? After Fisher's fleet redistribution, the first time in which the Foreign Office was affected by the lack of a British ship in the Caribbean was the Cuban revolution of 1906, and here a good case can be made for Fisher's views. When the British vice-consul first called for a ship to protect British property from the insurgents, the Foreign Office found there were no British vessels in the West Indies. As the closest ship was in Bermuda, 1500 miles away, and in need of a change of crew, the Foreign Office was forced to ask the United States for protection. The State Department not only responded, but the Foreign Office soon found that the appeal for American protection was actually a blessing in disguise. When the Spanish government made a rather vague and feeble attempt to put together a European concert to deal with the situation in Cuba, Grey was able to evade the subject on the grounds that Britain had already asked the United States to protect British lives and property.[49]

The Foreign Office certainly could not complain about the practical results of relying on the Americans during the Cuban revolution, but did the American intervention and the protection of British interests there mean that there was no real need for British ships in the Caribbean to cope with revolutionary disorders in countries that were not American protectorates? Events in Haiti in 1908 seemed to indicate otherwise.

British worries over the revolutionary disturbances in Haiti in 1908 did not result from any large economic interests. The United States, France and Germany all had greater economic stakes there than Great Britain. But even here the Foreign Office could not ignore the dangers of revolution, for there were a considerable number of British subjects from the British West Indies living in the turbulent little republic. Thus the problems of empire extended even into this primitive country where British commercial and financial interests were minute, and since American tutelage had not yet been imposed on Haiti, the Foreign Office was faced with a familiar problem when a revolution broke out in January of 1908 against the government of President Nord Alexis.

When Consul General Alexander Murray warned that foreigners would be in danger if the revolution continued to spread, the Foreign Office made the usual request to the Admiralty for a British man-of-war. The Admiralty ordered HMS *Indefatigable* to Port au Prince, but as the ship was awaiting a new crew in Bermuda, the Foreign Office had to ask the United States to extend protection to British subjects pending her arrival. "If an American ship had not been on the spot," Hardinge noted, "the situation would be very unpleasant, but it is wrong that we should have to depend on foreign vessels." The Foreign Office wasted no time issuing a complaint to the Admiralty about the "somewhat undesirable position" into which it had placed the government.[50] The years of criticism finally had their effect. Although a rather testy answer to the Foreign Office was drafted in the Admiralty, it was cancelled, and throughout the remaining year the Admiralty's responses to requests of the Foreign Office were quite prompt and cooperative.

The January revolution against Nord Alexis was unsuccessful and by the time the *Indefatigable* arrived the uprising had been suppressed. But the end of the revolution did not bring an end to the fears of the diplomatic corps at Port au Prince. Following an unwritten law or custom of Haitian politics, many of the unsuccessful insurgents sought asylum in foreign legations. Although the United States came out against the traditional practice and expelled a number of Haitian refugees from one of its consulates, the French and the Germans refused to surrender the refugees under their protection without a formal understanding from the vengeful Nord Alexis that their lives would be spared.[51] On March 16th Murray again called for a ship, claiming that a massacre of all Europeans was imminent. Although the Foreign Office thought the danger was probably exaggerated, two British ships were sent to Port au Prince where they joined a gathering of American, French and German vessels. The Foreign Office was careful to inform the State Department that Murray and the British ships were under orders to do nothing to interfere in the internal politics of Haiti.[52]

The problem of the refugees was settled temporarily when they were embarked from Haiti on French and German ships, but Murray and his French and German colleagues thought it absolutely necessary that "at least one foreign ship" remain as long as Nord Alexis was in power and that it would be best "to take turns." Hardinge thought a permanent arrangement for the protection of Europeans would be "a great bore . . . but it is difficult to see what else can be done."[53] The Admiralty did not object to the planned rotation of ships, and the diplomats at Port au Prince began making the necessary arrangements while waiting for their governments' approval.

Grey, of course, was unwilling to sanction any guardship arrangement that might not be acceptable to the United States, but before Bryce could sound out the State Department Assistant Secretary of

State Bacon sent for Howard to talk about the Haitian situation. Since the United States had ships available at Santo Domingo and Cuba, Bacon thought the presence of a warship at Port au Prince was "quite unnecessary." The State Department did not believe that the Haitian situation posed any danger "to whites," and they were opposed to any arrangement for cooperative police duty.[54]

When asked by the Foreign Office if he still thought warships were necessary, Murray was even more emphatic. The British ship captains and the British colony agreed with him that a ship, other than American, was needed for the safety of foreign subjects. Murray was sure that Henry Furniss, the Negro American Minister, was "in league with the Haytian Government," and had given the Haitians the impression that the United States would protect them against any action by Europeans. The Foreign Office knew that Murray was intensely anti-American, but they had no way of knowing that his charges against Furniss were unfounded. Murray's telegram was "unpleasant reading" and it convinced Grey's advisers that under the circumstances Britain would not be justified in leaving the protection of British subjects to the United States.[55]

Grey personally drafted orders to Bryce to ask the American government what their intentions were, "whether they are prepared to undertake the protection of foreign subjects, and whether, in the event of no British ship of war being present, British subjects may rely upon United States ship being on the spot and giving adequate protection, or whether the United States would prefer that we and other foreign Governments should take our own measures, or should concert with United States' naval officer." Root obviously did not want to make a firm commitment. He still thought there was no danger to foreigners in Haiti, but the United States did intend to keep its ships there for a while. The United States would undertake "for the present at least" to protect British subjects. Root promised to send a letter "stating fully his views," but seemed doubtful about any cooperative naval measures.[56]

American opposition to the guardship arrangement was enough to scuttle that proposal as far as Grey was concerned but, on the other hand, Root's answer had not been wholly satisfactory regarding the protection of British interests. The only solution was to reject the guardship plan but keep a British ship at Port au Prince. As Grey instructed Murray:

> His Majesty's Government prefer not to take part in scheme for international guardship. His Majesty's ship will remain for the present in Haytian waters. In view of United States susceptibilities, the greatest caution should be used, and no landing party should be permitted unless danger is urgent and American marines are unable to afford sufficient protection.
>
> We must avoid all appearance of international combination in opposition to the United States, whose interests are more considerable.
>
> You should, however, merely inform your colleagues that His Majesty's Government will not take part in international guard, without mentioning reasons, and are for the present retaining a ship in Haytian waters.[57]

Grey's solution was undoubtedly a wise one. With Bacon expressing himself in "strong terms" against Germany and dwelling "upon the difference between the attitude and methods" of the British and those of the French and Germans,[58] British cooperation with the European powers would have been extremely foolish. Even the pessimistic Murray was able to find solace in the fact that the British ship remained at Port au Prince when the French and German vessels left "because, the Americans of the ships were boasted, 'Uncle Sam' told them to get." When the *Indefatigable* departed on May 19th, Murray was sure British prestige had been increased. The extended presence of the British ship had made the Haitians think that the British as well as the Americans were to be considered, "and the change in the behavior of the officials and of the people towards me and other British subjects lately has been very marked."[59]

But what of the future? Was the United States planning to intervene in Haiti? According to Murray, the "general local opinion" at Port au Prince was that the Americans were determined to take charge of Haitian finances as in Santo Domingo. However, Bryce was convinced that this was exactly what the State Department was trying to avoid. The Foreign Office had no objections to American intervention. As Hardinge put it, any interference "whether American or other would be preferable to the horrible condition of affairs prevailing in the island." With "so little trade" with Haiti, Britain had "little to lose."[60] But the United States was not ready to intervene in 1908, and the Foreign Office was again faced with the problem of protecting British interests when a new revolution broke out in late November.

Once again thinking that Nord Alexis intended a general massacre, Murray called for a British warship to join the American and French ships that were at Port au Prince at the time. The State Department agreed to extend American protection to British lives and property until a British cruiser could arrive from St. Lucia. The successful revolution was over within a few days, and Nord Alexis took refuge aboard the French man-of-war, but not before a clash between Murray and Furniss led to the long awaited statement by Root regarding American protection.

Early in December, Bryce reported that the State Department had sent him "without comment" copies of recent telegrams between Washington and Haiti. According to Furniss, a meeting of foreign representatives on December 3rd had agreed that parties should be landed from all foreign ships, but that Murray had refused to agree to a British landing force because the United States had told Great Britain the previous spring that they were "not pleased with British interference in Hayti, and that [the] British Government had informed him that for the future [the] United States Government should be permitted to take charge of foreign interests." Root's answer to Furniss of December 4th emphatically pointed out that the understanding of last spring was "incidental" to the withdrawal of the British ship following the earlier revolution.

British vessel now being present, that understanding is no longer applicable, nor is there any such understanding regarding citizens of any other country. No such communication was ever made by this Government to Great Britain as the British Representative told you was made. If it is necessary for any naval forces to land it will be for the protection of American life and property, and the relations of such landing force to other national forces which may be landed will be that of friendly cooperation and concurrent action so far as necessary, but not of joint action or under any joint commander.

The following day Root supplemented these instructions with the policy that American naval forces would give "temporary protection" to Europeans whose countries did not have ships present "upon urgent occasion or request for protection of life and property," but it was clear that Root was opposed to any assumption that the United States was responsible for any blanket protection of European interests.[61]

The Foreign Office naturally asked Murray to explain Furniss' report. According to Murray's account, the Americans on the scene had not extended the promised protection. Furniss told him that the USS *Tacoma* had made arrangements to land parties for each of the legations, but during the disorders of the night of December 2nd, the Americans did nothing "because, I understand, the American Minister and the American Captains, as usual, were afraid to take responsibility and therefore could not make up their minds to land any men." Murray had not attended the meeting of the diplomatic corps on December 2nd, and when the British cruiser arrived early on the 3rd, he made arrangements with the Captain for a British landing party, but by then the disorders were over. Thus when Furniss asked him at the meeting on the 3rd if the British would land men, Murray replied that it was no longer necessary.

He worried me to do so, and asked what foreign subjects without a warship should do if the disorders recommenced. I thought he would have us land first to avoid responsibility, and replied "They should address themselves to you—you have three men-of-war and we only one." Besides which, in the spring we were all led to believe that United States Government to undertake protection of life and property of foreign subjects, to which German Minister assented.

United States' Minister began saying that he had no instructions to annex Hayti, whereupon I went.

The following day, after receiving reports that two British subjects had been wounded and their stores pillaged during the night of December 2nd, Murray dashed off an ill-tempered note to Furniss. Since the United States had promised protection until the British cruiser arrived and there "was every reason to fear pillaging that night," Murray wanted the American minister to inform him "of the measures taken by the Commanders of the American Cruisers in harbour for the protection of British lives and property on the 2nd, inadequate as the measures unfortunately appear to have been."[62]

The Foreign Office was aghast at Murray's tactlessness. Grey hastily explained to the State Department that Murray had fully intended to land men from the British ship if necessary, and that his reply to Furniss had been caused by what appeared "to be undue persistence on the part of the U. S. Minister in saying that British force should be landed when no necessity existed." The British government fully realized that it was never contemplated that the understanding of last spring "would be of general application in the future." They, of course, entirely disclaimed "any desire to make the U. S. Govt. take control or assume responsibility for Haiti, but will always be grateful if United States, who generally have some force present, will give protection to British subjects in emergencies, when no British ship is on the spot."[63]

As for Murray, he drew a private reprimand over the note of December 4th to Furniss. Louis Mallet, the Assistant Secretary of State in Charge of the American Department,[64] warned Murray that it was "very important to get on friendly" with the American minister, and that his note might be "misconstrued."

> We are not in a position to come down on the Americans for protecting our lives and property. We ask them to do so as a favour and they comply, but if they do not carry out their undertaking we cannot abuse them. The most that you could do would be to point out the neglect in a very friendly manner and assume that it was due to ignorance of the circumstances. The next time we ask them to protect our interests they may refuse altogether. Our only remedy is to abstain from asking in future and this may prove awkward.[65]

Thus the Haitian revolution of 1908 did not provide any clear-cut answer to the question of the need of British vessels to protect British interests in the Caribbean. Mallet's warning to Murray shows that the British realized they would have to appeal for American protection in the future, but the Foreign Office still wanted Britain to act as her own policeman. When Murray complained that the abandonment of frequent visits to Haitian and Dominican ports had resulted in British subjects, "especially in Santo Domingo," being "looked upon as pariahs that anyone may illtreat with impunity," the Foreign Office, in January of 1909, tried unsuccessfully to get the Admiralty to commit themselves to an annual show of the flag there.[66] A few months later Lionel Carden, the British minister to Central America, also complained of arbitrary behavior on the part of government officials all along the Atlantic seacoast district of Guatemala, Nicaragua and Honduras, and the Foreign Office responded by getting a rather grudging promise from the Admiralty to make arrangements for annual cruises along the coast "if practicable."[67] The Admiralty continued to grumble on occasions over the Foreign Office's calls for ships, but the quarrel over gunboat diplomacy was waning by 1909. During the next few years British ships would be used to protect British interests during revolutions in Nicaragua, Honduras, and Mexico.[68]

None of these policies meant that the Foreign Office had forgotten their fears of the United States. For example, when Murray suggested that he visit Santo Domingo in the summer of 1908 aboard a British man-of-war to discuss certain unsettled claims, the Foreign Office refused. In like manner, Carden was rebuffed in 1909 when he urged that British ship captains be given instructions to hear grievances from British residents along the coast of Central America "and obtain their settlement when it depends on the action of the local authorities." The Foreign Office was in favor of a periodic show of the flag, but such a use of naval officers was objectionable for a number of reasons, not the least being the fear that it "might lead to complications & difficulties with the U. S."[69] The Foreign Office's continuing use of ships within the American "sphere of interest" did not result from any challenge to the United States, but rather from a combination of necessity and pride. American hegemony had not been extended to the degree of accepting any general responsibility for policing the entire area, and the Foreign Office felt that it was "wrong" to be always dependent on "foreign vessels."

By the end of the Roosevelt years, British policy in Latin America was still plagued by uncertainty. Roosevelt's actions had left little doubt that the United States was vitally interested in dominating the Caribbean, but at the same time the extension of American power had been limited and Root's early "good neighbor" policy had brought about a lull in the application of the "corollary" into new areas.[70] American policy regarding the use of force to settle claims was clarified a bit at the Hague Conference of 1907, when Root sponsored the "Porter Proposition" by which the signatories agreed not to use force to collect "contract debts" but which also left the door open to coercion "when the debtor state refuses or neglects to reply to an offer of arbitration, or, after accepting the offer, prevents any *compromis* from being agreed on, or, after the arbitration, fails to submit to the award." But Root's compromise between the interests of the Latin Americans and those of European claimants was not popular in Latin America.[71] Who was to say whether public opinion in the United States would raise the cry of the Monroe Doctrine even if a European power followed the Hague Convention?

Certainly the British statesmen were more than ever aware of the importance of the Monroe Doctrine. For example, when Grey became Foreign Secretary, he asked Durand what subjects of foreign policy were most interesting to the American mind. The British ambassador had no difficulty in answering: "the 'open door' for trade, and the maintenance of the Monroe Doctrine."[72] But what exactly did those terms mean? Cuban reciprocity had cast some doubts in Great Britain as to American devotion to the open door in Latin America, and just what that magic phrase "Monroe Doctrine" meant to Americans was still a matter of some conjecture. But whatever the meaning of the doctrine, the British were afraid that further controversies over it were not improbable. As the author of a secret Foreign Office memorandum of 1908 on Anglo-American relations warned: "The Monroe Doctrine is too convenient a substitute for argument to be abandoned by politicians of little experience in foreign affairs, and by a public opinion still at the primitive stage of devotion to traditional dogma."[73]

An uncertain Latin American policy was still viewed by the British as a small price to pay for cordial relations with the United States. When Roosevelt left the White House, the British government was more than satisfied with the results of their rapprochement with the United States. Even in Latin America no immediate crises were foreseen, and with the exception of Cuba the extension of American influence had not yet touched any significant British interests. It was trying at times not to have either a free hand in the Caribbean or the advantages that would derive from a general American protectorate there, but since 1903 the "impetuous" Roosevelt had been less of a problem to the Foreign Office than had the British Admiralty. On balance, the situation seemed favorable, but, in actual fact, the British were entering a much more trying period in Anglo-American relations brought about by the policies and tactics of those apostles of "dollar diplomacy," William Howard Taft and Philander C. Knox.

NOTES AND REFERENCES

1. Lansdowne to Durand, February 4, 1905. Lansdowne Papers, U. S., Vol. 28.

2. The training squadron that replaced the old North American and West Indies Squadron was based at Devonport, England. The South Atlantic and Pacific squadrons disappeared. In the Pacific only one ship based at Esquimalt, Canada, was left to show the flag on the west coast of North America and Central America. See Arthur J. Marder, *From the Dreadnought to Scapa Flow, the Royal Navy in the Fisher Era, 1904–1919*, Vol. I: *The Road to War, 1904–1914* (Oxford University Press, 1961), 40–42; Brassey's *Naval Annual* for 1905; Bourne, *op. cit.* pp. 369–71.

3. Fisher to Beresford, February 27, 1902. Arthur J. Marder, ed., *Fear God and Dread Nought, the Correspondence of Admiral of the Fleet Lord Fisher of Kilverstone* (Cambridge, Mass., 1952–59), I, 233–34.

4. The first public statement of the "corollary" was Root's reading of a letter from Roosevelt at a Cuban independence anniversary dinner in New York on May 20, 1904. See Morison, *op. cit.*, IV, 801.

5. See Roosevelt's annual message of December 6, 1904, *Messages and Papers of the Presidents*, XVI, 7053.

6. *Messages and Papers of the Presidents*, XVII, 7376.

7. Ibid., XVI, 7053.

8. Ibid., XVII, 7376.

9. In his earlier message to the Senate of February 15, 1905, Roosevelt did mention blockades and bombardments as well as seizures of customs houses.

10. C. of F. B. to F. O., February 15, 1911. F. O. 371/1132.

11. Roosevelt to Root, June 7, 1904. Morison, *op. cit.*, IV, 821.

12. In January of 1904 *HMS Pallas* did intervene at Puerto Plata to help maintain order and protect foreign property, but the action was taken in cooperation with the American ships there and at the request of the American commander.

13. The authoritative study of the Santo Domingo debt prior to 1905 is J. H. Hollander's *Report on the Public Debt of Santo Domingo* of 1905. The history of the Dominican debt from 1869 to 1947 is treated in some detail as one of the case histories in Edwin Borchard and William H. Wynne, *State Insolvency and Foreign Bondholders* (New Haven, 1951), II, 199–280. The original Santo Domingo loan was so scandalous that it was investigated by a committee of Parliament, along with loans to Honduras, Paraguay and Costa Rica.

14. Borchard and Wynne, *op. cit.*, II, 220–23; C. of F. B., *Annual Report*, 1900–1901, pp. 333–38. £351,400 worth of the 4% bonds of the 1897 issue were not sold, and in 1901 they were returned to the Dominican government, leaving £1,148,600 of 4% bonds outstanding.

15. This is the "very approximate" estimate of the Council of Foreign Bondholders. C. of F. B. to F. O., April 24, 1902. F. O. 23/99.

16. Santo Domingo was in a state of near anarchy during these years. From the assassination of Ulises Heureaux in 1899 until the coming to power of Ramón Cáceres in 1905, Santo Domingo had four presidents.

17. Lansdowne to Cohen, April 2, 1902. F. O. 23/99. For American policy in Santo Domingo during these years, see Munro, *op. cit.*, pp. 78–111, 116–25. Great Britain did not have a minister in either Santo Domingo or Haiti. The Consul General for both countries resided at Port au Prince, Haiti, and the only British representative in Santo Domingo itself was a Vice Consul.

18. Fremantle to Villiers, April 24, 1902, confidential. F. O. 23/99.

19. For the text of the protocol of January 31, 1903, and the arbitration award of July 14, 1904, see U. S., *Foreign Relations*, 1904, pp. 270–79.

20. The *modus vivendi* was in operation from April 1, 1905, to July 31, 1907.

21. The *South American Journal*, February 18, 1905; *The Literary Digest*, April 29, 1905, p. 436; see also Perkins, *The Monroe Doctrine, 1867–1907*, pp. 444–45.

22. Durand to Lansdowne, March 20, 1905. F. O. 23/106.

23. The only Foreign Office minute to Durand's despatch of February 17th, containing a copy of Roosevelt's message to the Senate of February 15th, was by Larcom: "The President has to some extent been moved to later action in S. Domingo by the decision in favour of our preferential treatment at the Hague, and the fear of U. S. interests being similarly relegated to a back place in some other S. A. Republic." F. O. 23/106.

24. Bax-Ironside to Lansdowne, February 2, 1905, and minutes by Larcom and Villiers. F. O. 80/470.

25. Larcom's minute to Durand's of March 30, 1905.

26. C. of F. B., *Annual Report*, 1904–1905, pp. 11–12.

27. C. of F. B., *Annual Report*, 1905–1906, pp. 14–22.

28. C. of F. B., *Annual Report* for 1904–1905, p. 11.

29. Avebury to Hay, January 26, 1905; Hay to Avebury, February 10. C. of F. B., *Annual Report*, 1904–1905, pp. 95–96.

30. Avebury to Hay, March 10, 1905. *Ibid.*, p. 97.

31. According to the Council, British interests in 1905 amounted to one-third of the sum covered by the award. As the bonds were to be retired at 50% of their nominal value by the award, the British holdings of Dominican bonds at this point would have a nominal value of £600,000.

32. O'Beirne sent his note to the State Department on May 26, 1905. The answer is in O'Beirne's despatch of July 1. F. O. 23/106.

33. Durand to Lansdowne, October 26, 1905. F. O. 23/106.

34. Howard to Grey, December 29, 1906, and enclosure of Hollander to Howard of December 24th; Howard to Grey, January 19, 1907. F. O. 371/265.

35. C. of F. B. to F. O., January 3 and 10, 1907. F. O. 371/265. However, Judge Otto Schoenrich, Hollander's secretary during the investigation of the Dominican debt, claimed that the British bondholders "had remained discreetly silent while the State Department was pressing" the Improvement Company's claim "thinking it completely American." Otto Schoenrich, *Santo Domingo, a Country with a Future* (New York, 1918), p. 371.

36. C. of F. B. to F. O., March 4, 1907. F. O. 371/265.

37. Bryce to Grey, April 11, 1907. F. O. 371/265.

38. Bryce to Grey, January 5, 1908. F. O. 371/466.

39. C. of F. B. to F. O., January 22, 1908. F. O. 371/466.

40. See C. of F. B., *Annual Report* for 1908, pp. 357–62. The more than 10% difference was caused by different treatment of interest arrears and the expenses of the negotiations leading to the protocol of 1903 and the award of 1904.

41. "Admiralty Policy, Replies to Criticism," October 1906, CAB 1/7/299, pp. 61–62; Fisher to Tweedmouth, October 4, 1906, Admiralty 116/942.

42. Durand to Lansdowne, April 13, 1905. F. O. 51/276.

43. Balfour memorandum of June 10, 1905. F. O. 51/277.

44. Durand to Lansdowne, June 26, 1905, and to Villiers, private, June 26th. F. O. 51/277.

45. Although nothing came of it, the French in 1905 did consider seizing a Venezuelan customs house, and when they notified Roosevelt and Root of the possibility they were asked to pledge that there would be no permanent occupation of territory. In 1908 Root also told the Dutch that the U. S. would not oppose forceful measures against Venezuela if there was no permanent occupation of territory. See Embert J. Hendrickson, "Roosevelt's Second Venezuelan Controversy," *The Hispanic American Historical Review*, L (1970), pp. 489–91, 495–96; and Dexter Perkins, *A History of the Monroe Doctrine* (London, 1960), pp. 244–45.

46. The *Naval Annual* for 1906, pp. 45–46. The Jamaica earthquake occurred on January 14 and the first British ship did not arrive until January 22.

47. Quoted in Marder, *From the Dreadnought to Scapa Flow*, I, 53.

48. "Admiralty Policy, Replies to Criticism," October, 1906, pp. 61–62. CAB 1/7/299.

49. The correspondence on the Cuban revolution of 1906 is in F. O. 371/56.

50. Hardinge's minute to Admiralty to F. O., January 18, 1908. F. O. to Admiralty, January 25th. F. O. 371/466.

51. There were no refugees in the British consulates, but in February the Foreign Office did authorize Murray to support the French and German representatives in their quarrel with the Haitian government. However, when it became obvious that the United States was opposing the practice of asylum, Grey modified these instructions and ordered Murray to refuse asylum to all political refugees who were not British subjects. See Grey to Murray, April 6, 1908. F. O. 371/407.

52. See F. O. to Murray and Bryce, March 18, 1908 F. O. 371/466.

53. Murray's telegram received March 19, 1908, and minutes. F. O. 371/466.

54. Grey to Bryce, March 27, 1908; Bryce to Grey, March 27th. F. O. 371/467.

55. Murray to Grey, March 29, 1908, and minutes. See also the report of the Commanding Officer of HMS *Cressy* in the Admiralty's letter to the F. O. of March 30th. F. O. 371/467.

56. Grey to Bryce, March 31, 1908; Bryce to Grey, April 1st. F. O. 371/467.

57. Grey to Murray, April 1, 1908. F. O. 371/467.

58. Bryce to Grey, April 1, 1908. F. O. 371/467.

59. Murray to Grey, April 30 and May 20, 1908. F. O. 371/467.

60. Murray to Grey, March 29, 1908; Bryce to Grey, April 1st; Minutes to Murray of April 30th. F. O. 371/467.

61. Bryce to Grey, December 6, 1908. F. O. 371/468.

62. Murray's telegram received December 4; telegrams of December 9 and 11; despatches of December 2 and 4. F. O. 371/468.

63. Grey to Bryce, December 15, 1908. F. O. 371/468.

64. Mallet became an Assistant Under Secretary of State in May of 1907 and succeeded Sir Eldon Gorst as supervisor of the American Department.

65. Mallet to Murray, private, December 26, 1908. F. O. 371/468.

66. Murray to Grey, December 26, 1908. F. O. 371/680.

67. Carden to Grey, April 26, 1909; Admiralty to F. O., July 6th. F. O. 371/609.

68. From 1908–1913 there were three British cruisers stationed in the West Indies and along the east coast of North America, and another ship was added on the west coast. By 1914 the entire Fourth Cruiser Squadron had been detached for service in the Western Atlantic. See *The Naval Annual* for 1908–1914.

69. Carden to Grey, April 26, 1909, and Mallet's minute. F. O. 371/609.

70. The limited extension of American power was not due to any change in Roosevelt's attitude toward the desirability of intervention. As he himself wrote in December of 1908, the United States had already "interfered in various different ways" in Cuba, Santo Domingo and Panama, and he "would have interfered in some similar fashion in Venezuela, in at least one Central American State, and in Haiti already, simply in the interest of civilization, if I could have waked up our people so that they would back a reasonable and intelligent foreign policy which would put a stop to crying disorders at our very doors." Roosevelt to William Bayard Hale, December 3, 1908. Morison, *op. cit.*, VI, 1407–08. Root had no doubts that the United States had the right and duty to intervene when necessary, but in practice his Latin American policy was more cautious and sympathetic. See Jessup, *op. cit.*, I, 493–99.

71. Unlike the Drago Doctrine, the Porter proposition applied to all "contract debts" not only external debts, but as it still allowed intervention under certain conditions, Venezuela refused to sign and seven other Latin American states accepted only with reservations.

72. Grey to Durand, January 2, 1906; Durand to Grey, January 26. Grey Papers, Vol. 42.

73. "Memorandum respecting Relations between Great Britain and the United States," 1908. F. O. 414/210.

CHAPTER V

Dollar Diplomacy in Central America,
1909-1910

The Taft administration's attempt to insure stability in Central America by means of American loans and control of the customs was almost certain to create diplomatic headaches for the British Foreign Office. The largest British financial stake in the area was the share of the external debts of the small Central American countries held by British bondholders. It was not a question of whether British interests would be affected by the techniques of "dollar diplomacy"; this was inevitable. The problem facing the Foreign Office was the way in which the American bankers and the State Department would handle these British interests. From the British point of view, the first two years of Knox's Latin American policy were not encouraging. The Foreign Office was trying to pursue a policy of cooperation with the United States, but the vexing debt problems and recurring fears for the "open door" were already building up an accumulation of distrust and irritation that was to have an unfortunate effect on Anglo-American relations.

During a discussion with Philander Knox about the unstable situation in Central America in May 1909, James Bryce found the new American Secretary of State to be "a man of few words, extremely cautious and guarded, and very unlike Mr. Root, who was fond of launching out on all occasions into what amounted to a philosophical or historical disquisition of the phenomena presented by these Spanish American Republics and the policy to be followed in dealing with them." But Bryce concluded from the conversation that the new administration would be extremely cautious in their relations with the suspicious small states of Central America. He advised the Foreign Office:

> This attitude of prudence and non-intervention is likely to be maintained by the present United States Administration. Mr. Roosevelt would, had he followed his own impulses, have been less guarded. Mr. Root and the Senate, and his knowledge of the general public opinion of the country held him back. Mr. Taft and Mr. Knox have no desire to go forward.[1]

It was a poor prophecy by the usually perspicacious observer of the American scene. By the time his despatch had reached London, the Foreign Office was already mulling over the meaning of the new administration's move to block a British debt settlement with Honduras and their attempt to stop the flotation of a Nicaraguan loan in London. Whatever their original desires, it soon became clear that Taft and Knox did intend "to go forward," and that they not only accepted the principles of the Roosevelt "corollary" but were to elaborate upon them and attempt to extend them to some of the small independent nations in the crucial area of the future canal.

The Taft administration's first attempt at "dollar diplomacy" in Latin America was actually precipitated by a British plan to end the long-standing debt default of Honduras. Of the three Latin American states—Honduras, Costa Rica, and Guatemala—still in default on their external debts at the beginning of 1909, Honduras had the unenviable distinction of having the oldest of the unserviced debts. After forty years of default on its portion of the debt of the old Central American Federation, Honduras floated a conversion loan in 1867, followed by three sizable railway loans issued in London and Paris from 1867 to 1870. Less than sixty miles of railway was even constructed, and by 1872 all four of the loans were in default. By the end of 1908 little Honduras, the most backward nation in a backward region, was saddled with an external debt of £5,398,570 principal and the staggering sum of £16,681,127 of unpaid interest. As most of the Honduran debt was held in Britain, the Council of Foreign Bondholders had been trying for years to find an arrangement that would salvage some return for the holders of these almost worthless bonds.

One of the securities for the Honduran loans had been a mortgage or lien on the railway and its revenues. Despite this provision, in the 1890s the railway had fallen into the hands of American interests, and the Council had failed in its efforts to make some refunding agreement with them. In 1903 Honduras cancelled the American syndicate's concession, but nothing was done to satisfy the British bondholders, and, in 1908, despite protests from the Foreign Office, Honduras leased the line to Washington S. Valentine, an American resident in Honduras.

Although the railroad was again in American hands, the struggle for its control continued behind the scenes, for Valentine's contract contained a stipulation that the lease was revocable if a settlement of the external debt was reached on the basis of a transfer of the railroad. Lionel Carden, the British Minister to Central America, was afraid that more protests from the Council of Foreign Bondholders to Honduras would only hurt their chances for a settlement. While in London on leave in 1908 he persuaded the Council that their best hope was to submit to the Hondurans a new proposal for resuming their debt payments. Before returning to Guatemala City,[2] Carden and the Council had worked out the bases for the new plan. Early in 1909, Carden received permission from the Foreign Office to go to Tegucigalpa for unofficial discussions with the Honduran government. The talks were seemingly successful. On March 11th, President Miguel Dávila gave Carden a written acceptance of the new scheme and an invitation to the Council of Foreign Bondholders to conclude a definitive contract.

According to Carden's plan, Honduras was to recognize a total debt of £452,000 at 8.86% per year for interest and sinking fund, to be paid at the rate of £40,000 per year for a period of forty years. As security, the government was to hand over to the bondholders the existing railway and the wharf at Puerto Cortes for the duration of the debt.[3] For their part, the Council of Foreign Bondholders was to make the necessary arrangements for the issue and sale of £100,000 of new 6% bonds, the proceeds to be used to repair and re-equip the decrepit railway. The total debt would then be serviced by a first charge on the railway receipts and 15% of the Honduran customs duties.

The Foreign Office had taken no direct part in the negotiations but Carden's superiors were undoubtedly happy at the apparent solution of one of the troublesome Central American debt problems. However, the problems of the Foreign Office were in reality only beginning, for in March unwelcome news arrived from Carden that the American Minister, Philip M. Brown, had made an official protest to Honduras against any financial arrangement "which does not embrace interests of all other creditors." Such an arrangement, according to Brown, would be considered by the United States "as an act inconsistent with friendly relations existing between the two countries." Carden of course was furious and quite predictably in favor of a strong stand:

> Strongly recommend that the attention of U. S. Govt be at once drawn to such an unjustifiable interference with the right of a British Corporation to negotiate freely with the Honduras Govt. about matters affecting their interests, or of H. M. Minister to assist such negotiations by all legitimate means. Failure to take some such action may jeopardize arrangement when I leave here by making Honduras Govt. think they will embroil themselves with U. S. Govt. and receive no support from us.[4]

The Foreign Office had no intention of supporting Honduras against the United States, but they could hardly ignore Brown's protest. Grey immediately ordered Bryce to find out why the protest was made and to try getting the State Department to order Brown to end his opposition. When Alfred Mitchell Innes, the Councillor of the British Embassy, talked to Knox, the Secretary of State was evasive, claiming that he did not have enough information as yet to make a definite statement. Knox first had to "make himself acquainted with the financial situation of Honduras," for the United States was "deeply interested in the political and financial stability of Central America, and their policy is to help them to maintain those conditions." Perhaps a conference of interested nations would be advisable. In any event, there was no possibility that Honduras would be allowed to play off the United States against Great Britain.[5]

Grey warned Bryce to avoid reference to an international conference "which, if held, might tend to identify His Majesty's Government with the interests of the bondholders more closely than would be desirable or convenient."[6] But Grey need not have worried, for the United States had no intention of allowing any interested European nation to share in determining the future of Honduras. The planners in the State Department were already thinking of applying some form of financial control over Honduras. As early as January of 1909, Valentine had suggested a new loan to the Central American republic that would be secured by a Dominican style customs collectorship. Although the Hondurans rejected the idea, it had been viewed with some interest at Washington.[7] Brown had acted on his own initiative in opposing the British plan, but the State Department was more than willing to support him in blocking a settlement that would have frustrated any hopes of American control of Honduran finances. Thus, the imminent success of the British scheme forced the new American administration to look for an alternative, and the Foreign Office, in accord with its policy of deference towards the United States in the area, could only wait until the American plans for Honduras were formulated.

Meanwhile the Honduran government and the Council of Foreign Bondholders took steps to bring the Carden plan to fruition. An arrangement between Honduras and Valentine to turn over the railway and the wharf to the government made these properties available for security.[8] The Council, for its part, was trying to interest Weetman D. Pearson's influential engineering firm, S. Pearson and Sons, to undertake the renovation of the railway. Carden was most impatient about the slow pace of events. Seeing chances for the success of his plan dwindling, he wanted to facilitate the Council's negotiations by expressing to Honduras the British government's satisfaction over the proposed settlement. But with the embassy in Washington having little success in getting the State Department to take a definite position, the Foreign Office remained passive.

On May 29th the State Department finally stopped stalling and stated flatly that the United States was opposed to any partial arrangements of the Honduran debt. A group of New York bankers was working on a general refunding scheme, and the American government had hopes that Honduras would appoint an American "financial adviser." The Foreign Office knew the "special importance" the United States attached to Honduras, for Bryce wrote on June 1st:

> It is, they say, due to the fact that Honduras lies between the two troublesome states of Guatemala and Nicaragua, so that it is a natural battleground between these republics, and that the manner in which it conducts its government may be expected to influence for good or evil the governments of its two neighbors. It is, therefore, so they argue, only natural that the United States Government should take more than ordinary interest in the political situation in Honduras, and consequently in the financial situation on which the political situation so largely depends.[9]

The Council of Foreign Bondholders' reaction to the news from Washington was as expected. Complaining that "for some years past" the U.S. had shown "a marked want of regard" for the rights of the British bondholders in Latin America, the Council distrusted any American plan for Honduras until justice was done for the British holders of Dominican bonds. They did not know the details of the New York financial plans, but it seemed doubtful that Honduras would submit to American control. What was the attitude of the British government? Should the bondholders withdraw from the Carden scheme and cooperate with the United States?

The Foreign Office was by no means anxious to give such definite advice to the bondholders, but some action had to be taken. The United States would hardly withdraw its opposition to the Carden plan, but as Mallet pointed out, "if we acquiesce too readily in their veto, they will assume that we do not attach any great importance to the matter and the council will expect us to put up a fight." Bryce was ordered to use his "utmost endeavours" to induce the State Department to stop opposing the British arrangement.[10]

But before Bryce could use his "utmost endeavours," more definite American proposals reached the Foreign Office and the Council of Foreign Bondholders.[11] On June 24th, Mr. E. Grenfell, J. P. Morgan's representative in London, called at the Foreign Office and asked Mallet if the British Government would object to an Honduran debt settlement in which an American syndicate would take over the finances of Honduras "much in the same way as was done in S. Domingo." Mallet replied that the Foreign Office was only interested in fair treatment for the bondholders:

> I said that, so long as the interests of British Bondholders were safeguarded, & they received as good terms as the Honduranean [sic] Govt were now offering them, we should not object on political grounds, as we were not prepared to resist the growth of American interest in the Central American Republics. I said that we attached the greatest importance to the equitable treatment of the Bondholders, as in the case of S. Domingo, the indifference shown by the Americans to the interests of the British Bondholders had created great soreness of feeling.
>
> Mr. Grenfell said that he was aware of this & thought that the terms wh. would be proposed would probably be better than those now under consideration and that into the bargain, he might be able to throw a sop to the Dominican Bondholders.[12]

Morgan promised the Council of Foreign Bondholders that if an arrangement for financial control could be arranged between the governments of Honduras and the United States within one year, the American banking firm would purchase the British bonds outright for 15% of their face value. It would mean a further reduction of the principal of the debt, but payment would be immediate rather than spread over a forty year period. But would the American government be able to persuade Honduras to accept their financial tutelage? If the British cooperated with the Americans and the plan failed, what chance would the Council of Foreign Bondholders have in future negotiations with Honduras? On the other hand, was Honduras likely to carry through the Carden plan in the face of American opposition? And if Honduras in the end accepted American control, would Morgan renew his offer if the Council now refused it? The situation was too uncertain for the Foreign Office to give any definite advice. "We must in any case," Mallet advised Grey, "avoid being put in the position of backing Honduras against America & we must avoid giving advice to the Bondholders officially & limit ourselves to letting them know the pros & cons."[13]

After wrestling with the "pros and cons," the Council decided to cooperate with the American bankers. While the Council had been prepared to recommend that the bondholders accept the Carden proposal, it now seemed doomed because the British government "have intimated that they do not see their way to combat" the American opposition. On the other hand, the New York bankers had promised the Council that there was "good reason" to believe that the American government would succeed in getting a treaty with Honduras. Despite their reluctance to advise the bondholders, this was obviously the answer the Foreign Office wanted. To Mallet, the decision was "very satisfactory," especially as it was "entirely their own."[14]

Carden had lost another round in his crusade against expanding American influence in the Caribbean. If the decision was satisfactory to the Foreign Office, it was a taste of wormwood to the British Minister. He felt betrayed by the Council and his own government's supine attitude towards the United States. He was particularly galled at his instructions to suspend his negotiations with Honduras and adopt "a friendly attitude to the American proposals." When the Foreign Office complied with a State Department request to instruct Carden to tell the Hondurans that the British government was in favor of the success of the Morgan plan, his humiliation was complete.[15]

The Foreign Office had been cooperative with the Americans in Honduras, but Honduras was not the only country in which the

United States was showing an exceptional interest in 1909. As the situation in Honduras was coming to a head, the Foreign Office had another opportunity to follow the lead of the State Department in Central America, this time in Nicaragua.

Whereas the problem in Honduras was primarily one of liquidating a long-standing default on the best terms possible, the difficulties in Nicaragua arose from the influx of more British capital into Central America. In spite of the dismal record of defaults in the area, British investors were still active, and both Salvador, in 1908, and Nicaragua, in 1909, were able to float loans in London. Although the Salvadoran loan did not develop into "a case" as some in the Foreign Office feared, the loan to President José Santos Zelaya of Nicaragua was embarrassing because of the opposition of the new American administration.

Like Estrada Cabrera of Guatemala, Zelaya of Nicaragua had a long and unsavory career. Both maintained their power at home by harsh methods and interfered in their neighbors' internal affairs during their rivalry for influence in Central America. But while Estrada Cabrera was usually careful to avoid antagonizing the United States, Zelaya became more and more anti-American in his domestic and foreign policies. After coming to power in 1893, he became the dominant political leader in Central America and a loud advocate for reunion of the five republics. Angry at the United States for the collapse of negotiations for a Nicaraguan canal, he greatly resented the growing American influence in Central America during the second Roosevelt administration. By the end of 1908, American-Nicaraguan relations had almost reached the breaking point.

Any European loan to Zelaya was bound to be resented in Washington, but European investors were more impressed by the fact that Nicaragua had not defaulted on her external debt since 1895. The Nicaraguan external debt in 1908 consisted of £235,300 of outstanding bonds of an 1886 issue. In addition to this sterling debt, Zelaya had secured a $1,000,000 loan from a New Orleans financier in 1904. With a better credit rating than most of his Central American neighbors, he now turned to the European money market and in 1905 started negotiations with the "Ethelburga Syndicate" of London for a new loan. Although the issue was not carried through, in the fall of 1908 the Nicaraguan Congress authorized a new attempt to raise a European loan of £1,250,000.

The proposed Nicaraguan loan first became a matter of concern to the Foreign Office late in May of 1909 when Knox asked if the British government "could do anything in their power to discourage the raising of a loan in London by Zelaya, who is the general disturber of peace in Central America and guilty of shocking cruelties." Although the proposed loan was ostensibly for public improvements, the State Department viewed it as the Nicaraguan dictator's attempt to get money for arms and munitions to maintain his tyranny over the Nicaraguan people and to attack his neighbors. The French government had "spontaneously stopped the flotation" in Paris; did the British government have the power to do the same?[16]

It was an unusual request, but Mallet thought that a "private hint" to the bondholders would not be out of order and passed it on to Lord Avebury, the President of the Council of Foreign Bondholders.

> It is not the practice of His Majesty's Government to interfere officially in such matters but in the present instance they agree that it is undesirable that the President of Nicaragua should be supplied with money.
>
> They would therefore be obliged if you, in your capacity as President of the Council of Foreign Bondholders, could take any action in the sense desired by the United States Government.[17]

According to Avebury the Nicaraguan loan was a *fait accompli*. Subscriptions to the new bonds had already been publicly invited in both London and Paris. In any event, the Council had no intentions of cooperating with the American government to block a legitimate loan to Nicaragua that was to be used for debt conversion and railway construction. The Ethelburga syndicate had offered to exchange the bonds of 1886 on advantageous terms, and a public meeting of the British bondholders had unanimously approved the offer.[18]

However advantageous the Ethelburga loan may have been to British bondholders, the Foreign Office was determined not to become involved in any way. Not content with the extensive securities offered by Nicaragua, the English syndicate had attempted to give the loan some quasi-official status by adding a provision that copies of the contract were to be deposited by Nicaragua with the British and American governments. Despite vigorous pleas from the Council of Foreign Bondholders, the Foreign Office refused to accept the contract. The United States of course did the same, and Knox expressed "his gratification" at the British rejection.[19] Needless to say, the British bondholders were far from gratified.

Although the British government had divested itself of any responsibility regarding the Nicaraguan loan and the bondholders were seemingly in line for a settlement in Honduras under the Morgan plan, the Foreign Office was embarrassed by the bondholders' complaints. Inevitably the onset of "dollar diplomacy" caused some debate within the Foreign Office and the diplomatic corps as to the meaning of the new vigor shown by the Americans in Central America. Mallet refused to admit that the failure of the Carden plan for Honduras meant any change in British policy. He told Carden the British government "will continue to maintain British interests" in Central America "and cooperation with the United States Government which we sincerely desire can only exist on the understanding that British interests, in the widest sense, profit and do not suffer thereby."[20] These were brave words, but there were already nagging doubts in London. Would the new American activity in Central America really benefit British interests? What, if anything, should the Foreign Office do? Was it possible to formulate a general policy to cope with the expansion of American influence?

The debate was set off in July of 1909 when Lionel Carden sent the Foreign Office a long analysis of the situation. Carden was never one to underestimate the perfidious Yankees by taking the short view. He had no doubts that the American opposition to his Honduran debt scheme was only part of a concerted effort by the United States to dominate all commercial and financial enterprises in Central America. He feared that steps were underway for a debt settlement in Guatemala that would be disadvantageous to the British bondholders, and the recent denunciation by Salvador of her commercial treaty with Britain seemed to him to be the first step in a new American drive for Latin American reciprocity treaties. According to Carden, the United States in the future would try to dictate all debt settlements, discourage the investment of European capital, divert European trade to the United States, and prevent the granting of public works concessions in Central America to all non-Americans.

What could be done? For Carden, there were only three possible courses open to Britain: opposition, servile acceptance, or some formal understanding with the Americans.

1. To resist the pretentions of the United States Government, either separately or in combination with others, which would inevitably bring about serious friction.

2. To accept the situation passively, refraining from entering upon negotiations with the different Republics without first ascertaining the views and wishes of the United States, and generally avoiding anything which might remotely conflict with their projects for the future. The adoption of such an attitude would hasten the extinction of our interests by the loss of influence with the Governments of those countries entailed.

3. To endeavour to arrive at an understanding with the United States Government which would have for its object the conservation of our existing interests.

Carden wanted to explore the third suggestion. As the British government was admitting the right of the United States to special influence in Central America, and as the commercial and financial interests of the British there might not be considered great enough to warrant a defense at the risk of constant bickerings and disagreements with the United States, might it not be worthwhile to come to some arrangement with the Americans that would avoid friction and still safeguard at least the existing interests of Great Britain? Had not the great powers made agreements from time to time recognizing spheres of influence? The circumstances might not be "entirely analogous," but "the principle does not appear to be wholly inapplicable to the position of the United States in these Republics." It would be "premature" to discuss the exact form of such an understanding until the Foreign Office accepted the idea.

> But I may be permitted to point out that the aspirations of the United States in this direction are regarded with so much suspicion, and have to be so carefully concealed, that a friendly undertaking to take no steps which might encourage resistance to their influence would not be dearly bought by a promise not to discriminate against our trade by means of Reciprocity Conventions, nor to interfere with the free exercise of their rights by British subjects in the recovery of debts due them.[21]

Carden was certainly given to exaggeration, but at the same time had an embarrassing habit of exposing the vagueness and the inadequacy of the Anglo-American "entente" in Latin America. The Foreign Office was by no means opposed to the idea of an Anglo-American agreement over Central America, but they were sceptical that it could be achieved. As Larcom noted, the idea of an entente "is no doubt desirable and what we are in a sense strong for already," but he doubted that any *"definite agreement* with the U. S. either on the basis indicated by Mr. Carden . . . or otherwise is practicable or would be accepted by them."[22] Mallet decided to send Carden's letter to Alfred Innes, who was in London at the time, to get some observations from a member of the Washington Embassy.

In addition to the part that he had played in the Honduran debt question, Innes had already had a taste of "dollar diplomacy" regarding American loans to China, and he had formed some definite views on doing business with "the Yankees."[23] Both Bryce and he were disturbed by the "intriguing" over the Honduran debt, and now Innes took the opportunity to air his views to his superiors at the Foreign Office. According to Innes the Central American policy of the United States was "perfectly straightforward and sensible." Since the "barbarous little republics" were "a blot on the fair fame of America, and a standing menace to the Monroe Doctrine," the Americans were determined to "regenerate them."

Mr. Root had strong altruistic views and both he and Mr. Roosevelt believed in patience and moral suasion. The present Government is far more what we would call typically British and what they call typically American, more thoroughly practical and businesslike. Hence patience, forbearance, sympathy and moral forces appeal but little to them, and the sounder method of gaining the necessary influence seems to them to be the use of their immense wealth. Consequently they have virtually taken Mr. Pierpont Morgan into the Government.

The "ideal policy" for Britain to follow would be "to back up the United States all through," on condition that "they give us a fair deal." A "fair deal" would mean that the Americans "do not try to wrest us from Central America, that they offer us a fair equivalent for our bonds, and that, in return for past losses we obtain a fair share of future profits from financial operations." A conversion of old bonds into new ones at a lower rate of interest would be fair if English bankers were given the right to underwrite a proportion of the new loans and of all future loans, but Innes was opposed to accepting cash "which involves our expulsion from the financial market."

Innes realized that his "ideal policy" would mean a "diplomatic tussle" with the United States, but he did not think that the British had to fear any lasting ill feelings, for the Americans "are essentially good tempered and tolerant,—to bear malice or resentment against those who stand up for their rights is not in their nature." But as the Americans were also "terribly tenacious and pugnacious, and will fight every point hard," it would be necessary to plan each move with care. The Foreign Office would have to drop its traditional policy of letting the bondholders make their own bargains. The Council could get satisfactory terms only by acting under the instructions of the government, for tradition "is a source of weakness in dealing with a country which has no traditions, and whose foreign policy is thoroughly elastic, using whatever weapon comes to hand."

Innes disagreed with all three of Carden's alternatives. There was no basis for a general understanding and the United States would refuse to listen to any such proposal, but he did not see why the British could not "steer clear of both the first two alternatives and arrive at some fairly satisfactory compromise of each case as it arrives."[24] And in a private note to Mallet, Innes emphasized careful planning:

> In my memorandum, I did not like to insist more strongly than I did on the importance of well-thought out tactics in negotiating with the American Govt. I imagine that, with the French Govt., for example, one can deal exactly as one gentleman deals with another, and the moves are not of much importance. With the present American Govt. one can't. Mr. Knox is a typical American, kindly, good natured, with a considerable touch of vanity. But he is as sharp as they make 'em, and if he gets our head in the lemon squeezer, so to say, it will emerge without a drop of juice in it. In time, I expect their attitude will soften down a bit, and if we could secure even a small victory now, it would help that desirable result.[25]

Neither Carden's nor Innes's suggestions resulted in a positive policy. Innes's advice against the acceptance of cash came too late for the Honduran bondholders, and the Foreign Office had little inclination to abandon its laissez-faire attitude towards debt negotiations. "It is very difficult," Mallet decided, "to lay down a principle beyond the very general one that we must endeavor to hold our own in C. A. so far as possible."[26] As for Carden's three alternatives, the first two were "clearly out of the question," and the third would be difficult to achieve. Carden had to be content with endeavoring "as each case arises," to maintain "British rights and interests and to use Gt. Britain's present position in order to force the best possible terms from the U. S."[27] Nor were the bondholders any more successful in getting Mallet to make any specific promises beyond this day by day approach to the problem. As he wrote in answer to one of the Council's complaints about the Nicaraguan loan contract:

> Since it is clear that the United States Government intend in the future to take a closer interest in the Central American Republics, the problem for His Majesty's Government is to maintain British interests in the Republics without arousing the political jealousy of the United States Government. I am to point out however that it is difficult to lay down any hard and fast line as to the manner in which this can best

be done and it will probably be best to consider in each particular case as it arises the best method of procedure.[28]

Thus the Foreign Office's Central American policy stated in the fall of 1909 was in the best British tradition of muddling through. There was even hope that the United States would arouse enough fears in Central America to save British interests without the Foreign Office doing anything. The Americans "will probably encounter a good deal of opposition before they gain complete control of the C. A. Republics," Mallet wrote, "& if they attempt to go too fast, they will play our game."[29] One thing was certain. Any half-hearted British opposition to the United States would only embitter Anglo-American relations without achieving any results. As Grey summed up his thoughts on Central America:

> These Central American Republics will only side with us so long as we do not press them for payment of British claims. If we press for payment they will quarrel with us. And they are not worth backing against the U. S. Govt. They can never be depended upon to stand up for themselves or to behave themselves. For us to give them active support would only precipitate U. S. intervention for which provocation is instantly forthcoming. As to earning any gratitude from them, the constant revolutions prevent any chance of that; anyone of their Govts. with which we make friends may at any moment be replaced by an opposite party.[30]

Grey's determination that Britain would not act as a counterweight to the United States in Central America did not free him from apprehensions over American expansion into the area. Britain would not support any of the little nations against the United States, but "at each step of American intervention," Britain had to "claim the open door & equal treatment for our claims."[31] Grey was always more worried about the future of British commercial interests than the problems of the bondholders, and his mention of the "open door" in 1909 was one indication that the spectre of a general exclusionary policy by the United States within their sphere of influence had not yet been put to rest.

The particular problem that bothered the Foreign Office in 1909 was the difficulty Britain was having keeping her most-favored-nation commercial treaties in Central America. Honduras had denounced her treaty with Britain, and Salvador and Guatemala were reluctant to conclude new ones. By the end of 1909 a treaty with Nicaragua was the only one in effect. What did this trend mean? Carden was sure that the Central American governments were reluctant either through fear of the United States or through a desire to clear the way for reciprocity arrangements with the Colossus of the North. When Carden reported his conviction that Salvador had refused to extend their British treaty to meet the wishes of the United States, Algernon Law of the Foreign Office's Commercial Department was worried enough to suggest that Carden be authorized to offer "a discreet opposition" to American reciprocity arrangements. Grey understandably feared this approach, but he was sufficiently disturbed to ask Bryce if he thought it desirable to ask the State Department, in view of their recent declarations "in favour of the open door elsewhere," if they would support an Anglo-Salvadoran most-favored-nation treaty.[32]

Bryce thought such a request would be most undesirable. It would be best to wait and see the effects of the new American tariff act that had been passed in August. The Payne-Aldrich tariff had terminated all existing reciprocity agreements except with Cuba and had turned to a two-schedule tariff system aimed at ending discrimination against the United States. Instead of authorizing the President to negotiate special reciprocity arrangements, the new tariff gave him the power to extend the minimum rates to countries that did not "unduly discriminate" against American imports.[33]

Although the United States had given up the policy of reciprocity, the Foreign Office was still worried. What was to prevent Congress from passing special legislation for a reciprocity agreement with Salvador? Salvador had rejected an American proposal that she lower her tariff in favor of American goods, but would she do so if the United States offered better terms? Grey accepted a Salvadoran promise that British trade would be treated on an equal footing with other nations even in the absence of a commercial treaty, and Bryce reported that the State Department had dropped its proposals to Salvador and had no intention of renewing them. But the Foreign Office was still not completely satisfied. Even if the United States no longer wanted reciprocity, some in London suspected that the Americans were still using their influence in Central America against the negotiation of commercial treaties with Britain.

These suspicions were reinforced by reports arriving from Guatemala. According to Carden, President Estrada Cabrera was making "no attempt to disguise" his reluctance to conclude most-favored-nation treaties with European countries because of his desire "to conciliate the goodwill of the United States." Guatemala had not received a reciprocity proposal from the United States, but the ever-suspicious Carden was taking no chances. He argued at some length with Estrada Cabrera about the dangers to Guatemalan independence that could result from close commercial ties with the United States and the decline of European interests in his country.[34]

It is highly doubtful that the wily Estrada Cabrera needed any lectures from Carden about American influence in Central America, but the British Minister was once again playing a rather dangerous game, for Carden's arguments were essentially the same Grey had been afraid to authorize in the case of Salvador. The Foreign Office wanted no repetition of the embarrassing charges of anti-Americanism made against Carden in Cuba. Carden's language to Estrada Cabrera was "generally approved" but he was warned that his negotiations with Guatemala for a commercial treaty should not "take the form of direct opposition" to American commercial policy in Central America.

I doubt the wisdom, except as a last resort, of warning the Central American Governments of the prejudice which is likely to result from the predominance of the United States, since they must be already aware of the probable results of their present policy and a diplomatic struggle between the Representatives of this country and those of the United States on the spot will probably endanger the relations between this country and the United States without gaining the object which we have in view.[35]

In retrospect, British fears over Latin American reciprocity during the Taft administration were baseless. Whatever intentions the State Department may have had in the spring of 1909, reciprocity never became one of the weapons of "dollar diplomacy" in Latin America. Taft's only attempt at reciprocity was the agreement of 1911 that was rejected by Canada, and there was little sentiment left in the United States for any general system of reciprocal agreements. As the American Tariff Commission put it in 1918, the Payne Aldrich tariff of 1909 "marked a distinct departure from the policy of seeking special favors by granting reciprocal concessions."[36] But British fears for the future of the open door lingered on, and the Foreign Office remained suspicious of American intentions despite Grey's desire to avoid a diplomatic tussle of any kind.

When a full-fledged revolution broke out against President Zelaya of Nicaragua in October of 1909, the British had another opportunity to ponder the implications of Taft's Central American policy. Although it is highly improbable that the State Department encouraged or instigated the revolt, there were some suspicions in London. The Foreign Office realized that Zelaya was the Americans' *bête noire* in Central America. Knox had strongly denounced the Nicaraguan President at the time of the Ethelburga loan, and assistant secretary Francis M. Huntington Wilson had told Bryce that Zelaya was a mere "ruffian" who stayed in power only because "no one was publicly spirited enough to risk his own life in killing him." The Foreign Office was sure, as Larcom put it, that the U. S. will certainly not *regret* the revolution, even if they have not promoted it—which seems not impossible as in Panama!"[37] There was little surprise in London when Taft broke off diplomatic relations with Nicaragua and made it clear that the United States was intent on seeing Zelaya removed from power.

British interests in Nicaragua were not large, and, with the United States showing keen interest in the revolution, the obvious policy for the British was one of complete impartiality towards the contending factions. At Carden's request, a British cruiser, the H. M. S. *Scylla*, was sent to the Atlantic coast of Nicaragua to protect British lives and property, but the move had no political implications. In January of 1910 the commanding officer of the *Scylla*, Commander Thesiger, did land a small force at Greytown where many British subjects were living, and his action seemingly prevented a rebel attack on the city, but it did not reflect any British desire to influence the course of the revolution.[38]

British impartiality during the Nicaraguan revolution did not mean that the Foreign Office had forgotten the susceptibilities of the United States. When the Nicaraguan Congress elected José Madriz Provisional President following the resignation of Zelaya in December of 1909, Grey authorized Carden to open negotiations on pending questions with Madriz's Minister for Foreign Affairs, but the British Minister was told not to raise the question of formal recognition as yet. The British had no objections to Madriz, but they first wanted to see what policy other countries, particularly the United States, were following.

In spite of the removal of Zelaya, the American government was still not satisfied. Fearing Madriz was too closely connected with the former dictator, Taft now refused to recognize the new president. On learning from Bryce in March of 1910 that the State Department had "no present intention" of recognizing Madriz, the Foreign Office continued to wait, but reports that the revolution was at an end soon made Grey impatient. On April 7th he told the American Chargé at London that there no longer seemed to be any reason for Britain to withhold recognition.

> When I had last enquired, the United States Government considered that the revolutionary party represented the real feeling in Nicaragua, and they were not prepared to recognize President Madriz. I therefore wished to know their present view before I took the step of recognizing him, for—although there seemed to be no reason for not recognizing President Madriz—I did not wish our recognition of him to be construed, either in Nicaragua or elsewhere, as a sort of political demonstration in opposition to the policy of the United States Government.[39]

When Knox expressed the hope that Britain would take no action "in this matter at present," Grey said it was "a little difficult" to defer recognition in light of reports from Nicaragua that the situation was stable, but he promised to "keep the matter open for some time longer."[40] Although a number of Latin American and European countries had already recognized Madriz, the British continued to defer recognition and to rebuff all attempts by the Madriz government to get Great Britain involved in their quarrel with the United States.

Although Grey followed the American lead on recognition, Taft's policy did cause some irritation in London. According to Carden, foreigners and Nicaraguans alike were suffering "incalculable" injury from the revolution, and two British agricultural companies had complained to him of very serious losses due to a labor shortage caused by the fighting. Carden had "no hesitation whatever" blaming the American refusal to recognize Madriz for all the loss of life and property since the resignation of Zelaya.[41] Impressed by Carden's report, Grey tried to reopen the question of recognition during a meeting with Ambassador Reid in June. As he informed Bryce:

> I told the United States Ambassador to-day that I was receiving complaints from British subjects engaged in trade in Nicaragua of the damage caused by the prolongation of the revolution.
>
> The statement made to me was that the revolution would come to an end at once if the United States Government would recognize the Government of Senor Madriz.
>
> I had no interest in promoting the success of one party or the other in Nicaragua, but it was very important, in our trade interests that the revolution should come to an end, and I should be very glad to hear what the United States proposed to do.[42]

The State Department showed little sympathy for Grey's complaint. and even questioned the accuracy of his information. According to their reports, there were no British traders "of any standing" in Nicaragua, only a few West Indian Negroes. As the leader of the revolutionary party, Juan J. Estrada, was "at least as worthy" as Madriz, the American government "saw no reason to change their views with regard to the situation in Nicaragua." With the exception of Carden's rather vague report, the Foreign Office really knew very little about the actual status of British trade in Nicaragua. Thus, Grey was forced to ask for further information from Nicaragua,[43] but by the time Vice-Consul Godfrey Haggard and Commander Thesiger of the *Scylla* had made their reports, the revolution was over. Estrada's forces had turned the tide, and by the end of August the Madriz government had collapsed.

The problem of recognition was ended but the British were still irritated. Haggard was only able to find one specific case of crop losses suffered by a British owned sugar plantation, but the Foreign Office was incensed at the treatment of the planters along the Escondido river as reported by the captain of the *Scylla*. According to Thesiger, the "Planters Association" of independent planters in the river valley was suffering heavy losses because of the monopoly of the carrying trade maintained by the American owned Bluefields Steamship Company. Some 250 members, or three-fourths of the association, were British subjects. As Thesiger described the case, the United States was responsible for the continuance of the monopoly:

> When the Planters complain to Estrada, he informs them that he quite agrees that they ought to be allowed to work, but that the United States of America have given him orders that they are not to do so, and, as he is absolutely under the United States of America, he has to do what they tell him.
> The Planters saw the American Consul about it, but all he would say was that, if they became an American company they would be able to start away at once. This the Planters absolutely refuse to do, stating that they would sooner lose everything than turn over to the United States of America.[44]

Was this an example of the treatment British interests would get if the United States were allowed a free hand in Central America? At least here was a tangible complaint, and the Foreign Office made the most of it. The State Department was asked to investigate the case, and if the facts were correct, the Foreign Office wanted the Americans to order their consul to stop intervening "& remove from S. Estrada's mind the impression referred to, as His Majesty's Government are convinced that the United States Government do not desire to encourage the inequitable treatment which has been experienced by the British Company."[45]

The touchiness exhibited by the Foreign Office over the plight of the Planters Association indicates the extent to which American policy in Nicaragua had revived their doubts as to the adequacy of British policy in Central America. Even before Thesiger's report arrived, Grey had expressed his uneasiness in a private letter to Ambassador Bryce:

> I wonder whether with the smaller Republics our accepting the political line of the United States of America so long as we get the open door is doing any injury to our commercial interests. It is no good our attempting to run these little Republics against the United States of America: we could never bolster them up and eventually they would turn against us; but I do not want to lose our commercial interests by excessive complacency to the United States of America, whose policy seems sometimes to be inspired by American adventurers.[46]

Grey was rather miffed at the fact that Knox could complain of the lack of British cooperation in maintaining the open door in China and Manchuria at the same time that Britain was having troubles in Central America. As the Foreign Secretary wrote Bryce in another private letter in January of 1911, he was ready to support the open door in Manchuria "in every way that I can with regard to existing arrangements," but there were "other parts of the world besides Manchuria." Besides the problem of British planters in Nicaragua, the Foreign Office was faced with getting commercial treaties in Latin America and was "constantly finding that the difficulty is caused by a belief among Central and South Americans that the United States are not favourable to the open door."

> I do not suggest that Mr. Knox has instigated this belief amongst Central and South Americans, though I think it possible that some of his representatives may have encouraged it.
> It would however be only fair that he should do his best to keep the

door open, and not allow it to be shut under cover of a suspicion that the United States resent it being open, when it is in the power of his representatives in Central America to remove the suspicion.[47]

Although the State Department never explained the conduct of their consul in Nicaragua, the case of the Planters Association was soon settled satisfactorily for the British. On January 30, 1911, the Foreign Office learned that President Estrada had instructed his governor at Bluefields to issue permits to anyone wishing to navigate the Escondido. This removed the only concrete British complaint against the United States in Nicaragua, and the Foreign Office's fears for the open door there tended to die down. But the ingrained British suspicion of American motives in general remained strong.

Grey was not the only one worried about the adequacy of British policy in Central America. The Foreign Office's difficulties in negotiating trade treaties in Central America were being criticized in the British commercial press,[48] and British bondholders were pressuring the Foreign Office again. Twice in 1910 during the civil war in Nicaragua, the Ethelburga Syndicate appealed to the Foreign Office for aid, complaining of expensive delay in the construction of the proposed railway and the cancellation by Nicaragua of the tobacco and liquor concessions that were to be transferred to English companies under terms of the loan contract of 1909. After the warnings issued at the time of the loan to Zelaya, Grey had scant sympathy for the problems of the syndicate and curtly refused to give the financiers diplomatic help.[49]

However, no sooner had the Foreign Office washed its hands of the Ethelburga Syndicate than the question of the Honduran debt arose once again. Morgan had negotiated an agreement with the Honduran government for a loan in December of 1909, but the State Department could not get the Hondurans to accept the necessary treaty for American control of the customs. When the one year agreement between Morgan and the British bondholders lapsed in August of 1910, the Council of Foreign Bondholders extended it for another six months, but they were unhappy about the delay. Their complaints to Grey brought no immediate reply, but the Council launched the

Foreign Office on another general review of the Latin American debt situation.

Grey now attempted for the first time to formulate a more positive general policy on defaulted debts in Latin America. In the past, Honduras had refused to arbitrate, yet arbitration had been Grey's first thought. Should not the United States help Britain in return for her cooperation in following the American political line? Grey now laid down the following prescription:

> Where negotiations fail ask for arbitration, when we can make a case for it & I do not see why if the U. S. A. cannot be made an actual party to an arbitration they should not, where they have intervened as in San Domingo & assumed control of the finances, be asked to support the request for arbitration & to agree to support the execution of the award.
>
> In other cases where to fall in with a U. S. scheme offers a prospect of fair settlement with our bondholders let us encourage that course.
>
> When this course is not open & separate negotiations by ourselves are feasible we should ask at Washington that the U. S. should not oppose.[50]

It was easier to state this policy than put it into effect, since the bondholders were now clamoring for immediate aid in Honduras, Santo Domingo and Guatemala, and complaining about new problems with Ecuador and Colombia, the alienation of securities by Nicaragua, and the fact that Costa Rica had not serviced her debt in ten years. One of the difficulties in Grey's prescription was determining when an American scheme offered "a prospect of a fair settlement" and the point at which negotiations with the Central Americans were a failure. In words that would have warmed Lionel Carden's heart, Rowland Sperling, one of the more anti-American clerks in the Foreign Office, argued that the Foreign Office required no action on Nicaragua, Colombia or Ecuador, but should demand arbitration in Costa Rica, Honduras, Guatemala, and possibly Santo Domingo. To Sperling, the "crux of the whole matter" was the belief of the Central Americans that, whatever the British say, they will do nothing "especially if the U. S. object." Thus the Foreign Office would have "to make it quite clear to the U. S. as well as to the Republics concerned that we meant to have the award executed."

I venture to think that if we were seen to be in earnest the Republics themselves would compete with the U. S. G. in the offer of reasonable settlements to the bondholders; the Republics because they would realize that if they did not pay the U. S. would pay for them and assume control of their finances; the U. S., because they would be anxious to maintain their predominance in Central America at all costs.

It may be said that such action would be deeply resented both by the U. S. & by the Republics. But, as far as I have been able to see, we have gained nothing at all by considering U. S. susceptibilities in these matters.

But Sperling's superiors were not yet ready to run the risk of American resentment. Mallet again studied what his predecessors had done to help the bondholders in the past, but he was in no mood to inaugurate a general policy of vigorous action in their behalf. The Council "treat us as if we were their agents & we cannot accept the role," he complained. "We can only help them unofficially if they help themselves."[51]

The only concrete action at this time concerned Honduras. When the British bondholders had agreed to extend the time limit on the Morgan offer, they had added the condition that Morgan give them compensation for the delay. The Council felt that the bondholders were entitled to a 5% per annum interest charge to date from the expiration of the original one year agreement. In September of 1910 Mallet wrote to Morgan's London representative supporting the compensation request and reminding Grenfell of their conversation in June of 1909, in which the banker had held out the prospect of some additional payment to the British holders of Dominican bonds. The resulting correspondence was polite but fruitless. Grenfell could not get assurances from Hollander on the Santo Domingo settlement, and Morgan could not agree to any compensation for the holders of the Honduran bonds. Nor were Innes's enquiries successful in October. The State Department merely told Innes that negotiations with Honduras were proceeding satisfactorily and that the Council and Morgan had agreed to extend the time.

Since Grey and Mallet did not want to disturb the arrangement between the Council and Morgan or to revive the Carden plan, they continued to press the United States on the matter of compensation instead. Mallet thought the Council "a wooden-headed lot" for insisting that the British government was responsible for the bondholders' decision to go in with Morgan, but the State Department's answer to Innes had been irritatingly vague and unsatisfactory. Mallet was even ready to threaten the Americans that it would "be difficult" for the British government "to maintain their neutrality vis-à-vis the U. S. proposals" unless the State Department used its influence with Morgan on behalf of the bondholders. Innes was able to dissuade him from making his "mild" threat, but Mallet insisted that the reluctant embassy at Washington try to get some aid from the State Department.[52]

On December 17th Huntington Wilson promised Innes that he would use his "good offices" with Morgan, but only more disillusionment resulted. In January of 1911 the United States finally completed its negotiations with Honduras for a treaty controlling Honduran customs, and the following month Morgan and Honduras signed a loan contract providing for a refunding of the Honduran debt. But no tangible gain resulted for British bondholders. When early in 1911 the Foreign Office told Bryce to remind Huntington Wilson of his promise, Innes reported that Huntington Wilson could not get Morgan to agree to the Council's proposal. Huntington Wilson promised to try again, but had little hope because "Morgan does not care for the whole job" and was "only taking it up to please the State Department."[53]

The State Department would not exert any pressure on the bankers that might jeopardize their grand plans. Morgan's loan contract with Honduras contained no provision for interest on the old bonds, and when Innes talked to William Doyle, the head of the Latin American Division of the State Department, the American said the problems of British bondholders had not been one of his primary concerns in his attempts to get the contract signed. Doyle had raised the question of interest once again, but the representative of the bankers "had given him no indication of whether he was willing to consider the request or not."

> Mr. Doyle frankly told me that he had not pressed the point. He had, he said, spent a week in New York negotiating the contract, and had met with many difficulties. He had, therefore, been more anxious to get the contract through than to raise questions on behalf of the bond-holders.[54]

The bondholders were probably unrealistic to expect more from the State Department or Morgan on the matter of compensation, for in Innes's words, "unlike good wine, the bonds of a defaulting creditor do not become more valuable by lapse of time."[55] But any settlement, with or without compensation for the delay, depended on the ratification of the American-Honduran treaty. After two years of "dollar diplomacy" in Honduras, the prospects for a settlement were still uncertain, and the persistence of the Council of Foreign Bondholders made it inevitable that the Foreign Office would continue to be bothered by this minor diplomatic headache.

By the beginning of 1911, Britain's policy of accepting American predominance in the Caribbean had undergone no basic change. As Grey noted in September of 1910, the small Central American Republics "must succumb to some greater & better influence & it can only be that of the U. S. A."[56] Despite his talk about arbitration and the defense of the open door, the Foreign Secretary was still committed to a policy of salvaging the best terms possible as each problem arose. By any objective analysis, the United States had little cause for complaint regarding the cooperative attitude of Britain in both Nicaragua and Honduras. The Foreign Office had done nothing to aid the Ethelburga Syndicate, and Grey had followed the State Department's lead on recognition during the Nicaraguan revolution. And, while the Foreign Office had not forced the Council of Foreign Bondholders to accept the Morgan offer in Honduras, they had made clear that they were not prepared to defend the British plan for a debt settlement negotiated by their own minister.

Yet there were signs of a deteriorating situation. The State Department under Taft and Knox did not encourage smooth relations. American replies to British representations and inquiries had usually been vague and sometimes blunt to the point of insult. The American assumption that British interests were secondary to the grand policy of the United States was understandable, but it could have been accepted much more easily by the Foreign Office if the American administration had tried to cooperate in return. Mesmerized by the opposition at home and in Central America to their policies, the State Department merely assumed British acquiescence and hardly thought of pressures on the British government. The British decision to push for interest compensation for Honduran bondholders and the strong protest in behalf of the Nicaraguan Planters Association both stemmed partly from the Foreign Office's disgust at the State Department's cavalier attitude rather than from a conviction that the issues were important.

British irritation brought on by the onset of dollar diplomacy was accompanied by a growing contempt for the abilities of Knox and his subordinates. Bryce and Innes would not encourage the Foreign Office to take a stand in Central America and the Caribbean against the United States, but the diplomats in Washington contributed indirectly to the deterioration of Anglo-American relations by their unflattering estimates of the Secretary of State and the State Department. By 1910 Bryce viewed Knox as "the *bête noire* of the whole diplomatic body, which continually asks why he was chosen for so important a post."[57] Innes found Knox "indolent" and his assistants "none of them men of mark." With the exception of its legal office, the entire State Department was "very deficient in ability."[58] Perhaps the most scathing criticism of all came in this letter from Bryce to Grey:

> The trouble with the Secretary of State is that he is hopelessly ignorant of international politics and principles of policy, and is either too old or too lazy to apply his mind to the subject and try to learn. Nobody in his miserably organized department is competent to instruct or

guide him. No country but the U. S. could get on under such conditions. As President Taft said a few days ago Providence takes care of children, lunatics and the United States.[59]

Representatives of the British Foreign Office had never used such unflattering terms to describe Hay or Root.

The first two years of dollar diplomacy in Latin America did not seriously threaten British interests, but a significant turning point in the Foreign Office's attitude towards the United States occurred. No one in London doubted that Taft and Knox were friendly to Great Britain, but the President did not inspire the feelings of awe in the British that the "Rough Rider" had aroused, and the loss of respect for the State Department was accompanied by an inevitable decline of fear. The British were still very apprehensive of the dangers of alienating the United States, but the extreme fears brought on by the traumatic experiences of the Roosevelt days were waning. This new mood, combined with the growing irritation caused by "dollar diplomacy," paved the way for a more independent defense of British interests within the American sphere of influence.

NOTES AND REFERENCES

1. Bryce to Grey, May 20, 1909. F. O. 371/609.

2. As Minister to Central America, Carden was stationed at Guatemala City and represented Britain in Guatemala, Honduras, Nicaragua and Salvador. Early in 1908 Costa Rica had been transferred to the British minister at Panama. The two ministers also served as consuls-general to the six republics. The only other salaried British consular officer in Central America at the time was a vice-consul in Guatemala.

3. Puerto Cortes was the terminus of the short railway. Valentine had held the wharf concession since 1896, but the lease had expired. In addition, Valentine's railway contract of 1908 had not been submitted to the Honduran legislature for approval as required by the Honduran Constitution.

4. Carden to Grey, telegram 4, March 13, 1909. F. O. 371/608. Brown's protest to Honduras was made on March 10th.

5. Grey to Bryce, March 13, 1909; Innes to Grey, March 25. F. O. 371/608.

6. Grey to Bryce, April 8, 1909. F. O. 371/608.

7. See Munro, op. cit., p. 218. When he asked for permission to go to Honduras in February of 1909, Carden stressed the need for speed because "other proposals" were before the Honduran government, but the Foreign Office did not know the nature of Valentine's plan until Carden's despatch of March 27th arrived. F. O. 371/608.

8. In return for $60,000 and payment for any improvements that had been made, Valentine was to turn over the wharf and railway on April 30th. However, the Honduran government was unable to make the payment, and, when they attempted to seize the properties in June, an American gunboat blocked the confiscation. Valentine remained in possession of both the wharf and the railway until 1912. See Munro, op. cit., pp. 219, 233; U. S., Foreign Relations, 1913, pp. 594–607.

9. Bryce to Grey, telegram of May 29, 1909, and despatch of June 1st. F. O. 371/608. For the development of Knox's Central American policy during the first months of the Taft administration, see Walter V. Scholes and Marie V. Scholes, The Foreign Policies of the Taft Administration (Columbia: University of Missouri Press, 1970), pp. 35–39, 45–50, 68–70.

10. C. of F. B. to F. O., June 16, 1909, and minutes; Mallet to Bryce, June 23rd. F. O. 371/608.

11. Bryce did send notes to the State Department on July 10th and 15th, but they were too late to have any bearing on the negotiations.

12. Mallet's memorandum to Grey, June 24, 1909. F. O. 371/608.

13. Mallet's minute to Carden of June 30, 1909. F. O. 371/608.

14. C. of F. B. to F. O., July 10, 1909, and Mallet's minute. F. O. 371/608.

15. Grey to Carden, July 13, 1909; Reid to F. O. July 22nd; Grey to Carden, July 28th. F. O. 371/608.

16. Bryce to Grey, May 30, 1909. F. O. 371/609.

17. Hardinge to Avebury, private, June 2. F. O. 371/609.

18. Avebury to Hardinge, private, June 7, 1909. F. O. 371/609. The French Government did prevent an official quotation on the bonds in Paris, but they did not stop the flotation. See Munro, *op. cit.*, p. 169.

19. Bryce to Grey, September 18, 1909. F. O. 371/609.

20. Mallet to Carden, August 24, 1909. F. O. 371/608.

21. Carden to Grey, July 26, 1909. F. O. 371/610.

22. Larcom's minute to Carden's of July 26, 1909. F. O. 371/610.

23. See Innes's letter to Bryce of July 6, 1909, in Bryce Papers, USA 29.

24. Innes memorandum of August 24, 1909. F. O. 371/610.

25. Innes to Mallet, private, August 26, 1909. F. O. 371/610.

26. Mallet's minute to Innes's memorandum of August 24, 1909. F. O. 371/610.

27. Mallet to Carden, September 8, 1909. F. O. 371/609.

28. F. O. to C. of F. B., September 7, 1909. F. O. 371/609.

29. Mallet's minute to Chalkley to Grey, October 30, 1909. F. O. 371/708.

30. Grey's minute to Chalkley's of October 30, 1909. F. O. 371/708.

31. Grey's minute to Chalkley's of October 30, 1909. F. O. 371/708.

32. Law's minute to Carden's of September 11, 1909; Grey to Bryce, October 15. F. O. 368/279.

33. Bryce to Grey, November 2, 1909. F. O. 368/279. U. S. Tariff Commission, *op. cit.*, pp. 31–32.

34. Carden to Grey, October 9, 1909. F. O. 368/279.

35. Langley to Carden, November 22, 1909. F. O. 368/279.

36. U.S. Tariff Commission, *op. cit.*, p. 31.

37. Bryce to Grey, May 30, 1909; Larcom's minute to Bryce's despatch of October 6, 1909. F. O. 371/609.

38. On hearing that Thesiger was determined to prevent any fighting within Greytown, Mallet told Carden that no British forces should be landed except in case "of urgent danger" to the British consul and in order to evacuate British subjects who wanted to leave. The instructions arrived too late, but Mallet was careful to inform the State Department of them. See Grey to Carden and Bryce of January 17, 1910. F. O. 371/835. In May of 1909, the British had also sent a cruiser to Nicaragua because of some disorders along the Escondido river, but here too they had made sure that the United States knew that Britain had no ulterior motives. See Grey to Bryce, May 8, 1909; and F. O. to Admiralty, May 27th. F. O. 371/609.

39. Bryce to Grey, March 23, 1910; Grey to Bryce, April 7th; F. O. 371/835.

40. Grey to Bryce, April 15, 1910. F. O. 371/835.

41. Carden to Grey, April 16, 1910. F. O. 371/835.

42. Grey to Bryce, June 16, 1910. F. O. 371/836.

43. Grey to Bryce, July 22, 1910; Grey to Reid, July 29. F. O. 371/836.

44. HMS *Scylla* to Admiralty, August 19, 1910, in Admiralty to F. O., September 26. F. O. 371/836.

45. F. O. memorandum to Reid, November 2nd. F. O. 371/836.

46. Grey to Bryce, private, August 11, 1910. Grey Papers, vol. 43.

47. Grey to Bryce, private, January 7, 1911. F. O. 371/1057.

48. For a scathing attack on the Foreign Office and Ambassador Bryce in the British press in the fall of 1910, see Percy F. Martin's letter to the editor of the *British Trade Journal*, printed in the *South American Journal* for September 3, 1910. Martin had been sent by a group of British trade journals on a fact finding tour of Central America in the fall of 1909. See also the *South American Journal*'s comments on Bryce in the same issue.

49. Ethelburga Syndicate to F. O., February 25, 1910; reply of March 9; Ethelburga Syndicate to F. O., May 2, and reply of May 13. F. O. 371/835.

50. Grey's minute to C. of F. B.'s letter of August 9. F. O. 371/837.

51. Minutes to C. of F. B. to F. O., September 13, 1910; F. O. 371/837.

52. Grey to Innes, November 29, 1910; Innes to Grey, November 29, 1910, and minutes; telegram 133, undated, to Innes. F. O. 371/837.

53. Innes to Mallet, February 14. F. O. 371/1056.

54. Innes memorandum of February 17, 1911, in Bryce to Grey of February 17. F. O. 371/1056.

55. Innes to Grey, November 29, 1910. F. O. 371/837.

56. Grey's minute to Tower's despatch of August 23, 1910. F. O. 371/928.

57. Bryce to Grey, March 28, 1910. F. O. 414/218.

58. Innes to Grey, October 25, 1910. F. O. 414/218.

59. Bryce to Grey, private, March 28, 1910. Grey Papers, vol. 43. For the views of Bryce and Innes, see also Scholes and Scholes, *op. cit.*, pp. 13–14, 17, 23–24, 27.

CHAPTER VI

The Decline of Anglo-American Cooperation

With Mexico in the throes of revolution and the Congress of the United States passing discriminatory tolls legislation for the Panama Canal, the British Foreign Office had more to worry about across the Atlantic during the last years of the Taft administration than the relatively minor problems of "dollar diplomacy." British interests in Mexico were not seriously damaged by the liberal revolution of Francisco Madero that ended the long career of the aged dictator Porfirio Díaz. In his claims report after the Madero revolution, Chargé d' Affaires Thomas Hohler was surprised that the British claims were "so extremely moderate." In his annual report on Mexico for 1911 the British minister, Francis Stronge, found it "remarkable" that foreign interests, especially British ones, were so little affected by a revolution of such extent and duration.[1] The Foreign Office was able to follow a policy of strict non-intervention, but the continuing disorders aroused much anxiety in London because the British economic stake in Mexico was greater than in any other country of the Caribbean area. Nor could Britain, the foremost of maritime nations, be indifferent to the plans being laid in Washington to favor American shipping in the isthmian canal now only a few years from completion.[2] There were no serious differences between Britain and the

United States over Mexico during Taft's presidency, but the Panama Canal Act of 1912 caused the first great crisis in Anglo-American relations since the Venezuelan intervention of 1902–1903.

British disillusionment with the United States over the canal tolls legislation can be fully appreciated only by considering the high hopes that were engendered by the proposed general arbitration treaty of 1911. In 1908 the United States and Great Britain had signed an arbitration treaty, but like all the Roosevelt-Root arbitration treaties, it did not apply to all cases affecting "the vital interests, the independence, or the honor" of the two countries or to those concerning the interests "of third parties."[3] Such an agreement caused little excitement, but when Taft became caught up in the peace movement in the United States and came out strongly in 1910 for true arbitration treaties that would broaden the scope of the former ones by removing the crippling exceptions, vistas of the millennium began to open up for the advocates of arbitration on both sides of the Atlantic.

Sir Edward Grey and the Cabinet responded eagerly to the American initiatives in the winter of 1910–1911, and in the following negotiations the British pushed for a treaty as unlimited as possible. Not only would this have a beneficial effect on Anglo-American relations, but perhaps the idea might spread to the great powers of Europe and have a great effect on the armament race and what Grey called "the 'morale' of international politics."[4] The British regarded the treaty as the two countries' definite renunciation of war as a means of settling disputes, and although the language of the treaty as signed in August of 1911 was not all that the British had hoped for, it was sufficiently broad to justify great optimism.

The new treaty provided "means for the peaceful solution of all questions of difference" which could not be settled by diplomacy. It was to apply to all cases "relating to international matters" in which the two countries "are concerned by virtue of a claim of right made by one against the other under treaty or otherwise, and which are justiciable in their nature by reason of being susceptible of decision by the application of the principles of law or equity." If the two could not agree on the "justiciable" nature of a particular case, a "Joint

High Commission of Inquiry" consisting of three members from each country would determine whether it fell within the scope of the treaty. If no more than one of the members dissented, the issue would be submitted to arbitration according to the provisions of the treaty.

The British treaty and a similar one that Taft negotiated with the French were enthusiastically received in the United States, but to the dismay of their supporters the treaties soon became bogged down in the Senate, the victims of poor timing and tactics, disunity in the Republican party, partisan politics, and the attacks of Roosevelt and his followers.[5] The senators had little difficulty in finding objections to unlimited arbitration. Under the new treaties, the Senate still could accept or reject each *compromis* or specific agreement for arbitration. But what effect would the decisions of the joint commission have on the cherished powers of the senators? Were decisions binding and thus an infringement on the constitutional rights of the Senate? Could immigration policy be arbitrated? What of those repudiated bonds of some southern states in the hands of the British bondholders? And of course what of the Monroe Doctrine?

In March of 1912 the Senate finally consented to the treaties but only after rendering them unacceptable to Taft and the two European governments. The Senate deleted the controversial clause giving the joint commission of inquiry the power to determine if an issue was "justiciable," and by reservations the Senators excluded immigration questions, the rights of aliens in education institutions, any questions affecting the territorial integrity or the alleged indebtedness of any state, and the Monroe Doctrine or "other purely governmental policy."[6] Although talk about new negotiations continued half-heartedly for a time, the movement for unlimited arbitration had come to an inglorious end. "The disappointment is too great to cause annoyance," Andrew Carnegie wrote to Ambassador Bryce, "or rather it falls like a heavy dull load of disaster which we must slowly surmount."[7] But greater disillusionment soon came for the advocates of arbitration in Britain and the United States, for the canal tolls controversy was to show how meaningless even the existing arbitration treaty was to most Americans.

The British government knew the central role that an American owned and operated Central American canal played in American foreign policy. When Taft's plans to fortify the vital waterway were being debated in the United States in 1910 and 1911, the British government prudently kept quiet. The Hay-Pauncefote Treaty of 1901 had said nothing about fortifications and by implication the British had waived the point. Now ten years later Grey wanted nothing more than to avoid any discussion of the subject. Realizing that the growth of the American navy had made it "almost impossible" for the British to command the sea in the area of the canal "unless the neutrality or friendliness of European nations were absolutely assured," the Admirality even thought that the fortifications might be of benefit to Britain.

> If we are ourselves at war with the United States we cannot expect to be able to use the canal in any case, and in the event of war under any other conditions the fortifications may assist the United States in preventing damage to or obstruction of the canal by either belligerent, and to that extent they may be useful to the world in general and to us in particular as the greatest users of the canal.[8]

When the matter of canal fortifications was raised in 1911, it was the United States rather than Britain that broached the subject. During negotiations for the arbitration treaty of 1911, Knox asked for a formal statement from Britain on fortifications that he could use when the treaty went to the Senate. Grey was reluctant because he did want to bind a future British government but when Knox continued to insist, Grey allowed Bryce to send a note stating that in the British government's opinion the treaty of 1901 did not bar American fortifications.

But if strategic considerations in Central America were a thing of the past, the effects of the administration of the canal on British commercial and shipping interests was another matter entirely. The British were prepared to fight tenaciously for the principle of equality in the use of the canal. Even Root's attempt to give Colombian warships free passage of the canal in the American-Colombian treaty of 1909 drew a protest from the Foreign Office that was not with-drawn until the State Department formally promised that the case could not become a precedent. Root's treaty was never ratified by Colombia, but even before Taft took office the British had demon-strated that they would be extremely touchy over the possibility of discrimination in the use of the canal.

The Hay-Pauncefote Treaty seemed unequivocally opposed to special treatment for American shipping. According to Article Three:

> The Canal shall be free and open to the vessels of commerce and of war of all nations observing these rules, on terms of entire equality, so that there shall be no discrimination against any such nation, or its citizens or subjects, in respect of the conditions or charges of traffic, or otherwise. Such conditions and charges of traffic shall be just and equi-table.[9]

But by 1911 discussions in the American press and Congress had made the British aware that many Americans were beginning to interpret the treaty in ways that would justify the exemption of American ships from the general rule of equality.

In the fall of 1911, a memorandum by Edmond Ovey, the Second Secretary in the Washington Embassy, touched off the first serious discussion within the British government of this disquieting develop-ment. Ovey grouped the various proposals and suggestions on canal tolls that were being put forward in the United States into four classes: (1) free passage for all American ships through the canal, (2) free passage for American ships engaged in the coastal trade, (3) the use of subsidies to American ships using the canal, (4) the refunding of tolls paid by American ships.[10] Obviously American legal in-genuity was at work. Were any of these proposals compatible with the Treaty of 1901? Algernon Law of the Commercial Department of the Foreign Office and William Davidson, the Foreign Office's legal advisor, both believed that all of the four classes would violate the treaty. On the other hand, the Board of Trade doubted that any objections could be made to either subsidies or refunds, while agreeing that any exemptions were "clearly repugnant" to the treaty.[11]

The Foreign Office referred the issue to the Law Officers of the Crown, who replied in March of 1912 with an opinion that became the "official" view of the British government. In principle, the Law Officers argued, there was no difference between exemptions of tolls and refunds, and both would violate the treaty. Subsidies based on the use of the canal would "stand self-confessed as a colourable attempt to avoid the obligations of the treaty." The exemption of American coastal shipping was "a more difficult question," for only American vessels could engage in this trade.

> If the trade could be so regulated as to make it certain that only traffic which under United States law is reserved for United States vessels would be benefited by the exemption, it is not easy to see upon what ground objection could be taken. But it appears to us that this proposal may be combated on the ground that it would be impossible to frame regulations which would prevent the exemption from resulting, in fact, in a preference to United States shipping and consequently in an infraction of the treaty.[12]

While the British government was preparing a case to use if needed, news from across the Atlantic was increasingly gloomy. Taft's conversion to preferential treatment was particularly disturbing. In his message to Congress of December 21, 1911, Taft was "very confident" that his country had "the power to relieve from the payment of tolls any part of our shipping that Congress deems wise." "We own the canal," he trumpeted forth to the world. "It was our money that built it."[13] Taft's message drew an angry reaction from the British press, and pressure on the British government began to mount. Questions were asked in Parliament, and inquiries and memorials from interested groups and organizations began to arrive at the Foreign Office.[14] If any of the American proposals became law, Grey would be forced to vigorously defend British interests. The outlook was not encouraging for a government pledged to Anglo-American friendship.

When the House of Representatives passed a bill exempting

American coastal shipping, the Foreign Office had to take a stand. Grey ordered Innes to send Knox a note based on the Law Officers' opinion and to try to get further consideration of the bill postponed. On July 8th Innes launched "H. M. G.'s thunderbolt," and the following week Grey elaborated the British views to Ambassador Reid. Grey hoped his protest would help defeat or modify the bill, and he wanted to propose arbitration "only in the last resort." Although one British press correspondent in Washington complained that the protest was "as colourless as a young girl's invitation to tea" and doubted that it was intended to be taken seriously, Grey was in dead earnest in his opposition.[15] He rejected Innes's suggestions that the British abandon their protest in return for canal regulations that would minimize the bill's discriminating effects or for an agreement that would ensure a moderate rate on the tolls. Both the Foreign Office and the Board of Trade were convinced that their case was strong, and they had no intention of compromise until all other possibilities were exhausted.

There were some encouraging signs in the reports from Washington. The British note had aroused little Anglophobia in the American press, much to the relief of Innes, who had feared they would "indulge in the 'tail-twisting' which has in former years been a favorite pastime with the Americans." According to Innes the greater part of the "best papers" were on the British side. Public opinion was about equally divided, and the discussions in the Senate were friendly.[16] However, when the bill cleared the Senate and the conference committee in August, it retained the exemption for coastwise vessels and gave the President the power to discriminate in the setting of tolls on all American ships. According to the act, the President could fix tolls within certain limits: American coastwise shipping was exempted, and the tolls were not to exceed $1.25 per net registered ton, nor be less, "other than for vessels of the United States and its citizens," than the estimated proportionate cost of maintenance and operations of the canal. There were also some exemptions for the Republic of Panama.

Pessimism now pervaded the Foreign Office. Innes urged Taft to veto the bill, but was there any hope of this in an election year, particularly when both Roosevelt and Wilson were on record as favoring exemption? Taft did try to get Congress to pass an amendment that would allow foreign shippers to appeal their rights to the Supreme Court. But when Congress refused he signed the bill and even defended its controversial provisions in a long accompanying memorandum.

How did Taft defend the new law? How could the rule of equality in the Hay-Pauncefote Treaty be interpreted in a way that would not affect American ships? Taft argued that the treaty had been adopted by the United States solely to provide a basis for neutralization of the canal and was not intended to limit the power of the United States "to deal with its own commerce, using its own canal in whatsoever manner it saw fit." The article forbidding discrimination was an American declaration of policy that the canal would be neutral and that the commerce of all nations observing the rules adopted by the United States would be treated alike.

> In other words, it was a conditional most-favored-nation treatment, the measure of which, in the absence of express stipulation to that effect, is not what the country gives its own nationals, but the treatment it extends to other nations.

Taft's rebuttal to the British argument about there being no difference in principle between refunding and remitting tolls was that, if it were true, the treaty would restrict the United States from aiding its commerce in a way that other nations could. If other countries could extend favors to their shipping in any way they saw fit, the British protest would lead to the "absurd conclusion" that the United States had signed away a right by the treaty that other nations retained. Thus the United States would be discriminating against itself!

What of the particular law in question? It only favored American coastal shipping which was barred to foreign vessels, and even the British "seem to recognize a distinction" between this and discrimination for American ships engaged in foreign trade. The law "seems" to give the President the right to favor ships in the latter category, but, as it did not compel him to do so, there was no need to discuss this until he actually used his power to extend such favors. The exemption of ships in the coastal trade was really a government subsidy to encourage competition with America's transcontinental railroads.[18]

Was Taft arguing that the United States had the right to exempt all American shipping from the payment of tolls? In a conversation with the President in October, Bryce bluntly pointed out that his arguments on subsidies could go to that length.

> He admitted this, and added he thought the United States had a perfect right to exempt all their vessels, because the Canal was now theirs and the provision for equal tolls was only meant to prevent discrimination between the vessels of different foreign states. I traversed this contention, and asked whether he read the words "all nations" in the treaty as being equivalent to "all nations other than the United States." He replied this was the way he read the words. I expressed astonishment. . . .[19]

The next step was up to the British. Grey found Taft's view of the Hay-Pauncefote Treaty "quite outrageous." The arbitration treaty of 1908 was still in effect and it specifically referred to differences "relating to the interpretation of treaties." But would the United States agree to arbitrate? "If they refuse arbitration in such a point," Grey wrote Bryce, "it will put back the cause of arbitration 100 years. . . . It is a very serious prospect."[20] Grey's pessimism was well founded. Some "leading senators" told Innes that the Senate would probably refuse to arbitrate under the 1908 treaty until the British could complain of some overt act of discrimination, and by then the treaty would have expired.[21] Taft proudly assured Bryce that he personally would be the "last man in the world" to refuse arbitration, but the President also thought it probable that the Senate would refuse, perhaps on the grounds that canal tolls were a "vital interest" of the United States.[22]

Although neither arbitration nor a change in the law in the coming session of Congress seemed likely, an answer to the Americans was imperative. Grey and Bryce agreed that the best time to reply would be after the American presidential election in November but before the new session of Congress in December. Thus the British had ample time to consider the type of answer that would have maximum effect in the United States. In October the Cabinet agreed to refer the drafting of the reply to a five-man committee of the Cabinet headed by the Foreign Secretary.Grey in turn instructed Cecil J. B. Hurst, the Foreign Office's Assistant Legal Advisor, to draw up a proposed draft. The Cabinet again fully discussed the matter on November 13th and 14th. Hurst's draft was then sent to Bryce, who presented it to the State Department on December 9th after getting permission to make some changes.[23]

The British note aimed at refuting the American version of the rule of equality in the treaty of 1901. According to Grey, the true interpretation of the Hay-Pauncefote Treaty derived from the fact that it was a "corollary" of the Clayton-Bulwer Treaty of 1850. The treaty of 1901 had "superseded" the earlier one, but it had not impaired the general principle of equal treatment that had been the object of the pact of 1850.[24] In 1901 the United States had regained its freedom to construct a canal alone, but she was still limited by the principle of equality. This principle was repeated in the Hay-Pauncefote Treaty, and the meaning of "neutralization" as used there implied American subjection to the system of equal rights and was not confined to belligerent operations. If the rules of the Hay-Pauncefote Treaty gave Britain only most-favored-nation treatment, "the value of the consideration given for superseding the Clayton-Bulwer Treaty is not apparent to His Majesty's Government."

In addition to the rule of equality, there was the provision that tolls must be "just and equitable." Unless all vessels paid tolls, a fair rate based on the expenses of the canal could not be determined, and there would be no guarantee that the other ships would not pay more than their fair share. Therefore, "any system by which particular vessels or classes of vessels were exempted from the payment of tolls" would violate the treaty. The United States had the right to subsidize its shipping as long as the method chosen did not result in an unfair burden on others or any discrimination in the use of the canal. The exemption from the payment of tolls of certain classes of American ships would be a form of subsidy in violation of the treaty.[25]

Applying the rule of equality and the "just and equitable" provision to the Canal Act, Grey concluded that both the exemption to coastwise vessels and the power given to the President to fix lower rates for other American ships were infractions of the British treaty rights. The absence of foreign competition in the American coastal trade did not alter the situation. Other nations would still be injured by the shifting of the whole burden of upkeep of the canal on to the ships engaged in foreign trade, and by the fact that coastal shipping could not be "circumscribed" in such a manner as to prevent such vessels from benefiting at the expense of others. Because of its size, the British merchant marine would of course suffer from any such adverse results more than that of any other nation. The British government realized, Grey concluded, that "many persons of note" in the United States did not agree with the British interpretation. Therefore, if the United States preferred arbitration Britain was ready, but arbitration would not be necessary if Congress amended the Canal Act and removed the objectionable features.

The British made a powerful and well-constructed defense of their interpretation of the canal treaty, but at the same time the note was not bellicose. Considering English feelings of outrage against the action of the American Congress, it is little wonder that Knox seemed "to be a little relieved" that the note's "tone was so moderate" when it was read to him by Ambassador Bryce.[26] The moderation of the note of course was not intended as a means of relieving Knox's anxieties; it resulted from the fact that the British were aiming primarily at American public opinion. As Hurst explained his draft:

> The desire being that the dispute should be terminated by a spontaneous amendment of the law of Congress rather than by arbitration, I have borne in mind the conversation I had with Admiral Stockton and his view that there was a good chance of the law being altered if the British protest did not lead the jingo party and the yellow press to raise a clamour which would prevent the moderate section of the public in the United States from making itself heard.[27]

The British attempt to sway the administration and Congress by influencing American public opinion had no immediate results.

Grey's note encouraged support in that part of the American press already opposed to the law, but Elihu Root and other opponents of the exemption clause were unable to muster enough votes for repeal in the new session of Congress. As for arbitration, Taft's only suggestion was the possibility of referring the dispute to a joint Anglo-American commission similar to the one that decided the Alaskan boundary controversy, but the British wanted nothing to do with this arrangement. Grey still preferred a diplomatic settlement or a modification of the Canal Act, but as he instructed Bryce in January, 1913, if arbitration became necessary Britain wanted to use the existing arbitration treaty and refer the matter to the Hague Court, "seeing that the point to be decided is legal, is specially provided for in the treaty, and eminently suitable for settlement by that tribunal."[28]

In his reply to the British protests of July and December of 1912, Knox attempted to dismiss the matter on the grounds that there was nothing as yet to arbitrate. The Canal Act of 1912 had not set the tolls, and Taft's proclamation of November 13th setting the rates had not discriminated in favor of American ships engaged in foreign trade. Thus any discussion of American obligations under the Hay-Pauncefote Treaty would have to wait until the British could complain of a concrete injury. As for the coastal trade exemption, Knox claimed the British had conceded that such exemptions might not violate the treaty and he ignored the elaborate British arguments against them. The most Knox offered was the suggestion that a joint commission of inquiry might be used to examine the case if Britain, after studying all the facts, still thought there were important differences of opinion.[29]

An impasse had been reached. In February, 1913, the British denied the necessity under international law of waiting for an actual infringement of a treaty before complaining about a law that had violated it, and they still insisted that it was a suitable case for the arbitration treaty of 1908.[30] In fact, the British had long given up any hope for a settlement with the lame-duck Taft administration. There were already signs that President-elect Woodrow Wilson would be more receptive than Taft to the British views. Bryce delayed his resignation hoping that a speedy settlement could be reached as he knew from various sources that the President-elect was changing his position on tolls. For domestic reasons the new administration was unwilling to act in 1913, and Bryce was unable to get any commitments from either Wilson or Bryan. However, before he left Washington in April of 1913, Bryce was convinced that Wilson would do his best to bring about a settlement satisfactory to the British. Wilson would eventually succeed in pushing a bill through Congress repealing the discriminatory legislation in the summer of 1914, but when Taft left the White House in March of 1913, Anglo-American relations were more strained than they had been in over a decade.

The canal tolls controversy was not the only issue straining Anglo-American relations during the last years of Taft's presidency. To understand the degree to which Anglo-American cooperation had deteriorated by 1913 it is necessary to return to the story of the Foreign Office's reaction to "dollar diplomacy" in Central America. On the surface, British policy toward the United States and the small Latin American countries remained the same. When in November of 1911 Lionel Carden sent another direful warning about the dangers of American activity in the area, Sir Edward Grey replied in much the same terms he had used in 1909 and 1910: British interests were to be defended, but nothing could be done to check the expansion of American influence. However, the Foreign Office in 1911–1913 was working more vigorously than before to settle British claims in the Caribbean, and in Nicaragua and Guatemala this more independent policy came into conflict with American "dollar diplomacy."

The British government was always more willing to give diplomatic aid to British subjects having general claims against Latin American nations than it was to extend help to the British bondholders. During the Taft administration the Foreign Office was relatively active settling these claims.[31] From the viewpoint of Anglo-American relations, the most significant of these negotiations occurred in Nicaragua when Great Britain for the first time openly refused to cooperate with one of the plans of the State Department.

Although Taft's policy during the Nicaraguan civil war of 1909–1910 had caused irritation in London, the British were not opposed to the establishment of an American financial protectorate in Nicaragua. But when in 1911 American plans for the control of Nicaragua included an American-Nicaraguan Claims Commission that would have sole jurisdiction over all claims against the Central American government, British suspicions of the United States flared up once again. The British claims against Nicaragua were not large, but the Foreign Office instinctively balked at the idea of consigning them to the tender mercies of an American dominated commission. As Sperling argued, it "would certainly be hard to believe" that such a commission would be impartial, as the United States "wish to pose as the protectors of the C. A. Republics & would welcome a chance of doing so at our expense by whittling down our claims to the lowest possible point."[32]

In the usual style of the Knox era, the State Department did not bother to try getting prior acceptance of the Mixed Commission by the major European powers. When the proposed commission was formally announced in March of 1911 by the Nicaraguan government, the Germans, Italians and Belgians all protested, while the British and others simply ignored the decree. The ever-cautious British hoped that the opposition of the other powers would scuttle the plan, but Grey instructed Carden that British claimants were free to use the commission if they desired, "but in this case H. M. G. stand aside reserving their right to intervene diplomatically if not satisfied that justice has been done." As the Foreign Office explained to the French, the British government preferred a mixed Anglo-Nicaraguan commission if "other means of settlement" failed.[33]

By the time the new Mixed Commission was announced, Carden had already presented the pending British claims to Nicaragua, and the British decided to continue independent negotiations. Realizing that any personal move by himself in Nicaragua would be the same as waving a red flag in front of the American bull, Carden vetoed London's suggestion that he go to Managua. Well aware of the considerable opposition within Nicaragua itself to the commission, the British Minister preferred to take advantage of Consul Martin's "personal intimacy" with Nicaraguan politicians. When the Nicaraguan Minister for Foreign Affairs proposed that all British claims be referred to the new commission, Carden merely acknowledged receipt of his note, for at the same time Martin was reporting that his "private" talks with President Adolfo Díaz at Managua were showing definite promise.[34]

The inevitable clash with the United States was not long in coming. Unhappy over the European reaction to the claims commission, the State Department now decided to try to bring the British government into line. On September 21st, Assistant Secretary of State Huntington Wilson told Bryce of the State Department's "surprise and regret" on learning that Carden opposed British use of the commission, and, on the same day, the American Embassy at London gave the Foreign Office a memorandum calculated to clear up what Knox thought was "some little misunderstanding" on the part of the British.[35] A few days later Ambassador Reid personally called at the Foreign Office to boost the new commission.

According to the Americans, the British had no reason to fear using the commission. It was technically a Nicaraguan court, but its real aim was to safeguard litigants. The fact that two of the three commissioners would be Americans did not mean that the United States wanted "any exclusive advantage." The United States had insisted on such a composition, Reid professed, because "they were actuated solely by the desire to make it more acceptable to civilized nations, and to give it an infusion of ... Anglo-Saxon justice."[36] And if the lure of Anglo-Saxon justice was not sufficient, Huntington Wilson's note to Bryce bluntly pointed out that the United States expected British cooperation within its sphere of influence.

> Of course, the interests of British trade and of civilization generally must necessarily be on the side of the efforts this Government makes in Central America,—a part of the world where especially we should expect to count upon cooperation rather than opposition on the part of the representatives of Your Excellency's Government.[37]

American pressure was particularly distasteful and embarrassing to the Foreign Office, for the State Department seemingly assumed that Carden was acting on his own initiative. In spite of his attempt to work through Martin, the old charges of Carden's anti-American-ism were now revived. As early as April of 1911 Ambassador Reid had complained informally to Grey about the "anti-United States attitude of Mr. Carden," and now in September William Philips of the American Embassy told Under Secretary of State Campbell that the United States "could not help feeling" that London's views "were influenced to some extent at least by the hostility of Mr. Carden to all things American."[38] Carden had been a convenient scapegoat in the past in explaining away Anglo-American differences in Latin America, but now he had to be defended and the Foreign Office could do this only by admitting that their minister was acting on instructions from home.

While Grey was wondering how to reply to the American inquiries, news arrived from Nicaragua that President Díaz had proposed a direct lump sum payment of £15,800 for all the British claims. Although this meant scaling down some of the claims, the Foreign Office accepted the offer. In subsequent talks with Reid, Grey made no mention of these independent negotiations, but their seeming success enabled him to avoid a direct British refusal to use the commission. The British government would "not put an obstacle" in the way of British subjects' use of the commission, Grey assured Reid, but they could not accept it as "a bar to diplomatic intervention or eventual arbitration." Grey's reply was courteous, and he played down the importance of the "minor" difficulties between Britain and the United States in Central America, but he made no promises to force British claimants to use the commission in the future, and emphasized that Carden had not been acting on his own initiative:

> I am anxious that the State Department should realize that every step which Mr. Carden has taken has been on my instructions and if, at any time, his action has seemed in opposition to United States' views, it is not due to any personal feeling or to any hostile political intention either on his part or on mine, but to the obligation incumbent upon me to see that British trade and British claims are fairly treated.[39]

The British considered the Nicaraguan agreement binding, but unfortunately Díaz was presiding over a bankrupt government.

After months of haggling over possible partial payment plans, the Foreign Office realized that there would be no payment of any claims until Nicaragua could obtain enough funds to rehabilitate her finances. When the Knox-Castrillo Convention of 1911, providing for a customs receivership, failed to get the approval of the American Senate, Nicaraguan hopes for a large American loan also dwindled, and the Nicaraguan government was kept afloat only by smaller stopgap loans and arrangements with the American bankers and the State Department.[40] The mixed commission began acting upon claims in March of 1912, but Nicaragua had no funds to pay the awards. It is possible that the United States might have been able to get the Foreign Office to refer the recognized British claims to the commission if Nicaragua had had money for an immediate payment, but because of Nicaragua's bankruptcy there was no financial incentive for the British to change their mind.[41]

The American military intervention in the Nicaraguan revolution of 1912 on behalf of the Díaz government was generally welcomed by the British as the American marines protected foreign lives and property. But even this proof that the United States was determined to dominate Nicaragua brought no change in the British attitude towards the claims commission. When a new decree was promulgated late in 1912 that all claims from the latest revolution had to be submitted to the commission, the Foreign Office notified Nicaragua that they could not accept it as the sole means of settling claims, and Britain was able to get another Nicaraguan promise of £4,000 for the new ones.

Many small claims from British subjects were eventually handled by the Mixed Commission before it went out of existence in January of 1915, and even the "diplomatic claims" recognized by Nicaragua in 1912 were finally scaled down by another American dominated commission before they were finally paid in 1919.[42] But at the time the Foreign Office viewed Nicaragua's recognition of British claims as evidence of the wisdom of dealing directly with the small Central American states. This was hardly the type of cooperation that the State Department expected from Great Britain and the other European nations which had negotiated directly with the Nicaraguans. The British, however, made an even more startling show of independence in Central America before the Taft administration was over, for by the end of 1912 the United States and Britain were involved in a sharp "misunderstanding" over the Guatemalan debt.

In 1911 and 1912 the debt default situation in Latin America was better than it had been in decades. Costa Rica left the list of defaulting states in 1911 when the bondholders accepted a refunding arrangement negotiated by Minor Keith, and although Nicaragua defaulted on its external debt in January of 1912, the Council of Foreign Bondholders was able to reach an agreement with the American bankers that was accepted by the bondholders in June of 1912. These settlements helped the Foreign Office by reducing the number and intensity of the Council's complaints, but, since the British government had played no part in the negotiations, they did nothing to enhance the reputation of the Foreign Office as the defender of British interests. In any event, the remaining debt problems were more than sufficient to keep alive the vexing issue of aid to the bondholders.

An old problem that continued to plague the Foreign Office was the supposedly inequitable settlement in Santo Domingo. The Council of Foreign Bondholders had certainly not forgotten the matter— by their own count they had sent twenty-nine letters to the Foreign Office on the subject from 1906–1910—and their persistent complaints did lead to some new inquiries by the Foreign Office to the Dominican government. The reply was as expected: there was no basis for any British claims against Santo Domingo because the claims of the San Domingo Improvement Company had been settled in full, and the matter was solely one between the British bondholders and the now defunct company.

According to Grey's policy stated in 1910, arbitration was to be used to clear up such problems when negotiations failed. Was this such an instance? Did the bondholders have a sufficiently good case? And above all, would the United States support a request for arbitration and see that the award was carried out if it was favorable to the British bondholders? When asked to sound out the State Department, Bryce warned it was unlikely that the United States would cooperate. Before reopening the case, Bryce wanted the Foreign

Office to peruse Alfred Innes's report on the Santo Domingo debt.

Based on the State Department's detailed Hollander study of 1905, the Innes report of March, 1911, was a forceful attack on the Council's position. The British Councilor found that an "examination of the history of the Dominican debt is like raking in a muck-heap." There was hardly one of the financial transactions associated with it "with which an honourable man would care to have his name associated." Innes thought the activities of the Improvement Company were beneath contempt, and even if Englishmen had not taken a direct part in Dominican finances the bondholders deserved little sympathy. The worthless nature of the Dominican bonds "must have been apparent to any but a simpleton and the best that can be said for the voluntary investor in such trash is that he is gambling on the chance some Power may intervene, and that he may make a large profit." Nor was Innes convinced of the honesty of the Council's arguments that the bondholders were independent from the Company at the time of the settlement. In any event,they had received more than the bonds were worth and it was highly improbable that any arbitration could be successful.[43]

Innes's report ended any serious consideration by the Foreign Office of arbitration of the Santo Domingo debt. Nor did the Council of Foreign Bondholders ever ask for such a solution. Instead the Council tried to deal directly with the American government by sending their Secretary, James Cooper, to Washington. In April, 1911 Cooper discussed Santo Domingo and other debt problems with Thomas Dawson and other officials in the State Department's Latin American Division. He was able to get an American promise to aid the British holders of Ecuador's railway bonds which were in default at the time, but the meeting produced no change in the American view of the Dominican settlement.[44] The only immediate result of the meeting was an acrimonious dispute between the Foreign Office and the Council over Cooper's charge that his discussion with Dawson had supposedly shown the inadequacy of past measures taken by the Foreign Office and the British Embassy in Washington to defend the rights of the bondholders. In August, 1911, the Council was still vowing that they would not rest until justice had been secured, but as far as the Foreign Office was concerned the affair of the Dominican bonds was consigned to a well-deserved oblivion.

Another problem that could not be completely ignored was the still unsettled question of the Honduran debt. The American-Honduran treaty of January 1911 and Morgan's loan contract of February 1911 did nothing to help the British bondholders. Neither the treaty nor the loan contract ever went into effect because of the opposition in both Honduras and the United States to the Taft administration's plans for the little Central American nation. The failure of American "dollar diplomacy" in Honduras also meant the failure of British hopes for a settlement for the bondholders, but the uncertainty caused by the American attempts in 1911–1912 continued to agitate the Council of Foreign Bondholders and the Foreign Office.

In February, 1911, the six-month extension of the Council's original agreement with Morgan for the purchase of the British bonds came to an end. With the Foreign Office refusing to give any advice whatsoever, the Council had to content itself with devising another plan to get some compensation for the bondholders for the delay. As Morgan was adamant in his refusal to consider paying any interest on the bonds, the Council now suggested that one-half of any money saved by old bonds not being turned in during the proposed conversion should be given to the participating bondholders. The new proposal fared no better than the first. Cooper came away from his April visit to the State Department with the impression that the American officials "would do everything in their power to see that the Bondholders received compensation." According to Innes, the British Embassy received "the same kindly expressions of good will" from the State Department when they supported the Council's suggestion, but both approaches were equally fruitless.[45]

The Council should have known that appeals to the State Department were useless, but there seemed little else to do. In October, Cooper wrote directly to Knox, complaining that it was unreasonable to expect the British bondholders to wait without any information about prospects of the Morgan agreement being carried out in the near future, and pointing out that the Council was "constantly receiving complaints from the Bondholders, who insist that the United

States Government should not have imposed their scheme on them unless they saw their way to bring it to a successful conclusion." Cooper's letter was not appreciated at the State Department. In a conversation with Innes in January of 1912, William Doyle "denied emphatically" that the State Department had pressed for the adoption of the particular terms of the Morgan contract. The bondholders had accepted it "entirely on their own initiative" without any interference on the part of the American government.[46] By 1912 no one wanted to take responsibility for the bondholders' acceptance in 1909 of the ill-fated Morgan plan—neither the Council, the Foreign Office, nor the State Department.

In February, 1912, Morgan withdrew his Honduran loan agreement and his arrangement with the bondholders officially collapsed. "After waiting two and a half years for the consummation of the American scheme," the Council complained to the Foreign Office, "the bondholders hear that it has ended in nothing."[47] Not only had there been no compensation for the delay, but now there seemed little chance for any settlement whatsoever. There was little the Council could do independently, for the failure of the Morgan agreement did not mean that the American government had given up its plans for the financial control of Honduras. When Morgan withdrew, equally unsuccessful attempts were already underway for a refunding loan by a New Orleans group. In the end, Taft and Knox were unable to bring to fruition their own policy in Honduras, but their attempts at "dollar diplomacy" had frustrated any hopes for an independent British settlement.[48]

Throughout the inconclusive Honduran debt negotiations, the Foreign Office had never reached the point at which they were willing to strongly support the bondholders. Grey's suggestion of arbitration was never followed up, and neither the Foreign Office nor the Council made any attempt to revive the Carden scheme of 1909 in the face of the American plans and the uncertainty of the political situation within Honduras. The Honduran President with whom Carden made his arrangement in 1909 was no longer in power. Zelaya of Nicaragua had helped Dávila seize the Presidency in 1907 and had continued to support him. The resignation of Zelaya also meant the end of Dávila, who was overthrown in 1910. But, unlike the case of Santo Domingo, the Honduran affair did have a significant effect on the thinking of the Foreign Office regarding the desirability of cooperation with the United States in the Caribbean. Not only had American "good offices" been barren of results, but, above all, the Taft administration could not implement one of its cherished policies in the area. Even if the bondholders were not completely happy with the outcome, Roosevelt at least produced a settlement in Santo Domingo. Taft's complete failure in Honduras conditioned the reaction of the Foreign Office to the dispute between the British bondholders and Guatemala.

Despite continuing complaints from the Council of Foreign Bondholders, the Foreign Office had done nothing for the Guatemalan bondholders since the collapse of Lansdowne's efforts to apply pressure to President Estrada Cabrera in 1902. Guatemala not only remained in default on the external debt, but Estrada Cabrera continued to use for other purposes the special tax on coffee exports that had been pledged to the British bondholders.From 1903 to 1908 Guatemala used the coffee duty to get some sizable loans from a San Francisco syndicate represented by Adolfo Stahl, an American banker in Guatemala City. While the British bonds went unserviced, Estrada Cabrera made punctual payments to both his American and German creditors. The Council was outraged, but the Foreign Office was cautious, and by the beginning of the Taft administration there had been no official protests from the British government.[49] The ever-active Carden had been pressing Estrada Cabrera to resume payment on the debt, but during the early years of his stay at Guatemala the British minister succeeded only in getting vague promises and verbal assurances.

The situation was further complicated in 1909 and 1910 by the refunding projects put forward by three competing groups of American financiers. Carden correctly divined that Estrada Cabrera had no serious intention of accepting any of the American proposals, but the negotiations aroused British fears that an unsatisfactory settlement might be forced upon the bondholders. None of the American groups had consulted the Council of Foreign Bondholders, and no one in

London knew whether the American government was interested in any of the projects. In this delicate situation, Estrada Cabrera's stalling tactics and the continuing pleas for help from the Council produced another problem that the Foreign Office could not ignore.

By the end of 1910, Carden suggested that the British government make "strong representations" to Guatemala, and he had in mind a new general policy he had devised for helping the bondholders. Disenchanted with debt conversions, Carden now thought the British should limit their action toward defaulting governments to demands for a complete or partial resumption of interest payments, "holding entirely aloof from any refunding schemes, which are usually as futile in their results as they are detrimental to the real interests of the bondholders."[50] The Foreign Office was too pragmatic in its approach to such problems to accept Carden's advice as a general rule, but his analysis did become crucial in determining the British policy towards Guatemala.

Believing that the bondholders should decline any settlement in Guatemala involving a reduction of either principal or interest, Carden proposed that the British use Estrada Cabrera's negotiations with the American bankers as one of the proofs that Guatemala could afford to resume servicing the British debt. He suggested sending a formal note asking the President what provisions he was now prepared to make towards paying the current interest on the 1895 debt, and warning that "other steps" by the British government might be forthcoming. The Foreign Office realized that Carden's approach might lead to a possible conflict with the United States, for the British minister wanted to cite the proposed American project of George W. Young and Company and the Windsor Trust Company as one that would be harmful to the rights of the British bondholders. However, Mallet could see no other alternative, and, hopeful that "our opposition may lead to some compromise," he authorized Carden to send his note in February of 1911.[51]

The British pressure seemingly succeeded. In June of 1911 Carden secured a written promise from Estrada Cabrera to assign again the coffee revenues to the bondholders and resume interest payments on the December 31st coupons if the Council would consent to the issue of £600,000 in new Guatemalan bonds and get permission from the London Stock Exchange to quote them as part of the 1895 debt. Although they were sceptical of Estrada Cabrera's good faith and apprehensive that the United States might intervene as in Honduras, the bondholders decided to accept the Guatemalan offer, but in November the news arrived in London that the Guatemalan President had changed his mind and was not prepared "at present" to sign any contract relating to the foreign debt. The Council of Foreign Bondholders found Estrada Cabrera's "deliberate affront" to Carden "incredible" and wanted advice and help from the Foreign Office.[52]

Once again the Foreign Office was forced to decide how far to go in aiding the bondholders. Although Carden was convinced that Estrada Cabrera's change of mind was caused by his fear of the United States, no one at the Foreign Office wanted to drop the matter. The case was so "flagrant" and the British claim "so reasonable" that Spicer was sure Grey's arbitration formula of 1910 should now be used. Perhaps this would force the American government "to come into the open," and the Foreign Office could find out to what extent the American bankers were receiving official support. Mallet too thought that the British case was strong and "it should be well rubbed in." The Foreign Office and the Council decided to demand restitution of the coffee revenues to the bondholders within one month if Guatemala failed to pay the December coupons. If this did not succeed, they would demand arbitration.[53]

When Estrada Cabrera failed to resume the payments, Carden was personally very happy to be able to send his note of January 1, 1912, demanding return of the coffee revenues. The Guatemalan President now "has to face the music," Carden wrote privately to Spicer, and the British action "will have an excellent effect throughout Central America in showing that we at last intend to stand up for our rights."[54] The situation even seemed promising in Washington. The Foreign Office had not yet asked the United States for support, but reports from Bryce and Innes indicated that the State Department would not oppose British pressure on Guatemala. A few days after the British ultimatum, Doyle told Innes of his "indignation" at Estrada Cabrera's "knavery" in playing off the British and the American groups against each other. The Guatemalans could pay their debts, but would never accept any scheme "until obligated to."

> The United States Government, he said, were not in negotiations with Guatemala on the question of its finances, nor did he think that any Treaty such as had been negotiated with Honduras and Nicaragua necessary in this case. All that the United States Government desired was to see a fair settlement of the claims. The Government, Mr. Doyle declared, had taken no part whatever in the recent negotiations with American financiers, to each of whom Cabrera had said in turn that their scheme was the only one which did not contain fatal defects.[55]

Actually, the State Department was more interested in the subject than Doyle's statement indicated. The American government had been neutral regarding the three American projects, but the State Department certainly was not indifferent to the prospects of an American refunding of the Guatemalan debt. Since 1909 the State Department had been in contact with the American bankers and urging the Guatemalans to accept an American loan. After Carden delivered his "ultimatum" in January of 1912, the State Department urged the American bankers to take advantage of the situation and used the British demand as a means of putting more pressure on the Guatemalan government for an American financial reorganization.[56]

Estrada Cabrera of course was stalling everyone. He had once told Carden that the discussions with the American bankers about debt consolidation could be "regarded as so much waste paper,"[57] but he continued to prolong them as a means to fend off the British demands. His reply to Carden's note of January 1st was vague and without specific assurances. Carden now wanted to make a prompt demand for arbitration, but at this point the British pressure was suspended, not because of any reluctance on the part of the Foreign Office, but because of an offer to the Council of Foreign Bondholders from Minor Keith, one of the American bankers negotiating with Guatemala.

On January 19th the Foreign Office learned from the Council that Keith's representative in London had made a definite proposal to the

British bondholders. The Council did not like all the details of the offer, but they were anxious to negotiate with Keith because the arrangement promised better security and the implied support of the United States. Would it be possible for the Foreign Office to join hands with the State Department and combine the efforts of Carden and Keith?

This was not the type of Anglo-American cooperation that the Foreign Office now envisioned. Impressed by Carden's arguments against negotiating for a reorganization of the Guatemalan debt, the Foreign Office bluntly told the Council that the Keith proposal was "absolutely incompatible" with the plan to demand arbitration. The Council had to choose between two alternatives. If they wanted arbitration, the Foreign Office would officially demand it of Guatemala and ask the United States for support. If they wanted to negotiate with Keith, Grey could only ask the State Department "unofficially to do what they can to further the arrangement."[58]

It was not a choice that the Council was anxious to make. If the bondholders chose negotiations with Keith and were unsuccessful, would the Foreign Office then support arbitration? Were there any reasons for assuming that a demand for arbitration would be success-ful? When the Foreign Office refused to answer such "hypothetical questions," the Council's Secretary was once again sent to the United States to try the direct approach. Cooper did succeed in negotiating at New York an arrangement regarding the Nicaraguan debt, but did little to clear up the Guatemalan dilemma. He was disappointed when he missed meeting Keith in New York, and his talks with other bankers with Guatemalan schemes netted little information. His visit to the State Department was equally frustrating. One of Huntington Wilson's subordinates merely denied that the American government was participating in the present negotiations with Guatemala.

Thus by the summer of 1912, British pressure on Estrada Cabrera had been suspended because of a combination of the Council's in-decision and the Foreign Office's acceptance of the Carden policy of remaining aloof from negotiations for debt conversion. The rather ironic situation had been reached in which the usually reluctant Foreign Office was ready to give the bondholders strong support, but the Council was unhappy with the offer. Relations between the Foreign Office and the Council had reached one of their periodic low points. As Cooper told Bryce, the Council had no confidence in Carden, who was "not a business man." On the other hand, Mallet was convinced that Cooper was "of very inferior capacity" and that the President and Vice-President of the Council were too old. "The Bondholders interests are not well looked after & we get the blame."[59]

Carden's business talents may have been limited, but he took seriously his role as defender of British interests in Central America. Although his plans for Guatemala had been temporarily stymied, Carden was already hard at work on a new scheme to solve all Anglo-American difficulties in the area. In 1909 he had received little encouragement from London when he suggested an actual agreement with the United States for the protection of British interests within the American "sphere," but Knox's tour of Central America in 1912 gave the British minister an opportunity to revive his plan in a more precise form. Carden was heartily disliked at the State Department, but Huntington Wilson, hoping to put more pressure on Estrada Cabrera to make an arrangement with the American bankers, advised Knox to accept the British suggestion that he meet with Carden at Guatemala City.

When Knox and Carden met on March 16th, the British minister recounted his past woes in Cuba and Honduras and expounded his views on American reciprocity and the problems of the British bondholders. Knox of course defended the American record and avoided any promises, but at least on the matter of the British bondholders Carden was sure that his arguments had brought the American Secretary of State to regard the subject "in a totally new light." Knox's knowledge of some of the cases seemed to Carden "most superficial," but the Secretary of State radiated such interest and spoke in such a sympathetic tone that Carden thought the time had come to suggest a general Anglo-American understanding to cover all possible conflicts of interest in Central America.

I therefore invited Mr.Knox's attention to the great advantages which the United States Government would derive in the pursuance of their new policy in Central America from being in thorough accord with His

Majesty's Government, whereby these Governments would be prevented from playing off English against American influence. And I pointed out how few were the directions in which our interests might be expected to clash, and how easy it would be to anticipate any such possible differences by arriving at a friendly and permanent understanding on the subject.

According to Carden, Knox "welcomed the idea most warmly and said that something of the same sort had already suggested itself to him." There was not enough time to discuss the matter more fully, but Knox promised to take it up "promptly and actively" when he returned home. Upon learning that Carden soon was going to England on leave, the Secretary of State invited him to stop at Washington for more detailed talks.[60]

Although Carden's suggestion for a formal general agreement had been made entirely on his own initiative, the Foreign Office gladly allowed him to follow up at Washington. Carden arrived at the State Department with an outlined proposal, but when he talked to Knox on June 11th he found that the Secretary of State's views had suffered a sea change from Guatemala City to Washington. Although Knox's manner was "quite as friendly" as it had been in Guatemala, "the idea of a definite general agreement" on Central America "did not seem to appeal to him as strongly as it certainly did then." Carden was able to get only one interview with Knox, and after an exchange of letters, the British Minister left for home.

What, if anything, had been accomplished? For the British bondholders, Carden tried to get an official recognition by the United States that British rights would be protected in any American financial scheme in Central America. The British government would furnish Washington with necessary information on existing loan contracts and defaults, and the State Department would inform any American banking group that appealed for support of the conditions of the prior loans "so that they may be duly respected." In addition, the United States was to recognize the sum agreed upon by the Council and Morgan in 1909 "as a fair basis for a cash settlement" of the Honduran debt.

Knox denied that any "special recognition" of the rights of the

British bondholders in Central America by the United States was necessary since the American government would never support a scheme that was unfair to British investors, and he evaded the Honduras issue on the grounds that he did not have enough knowledge of the true value of the bonds. The most Carden could obtain was Knox's assurance that "legitimate British interests" would receive "all friendly consideration" by the State Department in their examinations of proposed financial plans.

In order to maintain the open door within his bailiwick, Carden also suggested a declaration by the United States that she had no intention of negotiating Central American reciprocity treaties "for the purpose of obtaining special advantages" over Great Britain. At Guatemala Knox had assured Carden that Cuba was a special case, and that in his own public references to reciprocity he had only been thinking of the advantages Central American republics would derive. But when Carden now argued at Washington that some formal statement in favor of the open door would allay British apprehensions, the whole matter received a cold reception. Knox dismissed the subject, saying that Carden's remarks were hypothetical and "do not commend themselves to me as adapted to lead to any useful discussion at the present time."

The only assurance Carden got from Knox that appeared to be "sufficiently clear and explicit" was that the United States would use its good offices to support British demands for arbitration. It was hardly a binding pledge, but in light of the British plans for Guatemala, Knox's words seemed promising:

> With relation to the question of American good offices in connection with just British contentions growing out of claims and grievances, without any more formal or specific understanding I think that your Government can safely count upon us to hold ourselves ready in a proper case to afford such good offices as might be desired, whether in the direction of arbitration or of some other mode of settlement.[61]

Carden had succeeded in hardly more than airing British grievances in more detail. His failure to get a general agreement caused no great stir at the Foreign Office for they had long suspected that the United States would balk at any formal arrangement in Central America, but there was some disappointment. As Mallet told Spicer, "I hardly think we need thank Mr. Knox who has done nothing but give Sir L. Carden[62] a short interview & has not committed himself in the smallest degree." However, both Mallet and Grey were hopeful that the meeting might have some good results, and the Foreign Office did have some grounds for expecting future American diplomatic support in Central America.[63]

An opportunity soon came to test Knox's "good offices." After Cooper's failure to solve the Guatemalan problem in the United States, the Council of Foreign Bondholders was ready to follow the Foreign Office's lead. After arriving in London, Carden bluntly told Cooper that if he asked for assistance again "he must leave matters in our hands & not allow himself to be led off into independent negotiations." There was little else that the Council could do, and in July they formally asked Grey to demand arbitration. On August 7th, the Foreign Office instructed Vice-Consul Haggard at Guatemala City to make the demand, and at the same time ordered Innes to remind the State Department of "the views expressed" to Carden in June and to ask for their support "by any means which they may consider appropriate."[64]

The State Department's reaction was encouraging. The previous May, Knox had already warned Guatemala about the necessity of a speedy financial settlement,[65] and now, after Innes's request for support, Huntington Wilson again upbraided the Guatemalan minister at Washington. When told that the time had arrived when the United States "could no longer interpose its counsel to influence Great Britain to desist in demanding the immediate arbitration of just claims," the Guatemalan begged Huntington Wilson to ask the British to consent to a delay of twenty days. The Acting Secretary of State agreed, but he warned the Guatemalan minister that the United States would "find itself absolutely unwilling further to intervene in the matter" if the promised settlement was not concluded within the twenty-day period. In his *aide memoire* of September 13th, Wilson even referred Guatemala to that part of the Hague Convention of 1907 that stated that the prohibition against the use of force in the recovery of contract debts was not applicable when the debtor nation refused an offer of arbitration.[66]

Although the American response to the British request seemed satisfactory, the cooperation was illusory, for the two governments were aiming at different goals in their pressure on Guatemala. The State Department wanted a general financial settlement through an American banking group, while the Foreign Office was following Carden's advice to avoid this arrangement. The British agreed to the twenty-day delay, but Bryce was told to "make it clear" to the Americans that the British government did not desire "a settlement of any kind" but rather the restitution of the coffee revenues to the bondholders.[67] The two goals were not compatible, and for any true cooperation either the British or the Americans would have to abandon their plans. The Foreign Office had committed itself to restitution or arbitration, and future cooperation depended on the State Department carrying out its threat to stop interceding in behalf of the Guatemalans.

As expected, Estrada Cabrera soon indicated that he would not refer anything to arbitration. When Haggard reported that the Guatemalans did not seem worried about the British demand, the Foreign Office began considering seriously the use of force against a Latin American state for the first time since the *Agnes Donahoe* controversy with Uruguay in 1905. The old British belief in gunboat diplomacy had been dormant rather than dead. As Sperling argued, the simplest plan would be to give the Guatemalans a fixed time in which to accept arbitration, and if that failed, to send a man-of-war to the most convenient port to collect the customs until the interest arrears were paid.

We should of course have to inform the U.S. Govt and in view of their assurances might in normal circumstances count on their (probably somewhat grudging) assent. At the present moment however one or other of the parties in the U.S. might, for electioneering purposes, raise the cry that the Monroe Doctrine was threatened. It would therefore be safest to consult Mr. Bryce on that point and, if he thinks that such a danger exists, to postpone any mention of forcible action until after the elections in the U.S.

Junior clerks such as Sperling were always more aggressive in their suggestions than were their superiors, but this time the idea of using force received considerable support. As Spicer pointed out, Bryce, if necessary, could give the United States "the most categorical assurances" that Britain had no "territorial designs" upon Guatemala. The perfidy of Estrada Cabrera so impressed Assistant Under Secretary of State Sir Walter Langley that he was willing to risk creating a precedent that the Council of Foreign Bondholders could use against the Foreign Office in other cases of Latin American defaults. Grey was seemingly the only one who had any qualms over using force to help people so foolish as to invest in bonds of "those dishonest & unstable little States." The Foreign Secretary reserved his opinion on the question of force, but was willing to ask Carden "what steps would be most quickly effective if we decided to go beyond diplomatic measures." His telegram of October 17 to Bryce asking for advice specifically referred to "the ultimate possibility of coercive measures, which might perhaps take the form of the temporary seizure of a custom-house."[68]

Carden immediately outlined what he considered the best course of action. If Estrada Cabrera could be convinced that Britain would use force, Carden was sure he would yield before any measures were taken. Two cruisers should be sent to Puerto Barrios; the commanding officers would then go to Guatemala City and with the British representative make "a peremptory verbal demand" for the restitution of the coffee revenues; if this failed marines would then land and occupy the customs house at Puerto Barrios.[69]

As usual Bryce was very cautious, and while he did not oppose the use of force outright, he obviously hoped that it could be avoided. Not only would it be unwise to mention the possibility to the United States until after the elections, he warned, but coercion would be undesirable as long as the Panama Canal tolls controversy "remains acute." Would it not be best now merely to point out to the State Department unofficially that the twenty-day period was over and refer them to the paragraph on the Hague Convention in Wilson's *aide memoire* to Guatemala of September 13th? Surely the United States would then be willing to put pressure on Guatemala "for the sake of avoiding fresh trouble in Central America." Impressed by Bryce's arguments, Grey merely told Haggard to define for Estrada Cabrera the points Britain wanted to arbitrate, and the Foreign Office sat back to await the American reaction to Bryce's informal representations.

The specific points of arbitration demanded were: 1) Does a government have the right to alienate revenues pledged as security for the issue of a loan on a foreign market and apply them to other purposes without the consent of the bondholders? 2) Can that government retain the use of the revenues for its own benefit? 3) Can that government allege that the revenues are not free, that is, re-pledged to a third party, when an official demand is made for restitution?[70]

The divergent goals of the British and American governments then came out into the open. The Seligman-Speyer group of American bankers was still negotiating with Guatemala, and once again Estrada Cabrera appealed to the State Department to restrain the "premature" British demands because a general settlement was imminent.[71] When Mr. Kerr of the British Embassy talked to J. Reuban Wright of the State Department's Latin American Division on the following day, he found the American very reluctant to even talk about arbitration. Instead Wright expounded on the "keenest interest" that the State Department had in the success of the Seligman-Speyer plan. The United States preferred a general settlement to arbitration and hoped for British cooperation. Would the United States support arbitration if the British bondholders did not like the American plan? Wright hoped that this problem would never arise, but if it did the American government "would have to reconsider" the "whole question from that standpoint."[72] This answer was hardly what the British expected after Wilson's warning to the Guatemalans in September.

When Seligman asked the British bondholders for their advance approval to the American refunding scheme, the Council replied that the interests of the bondholders had been placed "un-reservedly" in the hands of the British government and that they were "unable to entertain any outside proposals whatever."[73] Convinced that the bondholders had to have the coffee revenues restored before they could advantageously negotiate with the American bankers, the Foreign Office decided to stand firm and continue pressing the United States for support. As Grey now complained to Knox, the British were disappointed at being asked to suspend their action again after Wilson had encouraged them to expect active support from the United States. Considering past history, the present American proposal regarding Guatemala did "not appear to offer a fair prospect of a satisfactory solution." The British position was still restitution or arbitration, and Grey hoped that the United States would cooperate.[74]

In reply, Knox made clear the American view that Great Britain not the United States was supposed to cooperate in Central America. Restitution of the coffee revenues would only help the British bondholders, while the American plan was calculated to benefit everyone with interests in Guatemala. The British bondholders had just cause for complaint against Guatemala, but Knox argued that if the American government "is asked to assist the creditors of Central American states, it feels that they should be willing to consider favorably whatever equitable assistance it is most convenient for the United States to render them." The American plan was fair and the security was better. As everyone would benefit from it, Knox would find it "surprising and regrettable" if the British government should maintain its "apparently uncompromising attitude" because of past discouragements. The chances for the success of the refunding scheme were excellent if the Foreign Office would cooperate. If an agreement was reached, Knox promised his "best efforts" to see that Guatemala signed and ratified it within a reasonable period of time. If the American government was unable to do this, they would support the British demand for restitution.[75]

Knox's defense of the American scheme and his conditional offer of support made little impression on the British. Bryce and Innes tended to favor cooperation, but at the Foreign Office the reaction was completely negative. Carden was still in London successfully defending his policy, and by now he was preaching to the converted. "I think we must stick to our guns," Mallet advised, and to Spicer it seemed "that the time has come to consider whether we will not take action in our interests apart from the U.S. . . ." Although Grey was reluctant to consider the use of force to collect debts, his instructions to Bryce in late December still followed the previous line: the British government was interested only in restitution or arbitration, and the Foreign Office still hoped for the friendly offices of the United States as they wished "to avoid other measures."[76]

Knox and Huntington Wilson, arguing once again for "pre-eminent" American interests, continued to apply pressure on the British. Early in January, Knox sent Bryce a copy of the American bankers' preliminary loan agreement that had been signed late in December and asked him to "strongly urge" London to accept it, "pointing out the deep concern of this Government in the carrying out by this means of its broad policy with regard to Central America where its interests are necessarily of predominant importance."[77] The following day, the American Chargé at London, Irwin Laughlin, was instructed to urge Grey to study the contract "and to consider the question upon a broad basis of international policy." The United States expected the British government to consider the matter "from a broader and friendlier viewpoint than appears to have been the case hitherto, when doubtless the importance attached to the subject has not been clearly understood."

> In the course of your conversation it will doubtless occur to you to give point to the attitude of this Government by the discreet suggestion that the British Government would doubtless be amazed if in some country correspondingly within a sphere of special British interest the Government of the United States should press arbitrarily for a specific solution of a question involving American citizens without any regard for the broad interests and policies of the State, in such a case Great Britain, in whose sphere of special interest the controversy had arisen.[78]

Huntington Wilson now even denied that any promise had ever been made to support the British. When Innes argued that Britain was entitled to something more in the fulfillment of the American promise of September than the substitution of another scheme "as an afterthought," Huntington Wilson "indignantly repudiated the idea that any such engagement had been entered into." According to his rather tortuous reasoning, the United States was justified in refusing to support the British because the Seligman scheme was the same one on which Guatemala had been negotiating at the time she had requested the twenty-day delay. Now that a contract had been negotiated, the circumstances under which he had threatened to abandon the Guatemalans were no longer the same. The negotiations had taken longer than anticipated, but the United States was under no obligation to support the British demands if the Foreign Office was uncooperative.[79]

The American arguments and appeals continued throughout most of January, but the Foreign Office refused to budge. Grey's replies were polite and replete with assurances of friendly intentions on the part of his government, but the British position remained the same. Cooper told Carden that the Council of Foreign Bondholders was "quite content" to leave the matter in the hands of the Foreign Office, and the Foreign Office in turn maintained the convenient fiction that it could not advise the bondholders to accept the American arrangement. In any event, how could an "expiring administration" in the United States bring the Guatemalans around in a few weeks when they had failed for three years? On January 27, Grey sent his final refusal to the American government. With the Guatemalans putting forward unacceptable amendments to the bankers' contract at the same time, it was finally obvious to the State Department that the loan arrangement was dead. On February 7th Knox told the American ambassador at Guatemala that there would be "no further action" for the present.[80] "Dollar diplomacy" in Guatemala had failed.

The time had come for the British to decide on "other measures." Although the Americans were unaware of it, they had brought about a major modification of the Foreign Office's plans for Estrada Cabrera by their refusal to back the British demand for arbitration. Finding that there were now "insuperable objections" to coercive measures like the seizure of a customs house, Carden suggested as an alternative a threat to Guatemala of breaking off diplomatic relations and laying the matter before Parliament. As Estrada Cabrera would be uncertain what the British would do next, Carden thought that Guatemala would still yield. Grey had never committed himself to using force and was now more than willing to avoid sending cruisers to Puerto Barrios.[81] As Guatemala had already formally rejected arbitration, Grey instructed Carden in February to put his new plan into effect when he returned to Guatemala City.

With the overthrow of Madero by a military coup d'état in Mexico in February of 1913, the Foreign Office's American Department had little time to worry about the bondholders' problems with Estrada Cabrera. But the bondholders' interests were in good hands. Carden now finally had an opportunity to try the "independent" approach in Central America that he had so long advocated, and he proceeded to make the most of it. When Estrada Cabrera and Carden met on April 4th, the Guatemalan was "somewhat surprised" that Carden congratulated him for escaping the clutches of the American bankers. According to Carden, the only objection to a restoration of the bondholders' rights was now gone "since Mr. Knox's financial policy in Central America did not find favour with the new Government of the United States." Any more evasions could only lead to "certain steps which I trusted I might not be obligated even to refer to." Estrada Cabrera pleaded for a delay of three weeks to dispose of the American plans that were still before the Guatemalan Congress. He promised to resume payment on the external debt either by a simple restoration of the coffee revenues or according to the terms of the abortive proposal of 1911 to the bondholders.[82]

After unsuccessfully trying to bypass Carden by a direct appeal to the Foreign Office to wait until a Guatemalan financial mission could come to London, Estrada Cabrera was finally prodded by Carden into a decision to revert to the 1895 agreement with the bondholders and restore the coffee revenues.[83] Reports from Washington that Guatemalan agents were trying to get support from the American government only spurred Carden into applying more pressure. He drew up a draft agreement and forced a promise from Estrada Cabrera that it would be signed by May 10th. When Andrew Bickford, the Council of Foreign Bondholders' agent at Guatemala City, found that the Guatemalan Secretary of State wanted to negotiate for further concessions, Carden was adamant. If the agreement, he warned, was not concluded by May 10th at 6 PM he would deliver an ultimatum. If the Guatemalans did not comply within five days, he would close the legation and leave aboard a British warship.

Estrada Cabrera's last hope was more intervention by the United States, and his agents in Washington were diligently stirring up the press and the State Department. According to the Guatemalans, Carden had threatened that a warship would be sent "to compel the collection of the coffee tax for the bondholders" if restitution was not made by the end of April. The American Chargé in Guatemala, Hugh Wilson, immediately investigated the situation, and the Guatemalan Secretary of State claimed that Carden had not only threatened to break off relations but that "his Government will adopt the necessary measures to collect the revenues." Apparently the only information Carden gave Wilson during the first week of May was that a British cruiser had arrived at Belize in British Honduras.[84]

Had Carden made stronger threats to the Guatemalans than his reports to the Foreign Office indicated? Or were the Guatemalans deliberately trying to arouse the United States by exaggerating the British warnings? In any event, the State Department did not know exactly what the British were planning. In the exchanges during the last months of the Taft administration, the British had never specified what other measures would be taken, and the Foreign Office did not notify the new Secretary of State William Jennings Bryan of the coming action.

As Carden's deadline drew near, Estrada Cabrera again tried to use State Department influence to gain time. On May 12th, Bryan asked the British to postpone their action until the first of June as the State Department was "convinced" that Guatemala was making an "earnest effort" for a settlement. There may have been some lingering hopes in the State Department that Guatemala would still accept an American arrangement, but Bryan seems to have been motivated primarily by uneasiness over the possible reaction of the American public. On the day the State Department made its request for a postponement, Bryan promised the new British Ambassador, Sir Cecil Spring-Rice, "to urge [the] Guatemalan Government to meet their engagements, but spoke of [the] sensitiveness of public opinion here," and Spring-Rice in turn suggested that the Foreign Office tell the Americans exactly what measures against Guatemala were proposed.[85]

The British undoubtedly would have refused to extend the time limit, but it was unnecessary to rebuff Bryan, for by the time his request arrived Estrada Cabrera had finally capitulated. The Guatemalan President had stalled until the last moment. Carden's ultimatum of May 10th arrived at the Guatemalan foreign ministry at the same time as Bickford, who had been hurriedly called for at the last minute. Carden withdrew the note, the agreement was signed at midnight of the 10th, and Estrada Cabrera approved it on the 12th.[86]

After all the Foreign Office's fears of possible consequences from independent action in Central America, it is ironic that the British coercion of Guatemala aroused little interest in the United States. The Wilson administration did not protest the settlement, and neither Congress nor the American press exhibited any signs of alarm. Completely overshadowed by the canal tolls controversy and the situation in Mexico, Britain's role in the failure of "dollar diplomacy" in the little Central American state passed almost unnoticed. But for those in Britain with interests at stake, the affair was far from insignificant. Needless to say, the Council of Foreign Bondholders was "deeply grateful" for the action of the British Government.[87] After years of criticizing the passivity of the Foreign Office, the *South American Journal* applauded the "new departure" in policy which "should have a far-reaching effect on other defaulters."

Althought not entirely without precedent, for the British Foreign Office has on one or two previous occasions interested itself in the concerns of British investors in foreign Government loans, still the action of this country in bringing strong pressure to bear on President Cabrera is more or less an innovation, and distinctly a step in the right direction.[88]

The *South American Journal* was so surprised by the action that it completely misinterpreted the situation by assuming that the American government must have approved and aided the British venture.

Carden and the Foreign Office of course knew better. Although he was soon to suffer more defeats at the hands of the Americans in Mexico, Carden for a brief moment basked in the role of a prophet vindicated. "This is a triumph for Sir L. Carden," Grey noted when the arrangement was published, "for it is his advice on which we have acted & his forecast has come true."[89] Carden was sure that the success was "clearly attributable" to the fact that the negotiations had been carried on directly with Guatemala, "without invoking the intervention or good offices of the United States Government, which have up to now only served to confuse issues and to give rise to conflicts of interests." The capitulation of Guatemala, the ease with which he had arrived at an arrangement with Honduras in 1909, and the recognition of British claims by Nicaragua, "goes far to show the advisability of continuing to treat in this way all questions which may in future arise with any of the Central American countries." His superiors in London were in complete agreement. The United States was not only uncooperative in Central America but now she seemed impotent as well. "It is clear," Spicer noted, "that we get on better with Central American questions by acting independently of the U.S. who only interpose endless delays & have not the power, even if they had the will, to give us any real help." Mallet thought it would "be well to remember this in future cases," and to Grey it was "a valuable precedent."[90]

Britain's independent policy in Guatemala was the most striking instance of the decline of Anglo-American cooperation.[91] The British stake in Guatemala was relatively insignificant, and the pressure from the bondholders was no greater than it had been in the past. Not only had the Foreign Office overcome its distaste for strong action in such cases, but they followed a more independent course than the Council of Foreign Bondholders itself had originally wanted. The pleas and pressure emanating from the State Department delayed the British action and ended all talk in London about the possibility of using force, but the American arguments in favor of cooperation had fallen on deaf ears.

Why had the usually cautious Foreign Office taken the risk of a diplomatic clash with the United States? Undoubtedly the personal factor played a part. Estrada Cabrera's tactics were particularly infuriating, and Carden's manipulations and advice created a situation from which it would have been difficult to retreat. But in the last analysis the British action against Guatemala was basically the result of injured national pride. British deference to the United States in Central America was a slightly humiliating experience under the best of conditions, and the tactless style of Knox and his subordinates had only aggravated the situation. Feelings of irritation that had been accumulating for years finally found release in the case of the Guatemalan debt.

1. Hohler to Grey, July 7, 1911. F. O. 371/1148; Stronge to Grey, August 21, 1912. F. O. 371/1397. Despite the continuing disorders in Mexico during Madero's presidency, the Foreign Office was still not bothered by any serious British claims at the end of 1912. British exports to Mexico were higher than they had been before the revolution, and there was no pressure from the bondholders because Mexico did not go into default on its external debt until 1914. The British government definitely did not want Taft to intervene in Mexico to protect foreign interests. In fact one of the Foreign Office's greatest fears was that the United States would intervene and aggravate the situation. As for joint intervention, it was Taft, not the British government, who once suggested the possibility that Britain and the United States—and perhaps France and Germany as well—might intervene in case of anarchy. Nothing more was heard of Taft's suggestion but the Foreign Office was completely opposed to the idea. See Bryce to Grey, March 4, 1912, and minutes. F. O. 371/1392.

2. The canal was opened to commercial shipping in August of 1914.

3. See U.S., *Foreign Relations*, 1908, pp. 382–84. Root negotiated twenty-five treaties of this type.

4. Grey to Bryce, private, March 30, 1911. F. O. 414/225. For the relationship of the arbitrator treaty with the Anglo-Japanese Alliance, see Scholes and Scholes, *op. cit.*, pp. 10–11.

5. See John Campbell, "Taft, Roosevelt, and the Arbitration Treaties of 1911," *The Journal of American History*, LIII (September, 1966), pp. 280–87. Roosevelt himself did not fear such a treaty with Britain, but he was opposed to using it as a model for others. Taft originally envisioned only a British treaty but he felt unable to refuse the French when they asked for a similar one and he offered to negotiate treaties with any country that wanted one.

6. Jessup, *op. cit.*, II, 276; John Campbell, *loc. cit.*, pp. 286–87; Paolo E. Coletta, *The Presidency of William Howard Taft* (Lawrence: University of Kansas Press, 1973), pp. 170–73.

7. Carnegie to Bryce, September 2, 1911. Bryce Papers, U.S.A. 4.

8. Admiralty to F. O., March 23, 1911. F. O. 371/1176.

9. U.S. *Foreign Relations*, 1901, p. 245.

10. Bryce to Grey, September 20, 1911, with Ovey's memorandum. F. O. 368/562.

11. Board of Trade to F. O., November 11th. F. O. 420/254.

12. Law Officers to F. O., March 19, 1912. F. O. 420/256.

13. U.S. *Foreign Relations*, 1912, p. 468.

14. During 1912 protests and inquiries were received at the Foreign Office from the Chamber of Shipping of the United Kingdom, the London Chamber of Commerce, the Newcastle and Gateshead Chamber of Commerce, the British Imperial Chamber of Commerce, the Canadian Chamber of Commerce, the Royal

Steam Packet Company, the Department of Trade and Commerce in Ottawa, and the governments of Australia and the Union of South Africa.

15. Innes to Bryce, July 11, 1912. Bryce Papers, U.S.A. 33; Grey to Innes, July 14th and 15th. F. O. 420/256; U.S., *Foreign Relations*, 1912, pp. 469–71. Grey to Innes, July 30th. F. O. 371/256.

16. Innes to Grey, July 22, 1912. F. O. 420/256. For comments in the American press on the British note, see *The Literary Digest*, July 27, 1912, pp. 133–34.

17. See U.S., *Foreign Relations*, 1912, pp. 471–75.

18. The text of Taft's memorandum is printed in U.S., *Foreign Relations*, 1912, pp. 475–80.

19. Bryce to Grey, October 5, 1912. F. O. 420/256.

20. Grey to Bryce, private, September 8, 1912. Bryce Papers, U.S.A. 33.

21. The arbitration treaty of 1908 was due to expire in June of 1913.

22. Innes to Grey, August 28, 1912; Bryce to Grey, October 5th and September 20th. F. O. 420/256.

23. The original note is Grey to Bryce, November 14, 1912. F. O. 420/256. It is printed in its final form of December 9 in U.S., *Foreign Relations*, 1912, pp. 481–89.

24. For the text of the Clayton-Bulwer Treaty, see U.S., *Foreign Relations*, 1901, pp. 238–41.

25. Hurst's original draft specifically admitted the right of the United States to make refunds out of its general revenues as long as they were not regarded as part of the expenses of the canal. Following an opinion of Lord Haldane, the Lord Chancellor, Hurst stated that the United States could treat the tolls as part of its general revenue and could use such money for grants or subsidies to ships that have paid the tolls as long as the payment went into the accounts of the canal. This part of Hurst's draft was deleted when Bryce pointed out that such American defenders of the British position as Senators Root and Burton would be embarrassed if the British took a narrower view of their rights than the American Senators themselves had in their arguments against the bill.

26. Bryce to Grey, December 11, 1912. F. O. 420/256.

27. Hurst's memorandum in 47324, F. O. 371/1418.

28. Grey to Bryce, January 9, 1913. F. O. 371/1419. The British were aware of the virtual certainty of victory before an arbitral tribunal composed of interested powers. As a Foreign Office clerk noted after reading a despatch on the reaction of the German press: "We shall have to look to Switzerland or Bolivia for an umpire if this question ever goes to arbitration." Sperling's minute to Granville to Grey, September 4, 1912. F. O. 371/1418.

29. For Taft's proclamation on tolls of November 13, 1912, and Knox's note of January 17, 1913, see U.S., *Foreign Relations*, 1912, p. 481, and 1913, pp. 540–47.

30. *Ibid.*, pp. 547–49.

31. Great Britain even took part in a limited revival of the multilateral approach of applying pressure to reluctant Latin American states. From 1909 to 1913, the Foreign Office joined Germany and France in an unsuccessful attempt to get Cuba to arbitrate the so-called "insurrectionary claims" of 1895–1898. The British, French, Germans, and Italians were more successful in their joint pressure on Haiti in 1910–1912 for the payment of claims. There was never any intention of using force, and the United States even joined the Europeans in their demands on Haiti, but the mere fact that Britain was willing to act again in concert with other European nations in Latin America testifies to the new mood of independence.

32. Sperling's minute to Carden to Grey, April 28, 1911. F. O. 371/1058.

33. Grey to Carden, June 21, 1911, F. O. 371/1057. F. O. to Cambon, June 29, 1911. F. O. 371/1058.

34. Carden to Grey, September 2 and 18, and October 6, 1911. F. O. 371/1058.

35. Bryce to Grey, private, September 25, 1911, and enclosure Wilson to Bryce, private, September 21st; Philips to Grey, September 21st. F. O. 371/1058.

36. Campbell's memorandum of September 25, 1911. F. O. 371/1058.

37. Wilson to Bryce, private, September 21, 1911, in Bryce's of September 25th. F. O. 371/1058.

38. Campbell's memorandum of September 20, 1911, and Grey's minute. F. O. 371/1058.

39. Grey's reply to Reid was originally dated October 19, 1911, but it was temporarily suspended, presumably due to the Díaz offer. After Reid sent another note to Grey on October 23rd explaining the commission, an amended version was sent. F. O. 371/1058.

40. For the American loans and arrangements, see Munro, *op. cit.*, pp. 192–204, 211–14.

41. When the lump sum offered by Díaz was not forthcoming, Mallet began to consider the idea of offering a compromise to the United States by which the British would accept the commission in return for an American promise that the award would not be less than £15,000. But when he learned that the commission was not making immediate payments, the idea was forgotten.

42. The settlements were handled by the American controlled "Commission on Public Credit" set up in 1917. After prolonged haggling, the reluctant British eventually accepted £9,000 in cash and £4,000 in bonds for the claims recognized by Nicaragua in 1912. See U.S., *Foreign Relations*, 1919, pp. 659–71.

43. Innes to Bryce, March 10, 1911, enclosure to Bryce's of March 11. F. O. 371/1132.

44. See the correspondence in F. O. 371/1288.

45. Cooper to Avebury, April 26, 1911; Innes memorandum in Bryce's of June 30th. F. O. 371/1288.

46. Cooper to Knox, October 18, 1911, in C. of F. B. to F. O., December 7th. F. O. 371/1056; Innes memorandum of January 4, 1912, in Bryce's of January 8th. F. O. 371/1305.

47. C. of F. B. to F. O., February 20, 1912. F. O. 371/1307.

48. The Honduran external debt remained in default until 1926.

49. The Council was also unhappy over the fact that copies of two of Stahl's contracts were deposited in the American legation at Guatemala, and that the contracts gave the syndicate the right to ask for protection from the American government in case of default. When Cooper later complained about this to the State Department in 1911, he was told that the deposit "had been obtained in a more or less improper manner on the pretext of safe deposit," and that the American government "had formally repudiated" any connection with the loans. See C. of F. B., *Annual Report* for 1910, p. 211; Cooper to Avebury, April 26, 1911. F. O. 371/1288.

50. Carden to Spicer, December 10, 1910; Carden to Grey, December 14th. F. O. 371/1055.

51. Carden to Grey, February 27, 1911, and minute by Mallet; F. O. to Carden, February 17th. F. O. 371/1056.

52. Carden to Grey, November 2, 1911; C. of F. B. to F. O., November 6th. F. O. 371/1056.

53. Minutes to Carden to Grey of November 2, 3, and 26, 1911; F. O. to C. of F. B., November 30th and reply of December 5th. F. O. 371/1056.

54. Carden to Spicer, private, January 2, 1912. F. O. 371/1305.

55. Innes memorandum of January 4, 1912, in Bryce to Grey of January 8th. F. O. 371/1305.

56. See Munro, *op. cit.*, pp. 241–43; Scholes and Scholes, *op. cit.*, pp. 74–78; D.H. Dinwoodie, "Dollar Diplomacy in the Light of the Guatemalan Loan Project, 1909–1913," *The Americas*, XXVI (1970), pp. 239–47. For the State Department's attempt in 1910–1911 to take advantage of a dispute between Germany and Guatemala, see Dinwoodie, *loc. cit.*, p. 245.

57. Carden to Grey, August 7, 1911. F. O. 371/1056.

58. F. O. to C. of F. B., February 7 and 19, 1912. F. O. 371/1305.

59. Bryce to Grey, April 22, 1912; Mallet's minute to Carden to Spicer of February 2nd. F. O. 371/1305.

60. Carden to Grey, telegram of March 19, 1912, and despatch of March 18th. F. O. 371/1307. See also Scholes and Scholes, *op. cit.*, pp. 78–79; and Dinwoodie, *loc. cit.*, 247–49.

61. Carden's letter to Grey of June 29, 1912, from London, with enclosures: Carden to Knox, June 11th, and Knox to Carden, June 15th. F. O. 371/1307. See also Walter V. Scholes, "Sir Lionel Carden's Proposed Agreement on Central America, 1912," *The Americas*, XV (1959), pp. 291–95.

62. Carden had been made a K.C.M.G. in June of 1911.

63. Minutes by Spicer, Mallet and Grey to Carden's letter of June 29th. F. O. 371/1307.

64. C. of F. B. to F. O., July 24, 1912, and minute by Spicer; F. O. to Haggard of August 7th and to Innes of August 7th. F. O. 371/1305.

65. U. S., *Foreign Relations*, 1912, pp. 500–501.

66. Bryce to Grey, September 25 and 30, 1912; U.S., *Foreign Relations*, 1912, pp. 501–505.
    Guatemala signed the Hague convention of 1907, but she was one of the Latin American states that accepted it only with reservations. One of these reservations stated that public loans "with bond issues constituting the national debt cannot in any case give rise to military aggression nor to the occupation of the soil of American states." See Edwin Borchard, *The Diplomatic Protection of Citizens Abroad* (New York, 1916), pp. 318–21; Jessup, *op. cit.*, II, 73–74; Shea, *op. cit.*, pp. 14–15.

67. Grey to Bryce, September 26, 1912; Bryce to Wilson, September 29th. F. O. 371/1305. U. S., *Foreign Relations*, 1912, pp. 504–505.

68. Minutes by Sperling, Spicer, Langley, Nicolson, and Grey to Haggard's despatch of September 17, 1912, received at the F. O. on October 5th; Grey to Bryce, October 17th. F. O. 371/1305.

69. Carden's memorandum of October 21, 1912. F. O. 371/1305.

70. Bryce to Grey, October 20, 1912; Grey to Haggard, October 24th. F. O. 371/1305. Bryce's note to Wilson of October 25th is in U.S., *Foreign Relations*, 1912, p. 505.

71. Guatemalan Legation to State Department, October 25, 1912. U.S., *Foreign Relations*, 1912, p. 506.

72. Bryce to Grey, October 29, 1912, and despatch of October 30th. F. O. 371/1305.

73. C. of F. B. to F. O., November 6, 1912. F. O. 371/1305.

74. Grey to Bryce, November 11, 1912. F. O. 371/1305. Bryce to Knox, November 13th, U.S., *Foreign Relations*, 1912, p. 507.

75. Knox's memorandum of December 3, 1912, is in Bryce's despatch of December 5th, F. O. 371/1305, and in U.S., *Foreign Relations*, 1912, pp. 508–10.

76. Minutes to Carden's memorandum on Bryce's despatch of December 5, 1912; Grey to Bryce, December 23rd. F. O. 371/1305. U.S., *Foreign Relations*, 1912, pp. 510–11.

77. Knox to Bryce, January 6, 1913. F. O. 371/1583. U.S., *Foreign Relations*, 1913, p. 557. According to Innes, Huntington Wilson was "anxious" and "irritated" by the British refusal to consider the Seligman plan and had to be dissuaded from preparing a much stronger note. See Bryce to Grey, January 10th. F. O. 371/1583.

78. Knox to Laughlin, January 7, 1913. U.S., *Foreign Relations*, 1913, pp. 558–61.

79. Bryce to Grey, January 10, 1913. F. O. 371/1583; and Knox's instructions to

Laughlin of January 7th in U.S., *Foreign Relations*, 1913, pp. 558–61.

80. Grey to Laughlin, January 27, 1913. F. O. 371/1583; U.S., *Foreign Relations*, 1913, pp. 565–67; Munro, *op. cit.*, p. 244.

81. After the arrival of the text of Knox's note of December 3, 1912, Grey noted: "The weak point in our position is that we (at any rate I am) are reluctant to use force to collect debts. People who invest in bonds of these faithless republics must do so at their own risk. I prefer to reserve the use of force for some case such as ill treatment of a British subject." Minute to Bryce's despatch of December 5th in F. O. 371/1305. Knox's reply of January 6th led to Carden's alternative plan.

82. Carden to Grey, April 5, 1913; and Carden despatch of April 7th. F. O. 371/1583.

83. Carden's only concession to Estrada Cabrera was an agreement to ask the Council of Foreign Bondholders to accept a suspension of the sinking fund and a postponement of the interest in arrears.

84. U. S., *Foreign Relations*, 1913, p. 568.

85. Bryan to Laughlin, May 12, 1913. U.S., *Foreign Relations*, 1913, p. 569. Spring-Rice to Grey, May 12 and May 13. F. O. 371/1583.

86. The text of the agreement is printed in C. of F. B., *Annual Report*, 1913, pp. 180–81. The coffee revenues were returned to the bondholders and the interest payments resumed. Deferred certificates were exchanged for the coupons in default. The sinking fund was suspended for four years, and after four years the Council and the government were to negotiate as to the means of paying the interest arrears.

87. C. of F. B. to F. O., May 16, 1913; see also their letter of June 12th. F. O. 371/1583.

88. Editorials of May 17 and 24, 1913. The *South American Journal*.

89. Grey's minute to Carden's telegram of May 12, 1913. F. O. 371/1583.

90. Carden to Grey, May 17, 1913, and minutes by Spicer, Mallet, and Grey. F. O. 371/1583.

91. Britain's recognition of the Mexican government of Victoriano Huerta on March 31, 1913, was of course a much more fateful independent move within the American "sphere of influence." But it must be remembered that, although the United States had not recognized Huerta, Grey's decision was not made in the face of American opposition. The Taft administration's official explanation for withholding recognition was based on the necessity of settling pending claims and controversies, not on the character of the new regime. Nor did the Wilson administration make any objections when the Foreign Office informed the major powers on March 12th that Britain intended to recognize Huerta. Grey was perhaps foolhearty in taking the lead in a country in which American interests were predominant but he was not trying to thwart American plans, for Wilson simply had not formulated a definite anti-Huerta policy as yet.

CHAPTER VII

The Anatomy of an Entente

While it is generally agreed that Anglo-American friendship in the pre-World War I era largely depended on British concessions to the United States in the Western hemisphere, the impression still persists that the British Foreign Office was anxious to turn British interests in Latin America over to the benevolent protection of the United States. The Roosevelt "corollary" is usually viewed as a great boon to the British, who were now able to sit back and smugly watch the Americans police the Caribbean and collect British debts. In reality, in 1901–1902 Lansdowne and his subordinates wanted Britain to protect her own interests in the Caribbean. If any new policy was developing it was one of cooperation with other European powers in forcing claims settlements in Latin America. The unexpected uproar caused by the Venezuelan intervention of 1902–1903 ended this development and forced the British to pay homage to the Monroe Doctrine. The British never forgot the lessons of the Venezuelan fiasco, but in the following decade the Foreign Office became more and more dissatisfied with the one-sided nature of Anglo-American relations in the Caribbean. The coercion of Guatemala in 1913 was the culmination of that dissatisfaction.

From 1901–1913 Lansdowne and Grey were never able to formulate a Caribbean policy that could completely satisfy both the Americans and the Foreign Office's critics at home. Most Englishmen welcomed American imperialism at the turn of the century, but this enthusiasm was the result of emotionalism and racism as well as cool calculation. When the effects of American influence in Latin America were experienced, the British reaction was ambivalent. Many British investors, merchants and exporters benefited from American expansion into the Caribbean, but it was inevitable that others would feel that their interests were in jeopardy. The Foreign Office attempted to solve this dilemma by basing their Caribbean policy on a sharp distinction between British political and economic interests. The first could be sacrificed, while the second were to be defended. They would recognize the area as a sphere of American political influence and at the same time try to maintain a commercial "open door" and secure fair treatment for British claims.

It is difficult to see what other position the Foreign Office could have taken, but this was a policy that simply could not work in all cases. It was based on the assumption that the United States would make a similar distinction between her political and economic interests, and most Americans thought of the two as identical, or at least complimentary. As Carden once observed in a complaint about the impossibility of doing anything effective to protect British interests in Cuba without antagonizing the United States, "the political and commercial sides of the Cuban question are so interwoven that it is impossible to say where one ends and the other begins."[1]

During the Roosevelt years Britain could still avoid facing this dilemma. Cuba was an exceptional case, and bondholders' charges of discrimination in Santo Domingo were always slightly dubious. But what could be done with Taft's "dollar diplomacy," which was frankly based on the thesis that American political hegemony was to be achieved by economic domination of the area? An American policy aimed at creating political stability in Central America by ousting European capital may not have been anti-British in theory, but more often than not it was in practice. And if the British did attempt to protect their "non-political" interests they risked the charge of anti-Americanism. Could the British government protect its subjects in Venezuela, attempt to get a most-favored-nation treaty with Cuba, or refuse to cooperate with the United States in Nicaragua and Guatemala, without being anti-American? Was Carden suffering from "Yankophobia" or merely defending legitimate British interests? The semantic difficulties are obvious.

It did not take the British long to realize that the Anglo-American "entente" provided little reciprocity. Even before the problems caused by Taft's "dollar diplomacy," the author of a 1908 Foreign Office memorandum on Anglo-American relations felt obligated to explain why the Americans responded to British sympathy in the Spanish American War by refusing "to settle any outstanding questions except on a strictly business footing of taking all they could get." Critics of Anglo-American friendship had to remember that "in the United States business and sentiment occupy wholly different compartments of the brain, and men drive a hard bargain none the less because they were before the bargain, and will be after it, personal friends."

> Those who allow themselves to be irritated by the apparent absence of reciprocity in the American attitude, and by settlements of disputes based principally on British concessions, forget that the education America has received has not been such as to inspire a reverence for the Mother Country, while her traditions and her environment have failed either to induce a realization of the responsibilities to the world at large incumbent on a Great Power, or to introduce into her political institutions the men and machinery necessary for the proper conduct of national foreign policy.[2]

The British continued making extraordinary allowances for the diplomatic manners of their trans-Atlantic cousins, but such rationalizations for the inadequacy of the Anglo-American entente became increasingly hollow. There was certainly no "special relationship" between the United States and Great Britain in Latin America during the Roosevelt and Taft years. There is no evidence that the British received any considerations not accorded to other nations. The United States was not always uncooperative, but when the two countries coordinated their policies it was usually on American terms.[3] The State Department rarely notified the British of its plans, and requests for information were often answered in vague and unsatisfactory ways. The British from time to time took advantage of American naval power for the protection of British lives and property, but on the *ad hoc* basis in which it was offered to other nations as well.

The British liked the idea of a "special relationship" based on reciprocal advantages, and the Foreign Office approved Carden's attempt to secure one for Central America in 1912. But the United States was unwilling to make any firm commitments. The British were not content with American statements on the general benefits to all nations that would flow from a "Pax Americana" in the Caribbean. The Foreign Office had to appease its critics and wanted some diplomatic support from the U.S. in return for British recognition of an American "sphere of influence." The Foreign Office eventually became convinced that the United States was unwilling—or unable—to reciprocate.

The State Department's cavalier attitude towards the British stemmed partially from the Foreign Office's own timidity. Britain's Caribbean policy since 1903 was so passive that the United States came to expect automatic British cooperation on American terms. When the British finally did take an independent line in Nicaragua and Guatemala, the State Department was puzzled and indignant, having grown accustomed to British deference. Even over the Panama canal tolls Taft once expressed to Bryce "some surprise" that the British were taking "so serious a view of these points."[4]

Yet sometimes the State Department was simply unable to give any *quid pro quo* to the British. Since the United States did not pursue a consistent policy in the Caribbean and Central America during these years, neither Roosevelt nor Taft carried the "corollary" to its logical conclusion. Hampered by opposition at home and in Latin America, both administrations carried out a policy of sporadic intervention. The United States was only a part-time policeman in the Caribbean, and a bill-collector for some European debts but not for others.

In any event, the Caribbean policy of the United States was aimed at avoiding European intervention, not at securing "justice" for European creditors and claimants. The Council of Foreign Bondholders—the most persistent critic of American policy—made the mistake of accepting the Roosevelt "corollary" at face value and were inevitably disillusioned. Honduras was the only Latin American state in default on its foreign debt in 1913, and American policy and pressure had played a part in a number of the settlements. But this was not enough for the British bondholders. Had the United States not discriminated against them in Santo Domingo? Blocked a settlement in Honduras? Delayed the reckoning with Guatemala? The position of the Council of Foreign Bondholders is a classic example of British ambivalence towards the expansion of American power in Latin America.

Unlike the Council, the Foreign Office disliked references to the Monroe Doctrine. The doctrine, hanging like the sword of Damocles over every decision, could not be ignored, but the British statesmen much preferred to think in terms of an American "sphere" than to try to interpret the doctrine's meaning. After the Venezuelan blockade, the British Foreign Office was in much the same position as D. W. Brogan's "badly frightened citizen who, rescued from a lynching bee, protested: 'I didn't say I was against the Monroe Doctrine; I love the Monroe Doctrine, I would die for the Monroe Doctrine. I merely said I didn't know what it was.' "[5]

No one knew better than the British that the doctrine had a habit of expanding to the embarrassment of other nations. Take for example the back-stage manuevering between the two governments over the question of whether the doctrine should be mentioned in the arbitration treaty of 1911. While the negotiations for the treaty were underway in Washington, Ambassador Reid observed to Grey that attachment to the doctrine was "still very strong" and that the United States would at least "always adhere to it as far as Mexico and Central America were concerned." Grey saw no problem, for any questions "with regard to countries in that region" that the British would have for arbitration "would be only commercial questions."[6] When Knox and his counsellor, Chandler Anderson, asked Bryce a few days later if the doctrine was to be arbitrable, Bryce too had no desire to open this diplomatic Pandora's box. As he reported to Grey:

I replied that any such question that might arise as in their view affected by the "Doctrine" would be a question between ourselves and some other American State—not the United States—and that we should doubtless be willing to arbitrate such a question with that State, which was all they had asked for in the Venezuela Case of 1895-96. They did not, however, seem to be quite satisfied about this, and may possibly return again to the point.[7]

Bryce's fears were justified. The first American draft of the treaty did exclude "questions of national policy," and Anderson told Bryce "he was, as I had guessed, thinking of the Monroe Doctrine." Again Bryce objected to the reference, "pointing out how superfluous it was at all events in the present treaty, and indeed with everybody but Germany, with whom there was little likelihood that any treaty as wide as ours would be made."[8] Bryce's objections carried the day and the Monroe Doctrine and "questions of national policy" were not mentioned in the final draft, but once the treaty was before the Senate the issue was revived. Once again Bryce tried to avoid the inevitable. Remarking to Taft "on the vagueness" of the Monroe Doctrine, he bluntly asked the President how he defined it. Taft rather naively replied that "he took it to mean that the U.S. could not allow any European Power to invade an American Republic and establish therein a monarchical form of government." Bryce was still apprehensive:

> I observed that if that was all it meant, nobody would complain, but that a far wider scope had often been given and might be given again to it. Would the Senate be satisfied with such a definition? Was it not better to leave the matter alone?[9]

Grey was willing to accept Taft's definition and did not see how "we can object," but Bryce was convinced that it would be "impossible, and if possible, mischievous to define the 'Monroe Doctrine' " and he did not think Taft would try.[10] As it turned out the doctrine was neither defined nor left alone. The Senate merely excepted it from

arbitration in their changes to the ill-fated treaty and left the definition to future historians.

American vagueness, evasiveness and inconsistencies were not the
only reasons that the Foreign Office often found it difficult to evaluate objectively the Caribbean policy of the United States. Most of the
Foreign Office's information about events in Central America and
the Caribbean came filtered through a diplomatic corps still per-
meated by a great deal of anti-Americanism. It would be tempting
to blame Lionel Carden for most of the difficulties that arose—as
Americans never tired of doing; Carden had a knack for precipitating
crises, but merely blaming Carden would oversimplify the situation.
Other British representatives and consuls in Latin America shared
his feelings and suspicions.[11] Carden was unique only in the vigor
with which he defended British interests and in his apparent inability
to dissemble his true feelings.

Nor was the Foreign Office itself immune from anti-Americanism.
The clerks and advisors in the American Department, who partially
shaped British policy by their memorandums, minutes, and advice,
were always quick to suspect the worst of the United States. Few in
the Foreign Office had any diplomatic experience in the United
States. "I am sorry to say," Hardinge wrote to newly appointed Ambassador Bryce in 1906, "that we have not a soul in the F. O. who has
ever been to Washington except myself & it is 20 years since I left
so that my knowledge of the place is not worth having."[12] When
George Young, the First Secretary at the Washington Embassy,
visited the Foreign Office in the summer of 1911, he wrote to Bryce
about the "anti-American atmosphere."

> The office is so anti-American that it is always difficult to discuss
> American affairs with them and I don't find any change in this. The
> general sentiment is one of contempt, tempered with apprehension in
> proportion to the seniority of the subject.[13]

Luckily for the Foreign Office, certain key individuals in the diplomatic corps did much to keep Anglo-American relations on an even
keel. For example, one must be impressed by Sir Michael Herbert's

patience and good sense during negotiations with Herbert Bowen. During the crucial Taft years the Foreign Office fortunately had Bryce and Innes at Washington. Charges that they were willing to sacrifice British rights on the altar of Anglo-American friendship were exaggerated and unfair, but they were always cautious in their advice to London, tactful in their negotiations with the State Department, and sometimes even dilatory in carrying out instructions with which they disagreed. As George Young wrote in a letter to Bryce, the Embassy "under your regime has been a good non-conducting insulator" of the type of "insularity" Young deplored in the Foreign Office.[14]

As for the Foreign Secretaries, Lansdowne was more fortunate than skillful in his handling of Latin American affairs. He kept criticism of Cuban-American reciprocity within manageable proportions, but he and Villiers blundered into the Venezuelan affair, and a few years later they were even ready to send the navy against Uruguay. From the point of view of Anglo-American harmony, Grey soon made a serious mistake in recognizing the Huerta government in Mexico in March of 1913, but during the Roosevelt and Taft years he undoubtedly exerted a moderating influence on his subordinates. He took a firm stand during the canal tolls controversy but never forced the issue to the danger point. On the problems of "dollar diplomacy," he often modified instructions to Washington to make them more conciliatory and less blunt, and he seemed to be the only one in the Foreign Office to doubt the wisdom of using force against Guatemala when it was first discussed.

In the last analysis, however, the Anglo-American entente benefited most from the relatively small British commercial and financial interests in the Caribbean and Central America, that part of Latin America that bore the brunt of American activity during these years. British interests there were large only in Cuba and Mexico, and Grey's Mexican policy is proof of the fact that big interests can lead to big miscalculations and big crises. If the British stake in northern Latin America had been as great as that in the south, the "entente" certainly would have been much more difficult to maintain.

In addition, statistics show that even within the sphere of American activity, such prophets of doom as Carden were wrong. Far from being extinguished, British commerce and investments in Central America and the Caribbean were rising during the Roosevelt and Taft era. The investment picture can be seen by comparing J. Fred Rippy's estimates for 1890 with those of the *South American Journal* for 1913.[15]

Total nominal investment:

	1890	1913 (in pounds)
Mexico:	59,883,577	159,024,349
Cuba:	26,808,000	44,444,618
Venezuela:	9,846,219	7,950,009
Colombia:	5,399,383	6,654,094
Costa Rica:	5,140,840	6,660,060
Honduras:	3,888,250	3,143,200
Guatemala:	922,700	10,445,220
Nicaragua:	411,183	1,239,100
San Salvador:	294,000	2,224,700

Government Bonds:

	1890	1913 (in pounds)
Mexico:	20,650,000	28,596,510
Cuba:	24,412,000	9,687,000
Venezuela:	2,668,850	4,228,720
Colombia:	1,913,500	3,388,874
Costa Rica:	2,000,000	2,005,460
Honduras:	3,222,000	3,143,200
Guatemala:	922,700	1,445,220
Nicaragua:	285,000	1,239,100
San Salvador:	294,000	816,000

In commerce, figures from the Board of Trade show that the value of exports into the area was greater in 1913 in every country:[16]

	1901	1913
Cuba:	1,959,770	3,000,070
Mexico:	1,673,079	2,498,199
Colombia:	936,784	1,713,354
Venezuela:	513,680	839,268
Guatemala:	297,291	351,936
San Salvador:	225,805	333,296

Nicaragua:	114,568	249,731
Haiti and Santo		168,292 (Haiti)
Domingo	216,437	166,592 (S. D.)
Costa Rica:	158,880	246,590
Nicaragua:	114,568	249,731
Honduras:	57,919	128,662

Such figures of course do not reflect the feelings held by some that the British had too small a share, or that American and German competition would threaten that share in the future.[17] American domination of Central American commerce was very real—according to one estimate the United States controlled more than 63% to about 12% for Great Britain in 1913[18]—and although British investments in Central America, Colombia and Venezuela probably still exceeded those of the United States in 1913, the Americans had closed the gap and would soon forge ahead. But because of great opportunities for export and investment profits throughout the world, most British businessmen and financiers were not alarmed about an area of low potential and weak buying power. As Bryce told Carden in 1910, he had received the impression while in England "that our people there were rather slack in pushing into Spanish American countries. . . . Though the F. O. have not told me so, I suspect that they have not found British capitalists eager to obtain concessions or start exporting business in Central America; and therefore deem it not the promising field."[19]

This limited interest of the British business community led to the failure of Carden's plan to stimulate British trade by the creation of a special trade association of British merchants and industrialists interested in Central America, Colombia and Venezuela.[20] The Board of Trade took up Carden's idea, called meetings with representatives of interested firms in 1911 and the spring of 1912, and approved a draft plan for a "British Association for Central America" that would collect and publish information and act as an intermediary in informing the government of problems in the area.

The association died in the planning stages, partly because of apathy and partly because of jealousy of Lord Cowdray. In July of 1912, a committee of business representatives "reluctantly" reported to the Board of Trade that any further steps were "impracticable." The area to be covered was too limited, no large banking or financial concerns were interested, too many merchants were either apathetic or opposed, and the committee had been unable to form the necessary guarantee fund.[21] Although the Board of Trade was able to get a promise of a "substantial contribution" to the funds of the association for five years from Cowdray's S. Pearson and Company, the committee still recommended that the matter be dropped.

> This conclusion is due partly to the fact that British trade and industry is at present so active that merchants and manufacturers are indisposed to give any special attention to what is now, and is likely to remain, a somewhat restricted market; and partly to the opinion, on the other hand, that the inclusion within the scope of the proposed Association of Mexico (which was one of the conditions attached to Messrs Pearson's offer) is undesirable.[22]

Fortunately for the Foreign Office, the United States had successfully closed the "open door" only in Cuba, and even there it had little effect on British trade. There was enough uncertainty about future American policy to cause apprehension, but not enough present injury to cause serious problems for the Foreign Office in an area where the British capitalists themselves were "rather slack" in pushing. If the State Department had been as aggressive in violating the "open door" as it was in pushing American capital into Central America, relations would have been more difficult than they were, but American protectionist sentiment indirectly mitigated the effects of "dollar diplomacy."

In short, although the British bondholders of the day would have argued the point, Roosevelt's "big stick" and Taft's "dollar diplomacy" did not jeopardize any significant British interests in Latin America. Even the canal tolls issue—the one serious threat to British interests that did arise during these years—cost the British nothing but anxiety, for Woodrow Wilson was able to get the discriminatory legislation repealed before the canal was opened in 1914. Thus the Anglo-American "entente cordiale" in Latin America was able to survive the irritations and suspicions that were never far below the surface. It remained viable despite the lack of reciprocity during the Roosevelt and Taft years. So beneficial was American friendship to Britain in the world balance of power that the entente undoubtedly could have survived much more, but it was still fortunate for the British that they were able to prove their devotion to Anglo-American amity in an area of relatively small British interests. In a sense, Britain's Caribbean policy from 1901–1913 was a triumph of the head over the heart. For a brief period towards the end of the Taft administration, there were signs that British emotion and injured pride were replacing caution, but independence in the Caribbean was a luxury in which no British government could indulge for long.

NOTES AND REFERENCES

1. Carden to Villiers, January 15, 1902. F. O. 108/9.

2. "Memorandum respecting Relations between Great Britain and the United States," secret, 1908. F. O. 414/210.

3. The most notable area of Anglo-American cooperation was in Haiti. The Foreign Office in 1910 protested against some of the same provisions of the plan for a French-German dominated national Haitian bank that disturbed the United States. In 1911, after Haiti had refused to take part in a proposed international claims commission, the Foreign Office was able to get the State Department to join Britain, France, Germany and Italy in applying pressure on Haiti for settlements. The joint action was ultimately successful, and, in a clear departure from her usual policy, the United States even took part in a joint note with the European powers in 1911. However, American cooperation here seems to have made little impression on the British view that the State Department was uncooperative in such matters. Nothing was ever "normal" in Haiti.

4. Bryce to Grey, October 5, 1912. F. O. 420/256.

5. D. W. Brogan, *The American Character* (New York: Vintage Books, 1956), p. 156.

6. Grey to Bryce, private, April 3, 1911. Bryce Papers, U.S.A. 31. Latin American "commercial questions" were also the reason Grey opposed excluding cases involving the interests of third parties as in the treaty of 1908. As he explained to Bryce: "It is not impossible that subjects of difference may arise between the United States Government in the Central American Republics in connection with British commercial interests. Cuban questions again might give rise to difficulties. In fact, the words are capable of an interpretation so far-reaching as seriously to impair the value of the treaty." Grey to Bryce, June 20, 1911. F. O. 414/225.

7. Bryce to Grey, private, April 11, 1911. F. O. 414/225.

8. Bryce to Grey, April 28, 1911. Grey Papers, vol. 44.

9. Bryce to Grey, private, November 14, 1911. Grey Papers, vol. 44.

10. Grey to Bryce, private, December 2, 1911; Bryce to Grey, December 15th. Grey Papers, vol. 44. Bryce's personal views on the doctrine are reflected in his endorsement of Hiram Bingham's book *The Monroe Doctrine, An Obsolete Shibboleth*. See his correspondence with Bingham in Bryce Papers, U.S.A. 22.

11. Carden's anti-Americanism was actually mild compared to Alexander Murray's views of the Yankees. "It is curious," Murray observed in his annual report on Haiti for 1909, "that the Haytians, the mongrel descendants of the sweepings of Africa, should fall, as they inevitably will, into the clutches of the Americans, the mongrel descendants of the sweepings of Europe." Murray to Grey, December 17, 1909. F. O. 371/468.

12. Hardinge to Bryce, December 26, 1906. Bryce Papers, U.S.A. 27.

13. Young to Bryce, July 13, 1911. Bryce Papers, U.S.A. 32.

14. Young to Bryce, July 13, 1911. Bryce Papers, U.S.A. 32.

15. Rippy, *op. cit.*, pp. 37, 67. The *South American Journal* did not include Panama, Haiti, or the Dominican Republic in its 1913 estimates. According to Rippy, the *Journal*'s figures for Mexico, Cuba, and Guatemala are too high. But the general picture of rising investment values in Latin America is correct. The peak of British capital investment was not reached until 1928.

16. Great Britain, *Parliamentary Papers,* Cd. 2626 (1905) lxxx, C d. 7585 (1913) lxxxiii.

17. The Board of Trade was sufficiently interested in the area to appoint a special commissioner in 1911 to report on the situation. G. T. Milne's mission was completed in 1913, and his "Reports to the Board of Trade on the Conditions and Prospects of British Trade in Central America, Colombia and Venezuela" is printed in *Parliamentary Papers,* Cd. 6969 (1913) lxviii 421.

18. Max Winkler, *Investments of United States Capital in Latin America* (Boston, 1929), pp. 7–8.

19. Bryce to Carden, April 15, 1910. Bryce Papers, U.S.A. 30.

20. Carden seemingly devised his scheme in 1910. See Spicer to Mallet, October 8, 1910. F. O. 371/839. Carden's talk with Spicer also resulted in his promotion in 1911 from Minister Resident to Envoy Extraordinary and Minister Plenipotentiary, and in the appointment of more paid consular officers in his territory. It is probable that the Milne mission was also inspired by Carden.

21. Board of Trade to F. O., November 22, 1912. F. O. 368/660.

22. Board of Trade to F. O., December 4, 1912. F. O. 368/660.

Bibliography

Foreign Office Papers

Great Britain: Public Record Office, London

In addition to the regular correspondence for Central America,[1] Cuba, Guatemala, Haiti, Honduras, Mexico, Panama and Costa Rica, Santo Domingo,[2] and Venezuela, the following volumes of the Foreign Office Papers were found useful for this study:

A. America General: 1911.

B. Central America, Commercial: 1909 and 1912.

C. Confidential Prints:

    1. Correspondence respecting the Affairs of North America:1907–1912.

    2. Correspondence respecting the Affairs of South and Central America: 1908–1912.

    3. Correspondence respecting the Affairs of Venezuela: 1901–1902.

       Correspondence respecting the Affairs of Venezuela: January, February, and March of 1903.

    4. Memorandum respecting Relations between Great Britain and the United States: 1908.

    5. Uruguay 1, Correspondence respecting the Seizure of the British Schooner "Agnes G. Donahoe" by the Uruguayan Authorities: 1904–1909.

D. Cuba, Commercial Negotiations: 1901–1906.

E. Guatemalan Loans: 1901–1905.

F. Honduras: External Debt, 1898–1905.

G. Panama and Costa Rica, Commercial: 1911–1912.

H. Santo Domingo (filed under Dominica):

---

[1] The volumes for Central America from 1908–1913 contain the correspondence for all the Central American nations except Panama and Costa Rica.

[2] Before 1906, the correspondence for Haiti (Hayti) and Santo Domingo (Dominica) are filed separately. After 1906 they are filed together under "Hayti and San Domingo."

Commercial, 1896–1903.

Santo Domingo Debt. Claim of Santo Domingo Improvement Company, etc., 1903–1905.

I. Uruguay: Seizure of the Schooner "Agnes G. Donahoe" for Alleged Illicit Sealing. November 1904 to October 1905.

J. Venezuela:

British General Claims, 1896–1901.

External Debt, 1902–1905.

Claims. Coercion of Venezuela. 1902 and 1903.

Manuscripts

Arthur J. Balfour Papers. The British Museum, London.

James Bryce Papers, The Bodleian Library, Oxford.

Sir Edward Grey Papers. The Foreign Office Library, London.

Lord Lansdowne Papers. The Foreign Office Library, London.

State Department Records

United States: The National Archives, Washington, D. C.

A. Diplomatic Instructions:

The Central American States, Vol. 22, 1900–1906.

Cuba, Vol. 1, 1902–1906.

Great Britain, Vol. 34, 1902.

Venezuela, Vol. 5, 1900–1906.

B. Despatches from United States Ministers:

Central America, Vol. 46, Guatemala and Honduras, 1901–1903.

Great Britain, Vols. 205 and 206. 1902–1903.

Printed Documents and Government Publications

A Compilation of the Messages and Papers of the Presidents, 1901–1913. Washington: Bureau of National Literature.

German Diplomatic Documents, 1871–1914. Edited by Edgar T. S. Dugdale. Vol. III. London, 1928–31.

Germany. *Die grosse Politik der Europaischen Kabinette,* 1871–1914. Vol. 17. Berlin, 1922–27.

Great Britain. *The Parliamentary Debates,* 1902–1913.

Great Britain. *Parliamentary Papers:*
"Annual Statement of the Trade of the United Kingdom with Foreign Countries and British Possessions." 1905 (Cd. 2626), 1909 (Cd. 4784), 1914 (Cd. 7585).
"Exports to China and South America." 1906 and 1907.
"Reports to the Board of Trade on the Conditions and Prospects of British Trade in Central America, Colombia and Venezuela," by G. T. Milne. 1913 (Cd. 6969).

United States. Department of Commerce and Labor. *Statistical Abstract of the United States,* 1911, 1920. Washington: Government Printing Office, 1912, 1921.

United States. Department of State. *Papers Relating to the Foreign Relations of the United States.* 1901–1919. Washington: Government Printing Office.

United States. Tariff Commission. *Reciprocity and Commercial Treaties.* Washington: Government Printing Office, 1919.

Periodicals and Reports

Annual Reports of the Council of the Corporation of Foreign Bondholders for 1900–1913. London.

The Literary Digest. 1901–1913. New York.

The Naval Annual for 1899–1913. London.

The South American Journal. 1902–1913. London.

Articles

Blake, Nelson M. "Ambassadors at the Court of Theodore Roosevelt," *Mississippi Valley Historical Review,* XLII (1955), 179–206.

Campbell, John P. "Taft, Roosevelt, and the Arbitration Treaties of 1911," *The Journal of American History,* LIII (1966), 279–98.

Coker, William S. "The Panama Canal Tolls Controversy: A Different Perspective," *The Journal of American History*, LV (1968), 555–64.

Dinwoodie, D. H. "Dollar Diplomacy in the Light of the Guatemalan Loan Project, 1909–1913," *The Americas*, XXVI (1970), 237–53.

Grenville, J. A. S. "Great Britain and the Isthmian Canal, 1898–1901," *American Historical Review*, LXI (1955), 48–69.

Hendrickson, Embert J. "Roosevelt's Second Venezuelan Controversy," *The Hispanic American Historical Review*, L (1970), 482–98.

Holbo, Paul S. "Perilous Obscurity: Public Diplomacy and the Press in the Venezuelan Crisis, 1902–1903," *The Historian*, XXXII (1970), 428–48.

Kaufman, Burton, "United States Trade and Latin America: The Wilson Years," *The Journal of American History*, LVIII (1971), 342–63.

Livermore, Seward W. "Theodore Roosevelt, the American Navy, and the Venezuelan Crisis of 1902–1903," *American Historical Review*, LI (1946), 452–71.

Platt, D. C. M. "The Allied Coercion of Venezuela, 1902–3—a Reassessment," *Inter-American Economic Affairs*, XV (1962), 3–28.

————"British Bondholders in Nineteenth Century Latin America—Injury and Remedy," *Inter-American Economic Affairs*, XIV (1960), 3–43.

Rippy, J. Fred. "Antecedents of the Roosevelt Corollary of the Monroe Doctrine," *The Pacific Historical Review*, IX (1940), 267–79.

————"The British Bondholders and the Roosevelt Corollary of the Monroe Doctrine," *Political Science Quarterly*, XLIX (1934), 195–206.

Schoenrich, Otto. "The Nicaraguan Mixed Claims Commission," *The American Journal of International Law,* IX (1915), 858–69.

Scholes, Walter V. "Sir Lionel Carden's Proposed Agreement on Central America, 1912," *The Americas,* XV (1959), 291–95.

Seed, Geoffrey. "British Reactions to American Imperialism Reflected in Journals of Opinion," *Political Science Quarterly,* LXXIII (1958), 254–72.

Books

Allen, H. C. *Great Britain and the United States.* New York: St. Martin's Press, 1955.

Bacon, Admiral Sir R. H. *The Life of Lord Fisher of Kilverstone.* 2 vols. Garden City, N. Y.:Hodder and Stoughton Lmt., 1929.

Beale, Howard K. *Theodore Roosevelt and the Rise of America to World Power.* Baltimore: Johns Hopkins Press, 1956.

Bemis, Samuel F. (ed.). *The American Secretaries of State and Their Diplomacy.* Vol. IX. New York: A. A. Knopf, 1928.

Bernstein, Marvin D. (ed.). *Foreign Investment in Latin America, Cases and Attitudes.* New York: Knopf, 1966.

Borchard, Edwin M. *The Diplomatic Protection of Citizens Abroad, or the Law of International Claims.* New York: The Banks Law Publishing Co., 1916.

Bourne, Kenneth. *Britain and the Balance of Power in North America, 1815–1908.* Berkeley: University of California Press, 1967.

Bowen, Herbert W. *Recollections Diplomatic and Undiplomatic.* New York: Hitchcock, 1926.

Burton, David H. *Theodore Roosevelt: Confident Imperialist.* Philadelphia: University of Pennsylvania Press, 1968.

Callcott, Wilfrid H. *The Caribbean Policy of the United States, 1890–1920.* Baltimore: Johns Hopkins Press, 1942.

Calvert, Peter. *The Mexican Revolution, 1910–1914: The Diplomacy of Anglo-American Conflict.* Cambridge: Cambridge University Press, 1968.

Campbell, Alexander E. *Great Britain and the United States, 1895–1903.* London: Longmans Ltd., 1960.

Campbell, Charles S., Jr. *Anglo-American Understanding, 1898–1903.* Baltimore: Johns Hopkins Press, 1957.

Cole, G. D. H. *British Trade and Industry, Past and Future.* London: Macmillan, 1932.

Coletta, Paolo E. *The Presidency of William Howard Taft.* Lawrence: The University of Kansas Press, 1973.

Cumberland, Charles. *Mexican Revolution: Genesis under Madero.* Austin: University of Texas Press, 1952.

Dennett, Tyler. *John Hay, from Poetry to Politics.* New York: Dodd, Mead and Co., 1934.

Feis, Herbert. *Europe the World's Banker, 1870–1914.* New Haven: Yale University Press, 1930.

Fisher, H. A. L. *James Bryce.* 2 vols. New York: Macmillan, 1927.

Fitzgibbon, Russell H. *Cuba and the United States, 1900–1935.* Menasha, Wisc.: George Banta Publishing Co., 1935.

Gelber, Lionel M. *The Rise of Anglo-American Friendship: A Study in World Politics, 1898–1906.* London: Oxford University Press, 1938.

Grey, Sir Edward. *Twenty-five Years, 1892–1916.* 2 vols. New York: Frederick A. Stokes Co., 1925.

Harbaugh, William H. *Power and Responsibility: The Life and Times of Theodore Roosevelt.* New York: Farrar, Straus and Cudahy, 1961.

Healy, David F. *The United States in Cuba, 1898–1902.* Madison: University of Wisconsin Press, 1963.

234

Heindel, R. H. *The American Impact on Great Britain, 1898–1914.* Philadelphia: University of Pennsylvania Press, 1940.

Hill, Howard C. *Roosevelt and the Caribbean.* Chicago: University of Chicago Press, 1927.

Hoffman, Ross J. S. *Great Britain and the German Trade Rivalry, 1875–1914.* Philadelphia: University of Pennsylvania Press, 1933.

Hough, Richard. *Admiral of the Fleet: The Life of John Fisher.* New York: Macmillan, 1969.

Jessup, Philip C. *Elihu Root.* New York: Dodd, Mead and Co., 1938.

Karnes, Thomas L. *The Failure of Union: Central America, 1824–1960.* Chapel Hill: University of North Carolina Press, 1961.

Kemp, P. K. (ed.). *The Papers of Sir John Fisher.* London: Navy Records Society, 1960.

Link, Arthur S. *Wilson, the New Freedom.* Princeton: Princeton University Press, 1956.

Marder, Arthur J. *The Anatomy of British Sea Power.* New York: A. A. Knopf, 1940.

_____.(ed.). *Fear God and Dread Nought: The Correspondence of Admiral of the Fleet Lord Fisher of Kilverstone.* 3 vols. London: Jonathan Cape, 1953–1959.

_____ *From the Dreadnought to Scapa Flow: The Royal Navy in the Fisher Era, 1904–1919.* Oxford: Oxford University Press, 1961.

Monger, George. *The End of Isolation: British Foreign Policy, 1900–1907.* London: Thomas Nelson and Sons, Ltd., 1963.

Morison, E. E. (ed.). *The Letters of Theodore Roosevelt.* Vols. III–VI. Cambridge, Mass.: Harvard University Press, 1951.

Munro, Dana G. *The Five Republics of Central America.* New York: Oxford University Press, 1918.

_____.*Intervention and Dollar Diplomacy in the Caribbean, 1900–1921.* Princeton: Princeton University Press, 1964.

Neale, R. G. *Great Britain and United States Expansion, 1898–1900*. East Lansing: Michigan State University Press, 1966.

Nevins, Allan. *Henry White: Thirty Years of American Diplomacy*. New York: Harper and Brothers, 1930.

Perkins, Bradford. *The Great Rapprochement: England and the United States, 1895–1914*. New York: Atheneum, 1968.

Perkins, Dexter. *A History of the Monroe Doctrine*. London: Longmans, 1960.

———. *The Monroe Doctrine, 1867–1907*. Baltimore: Johns Hopkins Press, 1937.

Pringle, Henry F. *The Life and Times of William Howard Taft*. New York: Farrar and Rinehart, 1939.

———. *Theodore Roosevelt*. New York: Harcourt, Brace and Co., 1931.

Rippy, J. Fred. *British Investments in Latin America*. Minneapolis: University of Minnesota Press, 1959.

———. *The Caribbean Danger Zone*. New York: G. P. Putnam's Sons, 1940.

———. *Globe and Hemisphere*. Chicago: Henry Regnery Co., 1958.

———. *Latin America in World Politics*. New York: Crofts, 1931.

Rodriquez, Mario. *Central America*. Englewood Cliffs, N.J.: Prentice-Hall, 1965.

Schoenrich, Otto. *Santo Domingo: A Country with a Future*. New York: Macmillan, 1918.

Scholes, Walter V., and Marie V. *The Foreign Policies of the Taft Administration*. Columbia: University of Missouri Press, 1970.

Shea, Donald R. *The Calvo Clause*. Minneapolis: University of Minnesota Press, 1955.

Spender, J. A. *Weetman Pearson, First Viscount Cowdray, 1856–1927*. London: Cassell and Co. Ltd., 1930.

Sprout, Harold and Margaret. *The Rise of American Naval Power.* Princeton: Princeton University Press, 1942.

Stewart, Walt. *Keith and Costa Rica.* Albuquerque: University of New Mexico Press, 1964.

Tischendorf, Alfred P. *Great Britain and Mexico in the Era of Porfirio Díaz.* Durham, N.C.: Duke University Press, 1961.

Welles, Sumner. *Naboth's Vineyard: The Dominican Republic, 1844–1924.* New York: Harcourt, 1928.

Williams, Benjamin H. *Economic Foreign Policy of the United States.* New York: McGraw-Hill, 1929.

Winkler, Max. *Investments of United States Capital in Latin America.* Boston: World Peace Foundation, 1929.

Wynne, William H., and Borchard, Edwin. *State Insolvency and Foreign Bondholders.* 2 vols. New Haven: Yale University Press, 1951.

Index

Adams, Henry, 48
Adee, Alvey A., 6, 15
Admiralty: on isthmian canal, x; and Venezuelan intervention, 17, 33, 34, 38; quarrels with Foreign Office and Colonial Office, 100, 115–16, 117–18, 119–20, 126; on Panama Canal fortifications, 170. *See also* British navy
Agnes Donahoe incident, 116–17, 197
Alaskan boundary dispute, x, 99, 178
Anderson, Chandler, 218, 219
Anglo-American commercial treaty of 1815, 82
Anglo-French "Entente Cordiale," 100
Anglo-Japanese alliance of 1902, 100
Arbitration Treaty of 1908, 168, 175, 178
Arbitration Treaty of 1911, 168–69, 170
Argentina, xii, 62
Atlas Trust, Lmt., 29n
Australia, 209n
Austria, 19
Avebury, Lord, 143, 193

Bacon, Robert, 113, 120–21, 122
Bailey, James, 6
Balfour, Arthur J.: and Venezuelan intervention, 19, 36–49 *passim*, 56, 59, 60; on Monroe Doctrine, 61–62; and *Agnes Donahoe* affair, 116, 117
Ban Righ, 14, 17, 29n, 43
Barrington, Sir Vincent, 74
Belfast Chamber of Commerce, 74, 81
Belgian bondholders, and Santo Domingo debt, 104, 105, 107, 112, 115
Belgium, 3, 4, 6, 24, 63, 180
Bernstorff, Count, 22, 34, 44
Bickford, Admiral, 4, 5
Bickford, Andrew, 204, 205
Bigland, Alfred, 81–82
Birmingham Chamber of Commerce, 70, 74
Blackburn Chamber of Commerce, 81
Bluefields Steamship Company, 155
Board of Trade: and commercial treaty with Cuba, 71, 83, 93; protests U.S.-Cuban reciprocity treaty, 82; and Panama Canal tolls controversy, 171–72, 173; and proposed British trade association for Central America, 223–24; and Milne mission, 227n
Bolivar Railway Co., Lmt., 29n

Bowen, Herbert, 10, 19, 221; and *Suchet* incident, 15; on Monroe Doctrine, 20, 29–30n; as negotiator for Venezuela, 41–59 *passim*, 65n, 67n
Bradford Chamber of Commerce, 74, 81
Brazil, xii
British Association for Central America, 223–24
British Association of Chambers of Commerce, 73, 74
British Imperial Chamber of Commerce, 208n
British investments: in Latin America, x, xvin; in Caribbean and Central America, xi, 221–22, 223
British navy, strength in American waters, ix, xvin, 100, 118, 129n, 132n. *See also* Admiralty
British trade: with South America, x, xi; with Caribbean and Central America, xi, svin, 221–23; with Cuba, 69, 93–94. *See also* Open Door Policy in Latin America
Brogan, D. W., 218
Brown, Philip, 137, 138
Bryan, William Jennings, 179, 204–5
Bryce, James, 120, 121, 137, 138, 140, 160, 169, 170, 181, 193, 217 220, 221; and Santo Domingo debt, 114, 115, 184–85; on U.S. and Haiti, 122–23; on U.S. Central American policy, 134–35; on Honduran debt, 146; on Payne-Aldrich tariff, 150; and recognition of Madriz, 153, 154; on Knox and State Department, 162–63; and Panama Canal tolls controversy, 175–79 *passim;* and Guatemala, 190, 198–99, 200, 201; on Monroe Doctrine and arbitration treaty of 1911, 218–19; on British capitalists and Central America, 223
Buchanan, George, 11, 22, 35
Bulow, Bernhard von, 34
Burmuda, 100, 118, 119
Bury Chamber of Commerce, 74

Cabinet: and Venezuelan intervention, 18–19, 29n, 36–37, 38, 47; and *Agnes Donahoe* affair, 116; and arbitration treaty of 1911, 168; and Panama Canal tolls controversy, 176
Campbell, Francis A., 80, 182